# THE COMPLETE
## ENCYCLOPEDIA OF
# ANTIQUE FIREARMS

# THE COMPLETE ENCYCLOPEDIA OF

# ANTIQUE FIREARMS

**An expert guide to firearms
and their development**

**A. E. HARTINK**

© 2001 Rebo International b.v., Lisse, The Netherlands

This 2nd edition reprinted 2004

Text and photographs: A. E. Hartink
Editing and production: TextCase, Groningen, The Netherlands
Cover design: Minkowsky Graphics, Enkhuizen, The Netherlands
Layout: Signie, Winschoten, The Netherlands

ISBN 90 366 1488 0

# Contents

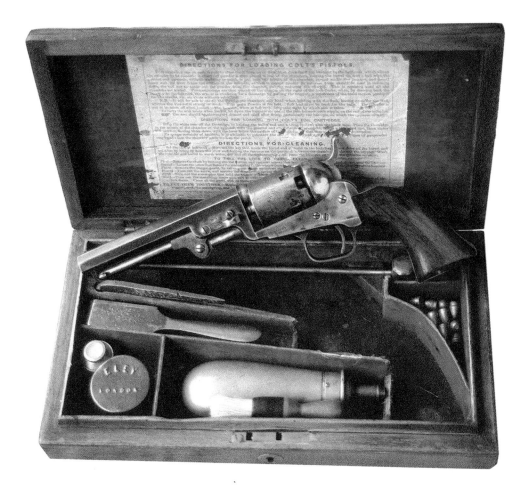

# The history of firearms

The history of firearms is closely related to the invention and the further development of gunpowder. The first references to a propellant for projectiles are found in ancient Chinese writings. A Chinese document from the year 618 B.C., which did not find its way into the Western world until the 15th century, referred to some form of gunpowder which was mainly used for fireworks, but also as a propellant for projectiles. The Great Wall of China, built some 200 years B.C. on the instructions of the Chinese Emperor Schi Huang Ti as a defence against Mongol raids, has also been found to have been built with special embrasures for the firing of guns. Then in the Greek era, fire was sometimes used as a weapon during wars and, some 200 years later, the Greek philosopher Aeneas wrote a dissertation on firebombs. This outlined the use of so-called 'Greek Fire', a mixture of oil, resin, lime, flax and sulphur. The oil allowed Greek fire to float on water, making it highly useful in naval battles. In this way Greek fire was successfully used to defend Constantinople against the Arabs from Palestine and Syria. In the early Middle Ages alchemists experimented with

*Old copperplate impression of the siege of a fortress, c. 1500*

the composition of this incendiary. Early documents refer to the ingredients charcoal, camphor, pitch, saltpetre, tartaric acid, salt and sulphur. During the conquest of Mekka in 630 A.D. Arab soldiers were alleged to have used firearms that looked like some form of cannon. Their knowledge of these weapons came from India and Persia, but the Indians may well have learnt what they knew about weapons in China. However, it was not until the end of the Middle Ages that gunpowder mixtures were commonly introduced to the Western world.

One theory claims that the secret was brought to Europe from China by Marco Polo, the famous Venetian merchant who travelled to Peking, crossing Europe, Russia and China, in the period 1271–1292 and gathered his knowledge of Chinese fireworks there. There are also theories that

say that gunpowder was discovered in Europe. These theories mention the names of Roger Bacon, a Franciscan monk, and Berthold Schwarz, also a monk, from Freiburg in Germany. The name of this latter monk is closely linked with gunpowder or 'black powder' (Schwarzpulver), as it is more commonly known now. However, this latter theory is not very plausible and it is more probable that Schwarz and Bacon already knew that gunpowder existed due to merchants' contacts with the Orient. The composition of black powder is roughly 75% saltpetre, 15% sulphur and 10% charcoal.

The development of firearms began in the early 14th century when it was discovered that black powder could not only be used to make attractive fireworks but to shoot heavy projectiles as well. The first handguns also emerged during this century. By the end of the 14th century various names for

*Engraving of mortar, c. 1550*

firearms had appeared, such as bombard, bombardelle (a small cannon) and mortar. Another version is the 'Hakbutt' or 'Arquebuse', a wooden stock with a short iron barrel on it. The stock had a vertical hook which acted as a brace to reduce the effects of recoil when the gun was fired. In the 15th century every city had its own iron or bronze cannon to defend the city walls. Initially pebbles were used as the projectiles for cannons, but soon ammunition was forged from iron.

Shortly after this the carriage-mounted cannon appeared. A good example of this is the cannon of Mons in Belgium which dates back to 1449. Up until Medieval times, knights were very well protected against

*Hakbutt around 1400*

spears and arrows by their armour. This however changed when the use of gunpowder increased. Their armour could be easily penetrated by the relatively simple projectiles of the time and lances, spears and swords proved to be no match for firearms. The technology has not stood still since that time, but the original principles still apply: an iron barrel, sealed on one side, with a small hole left open, or added later.

The gunpowder and the charge were driven down into the barrel through the open end. The gunpowder was then ignited and the projectile was forced from the barrel. Initially the powder was ignited by a glowing splinter of wood, but around 1415 this was replaced by slow matches which in turn were replaced by matchlocks.

## The matchlock

The simple slow-match ignition of around 1400 led to the development of the matchlock. The first evidence of this lock is found in writings, drawings and paintings of around 1470. The matchlock consisted of a curved iron arm that was fitted to the gun.

This arm, which was known as the serpentine, could pivot and was linked to an iron lever under the wooden stock of the gun. In fact this lever was the predecessor of the trigger. The loading procedure was as follows: the shooter would set his gun upright and pour a predetermined quantity of gunpowder into the barrel. The powder was then carefully rammed down and compacted by a rod. The projectile was then placed into the barrel and rammed home by the rod as well. Now the weapon was ready to be fired by holding a burning match to the touchhole to ignite the charge of gunpowder.

A later version of the matchlock had a priming pan at the rear of the barrel. The shooter placed a pinch of fine-grained

powder, the priming powder, in this pan. When the lever was squeezed against the stock the serpentine pivoted around its axis, moving the glowing match to the priming pan and igniting the powder in the pan. Next to this priming pan there was a small hole that allowed the fire to reach the main charge in the barrel. This fire would ignite the charge of gunpowder down in the barrel. The main charge would burn, generating a gas pressure that drove the projectile out of the barrel.

In later models the serpentine was fitted with a leaf spring. When the serpentine was tilted backwards, it was caught by a catch. When the catch was pushed, the spring would cause the serpentine to move forwards. In those days the firing lever was sometimes replaced by a pushbutton to trigger the firing catch. This was later replaced by a trigger. Reloading was strongly affected by the weather. A strong gust of wind could blow the fine-grained gunpowder out of the

priming pan and ignition was especially difficult in rainy conditions. This led to 7th century matchlock models being fitted with lidded priming pans. While the gun did not have to be fired, the priming powder was covered by a hinged lid. If the shooter had to fire the gun, he would swivel or tilt the lid off the priming pan so that the match could reach the gunpowder. As early as 1600, soldiers, known as musketeers, already wore bandoleers with containers that held the exact amount of gunpowder for every charge.

The use of the larger powder horns or flasks of gunpowder was not always very safe. In fact many shooters who used powder horns to reload their gun were seriously injured by burns caused by smouldering soot in their barrels igniting the gunpowder early. Gunpowder used in smaller portions was much safer to use. The wheel-lock was the next step in the development of guns. This firing system, which replaced the

the end of the 15th century. Their operation can be compared to that of an old-fashioned lighter.

A serrated wheel scraped a piece of mineral to create sparks. The serrated wheel of the wheel-lock was driven by a spring. Before the gun could be fired, the spring had to be first spanned or wound by turning a key and locked by a pawl, the sear. As the spring was wound the cock tilted back-

*Wheel-lock gun c. 1570*

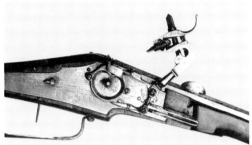

matchlock, was actually invented by Leonardo da Vinci. In the early 16th century he created the Codex Atlanticus which includes sketches of a wheel-lock. The first types of wheel-lock emerged by

*Engraving of a 17th century musketeer*

wards. When the trigger was pressed, the serrated wheel was unlocked and the cock with the piece of mineral hit the wheel. The wheel rotated at high speed due to the spring pressure and scraped the mineral, producing a shower of sparks that ignited the priming powder. The wheel-lock was a complex mechanism that was expensive to manufacture.

In addition it was easily affected by dirt which could cause the gun to jam. It may therefore come as no surprise that weapons from this period sometimes had two different firing systems. During the 16th and 17th centuries large groups of musketeers were formed to fight wars and it was quite a costly affair to issue them with weapons and other equipment. The search for a simpler and cheaper solution led to the development of the snaphaunce lock that, in turn, would soon be replaced by the flint-lock.

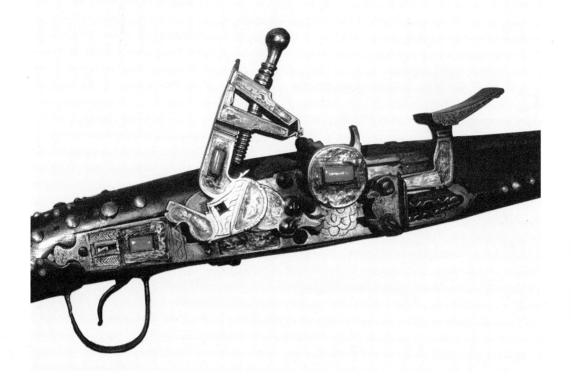

## The snaphaunce lock

The first snaphaunce lock was probably produced around 1545. The mechanism consisted of a cock with a piece of flint in it. When the trigger was pressed spring pressure would swing the cock forwards. A steel plate was mounted in front of the priming pan. The flint in the cock struck the steel to create a spark that would fall in the priming pan. The priming then ignited the powder charge in the barrel. Initially the priming pan was closed off by a hand-operated lid, as was the case with the later types of matchlock firearms. Later the pan lid was mechanically pivoted away when the cock struck forwards. A variation on this system was the 'Swedish snap-lock', which had a loose steel plate mounted to the priming pan lid. This steel plate could be pivoted away sideways, and acted as a kind of safety device. The shooter could carry the gun with the cock tensioned. Since the steel plate was not in position, the weapon could not be fired, whereas the lid on the priming pan would keep the priming dry.

## The flintlock

The first real flintlocks were produced around 1610. This lock was very similar to the snaphaunce lock, the main difference being that the steel plate and the priming pan lid were combined into one part. The priming pan lid of the flintlock had a vertically raised plate.

When the trigger was pressed, the cock struck forwards. The flint hit the steel which tilted forward together with the pan cover connected to it. This allowed the sparks created by the friction between the steel and the flint to fall in the uncovered

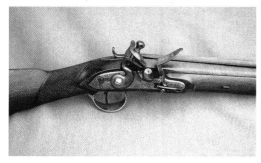

## The percussion lock

priming. The miquelet or Spanish lock is a variety of the flintlock. The main differences with the Northern flintlock were its serrated steel plate and the cock spring that was carried externally on the lock plate. Other varieties of the flintlock will be discussed in a later chapter.

As early as the 17th century scientists were already looking for methods to give more power to the gunpowder and to improve on the distance the projectiles fired could travel. Experiments were made with various substances including mercury and antimony. By the mid-18th century, the French chemist Berthollet developed the explosive silver fulminate.

In 1798, an Englishman, Edward Howard, found an easy method to manufacture an alternative substance, mercury fulminate. The real revolution in the development of firearms did not start until a Scottish clergyman, Alexander Forsythe from Belhelvie in Aberdeenshire, invented the percussion cap, or more accurately the principles for the

*Four-barrelled flint gun with a box-lock*

*Collection of percussion rifles from the American Civil War (Navy Arms replicas)*

*Collection of percussion rifles from the American Civil War (Navy Arms replicas)*

percussion cap. In 1799, he published a scientific treatise on a chemical compound, called fulminate, that could be ignited by a firm stroke. The credits for the development of the percussion cap were claimed by several gunmakers, including the English engineers Joseph Egg, Joseph Manton and James Purdey in 1816, the leading French gunsmiths Prélat and Deboubert in 1818 and the American Joshua Shaw in 1822.

The principle behind the system was simple. The weapon was loaded the same way as a matchlock firearm. Then the solid-nosed hammer (which replaced the cock) was tensioned. A hollow pin, the nipple, had been

screwed into the rear of the barrel. To shoot the gun, a small copper thimble filled with fulminate was placed on the nipple. When the trigger was pressed, a spring made the hammer strike the percussion cap. This created a bright flash that was transmitted to the flash hole by the hollow nipple to ignite the main charge in the barrel. This system was used in rifles, pistols and eventually in the more modern five- or six-shot black powder revolvers for quite some time.

## Ammunition

The development of the complete round started around the late 18th and early 19th century, simultaneous with the development of the so-called 'rifling': grooves cut into the barrels to give the bullet fired a more stable trajectory, so that the target could be hit more accurately. The next important step was the development of self-contained cartridges. The components – projectile, powder, cap and case (initially paper or cardboard, and later brass) – were assembled together into one cartridge.

These cartridges were no longer loaded via the muzzle of the barrel, but directly into the breech: the chamber at the rear end of the barrel. This meant that the gun had to be constructed so that the breech could be opened to load the weapon and sealed tight after loading the cartridge to withstand the gas pressure that was created when the powder was ignited. This system is called the

*Lancaster double-barrelled shotgun with percussion locks*

*Round musket bullets (Remington)*

14

*Cross-section of a .22 LR cartridge (Remington)*

*Detail of a single-barrelled pin-fire rifle. The pin of the cartridge fits into the slot in the breech*

'action' or 'breech-loading'. The development of cartridges went through various stages, such as needle fire, rim-fire cartridges and pin-fire cartridges. Rim-fire ignition was invented by Flobert, a French gunsmith from Paris, who built 6-mm Flobert calibre sporting rifles around 1845. In rim-fire cartridges the priming compound is not embedded in a brass thimble, but in the rim of the cartridge case itself.

Rim-fire ammunition is still quite popular for small-calibre weapons. Initially the priming compound, consisting of potassium chlorate, mercury and sulphuric antimony, was highly corrosive.

This did not change until 1927 when Remington introduced the 'Kleanbore' rim-fire cartridge. Its priming compound was a mixture of barium nitrate, lead dioxide and TNT. Rim-fire ammunition was marketed in many different brands, types and versions in the period between 1845 and 1940, varying from the 6-mm Flobert to the big-bore.56 Spencer cartridges. Another system where the priming compound was contained inside the cartridge case was the pin-fire cartridge. These cartridges were ignited by the hammer striking a pin that protruded from the side of the cartridge. The popularity of this system was however short lived.

*Collection of powder flasks (Hege)*

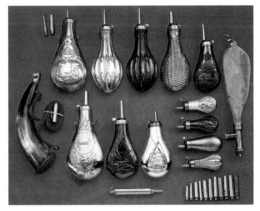

*Examples of targets from former times*

*Drawing of a pin-fire cartridge*

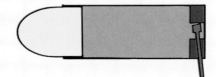

15

# Lock systems

The firing system of a firearm consists of the trigger mechanism and the lock. The lock is the mechanism with the springs, catches and pins on a mounting plate that connects the trigger to the hammer with the aim of moving the cock or the hammer forward to create a spark and fire the weapon when the trigger is pulled. Fifteenth-century lock systems were of simple designs, but the system gradually became more complicated as more and more inventions were introduced. Below is a detailed survey of the various lock systems as they were developed through the ages.

The first firearm was introduced to Europe around 1400. In the first century of its existence its technical development was slow, until around 1800 when it was intensified.

## The matchlock

One of the oldest recorded firearms is the Milemete cannon from the early 14th century which was ignited using a glowing splinter of wood.

Around 1350 the first handguns were introduced, some using rudimentary brass barrels. Then around 1400, people started using a loose match to ignite gun charges.

*Drawing of an early matchlock*

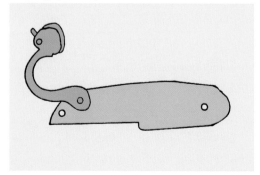

The first evidence of a mechanism used to attach a match to a firearm and to operate this system stems from 1415. These weapons have all been lost over the years, but there are many old sketches and drawings in existence to show how they worked. The matchlock period can be classified as follows:

1. the matchlock with a firing lever,
2. the matchlock with a pushbutton,
3. the matchlock with a lidded priming pan.

## The matchlock with a firing lever

This is the first type of matchlock, dating from 1415. This lock consisted of an iron or copper lock plate that was screwed onto the foremost end of the stock. A pivoting hammer, also called a serpentine, was connected to the plate. A slow match could be fitted in the serpentine. To shoot the gun, the glowing match had to be moved towards the priming pan by hand. The fine-grained powder, or 'primer', in the priming pan then ignited to set off the main charge in the barrel.

As it was quite difficult to hold and aim the weapon and operate the serpentine at the same time, the mechanism was further refined by around 1450. A firing rod was fitted to the serpentine, which in turn was connected to a long lever. This lever was mounted in parallel to the stock and served as a primitive kind of trigger. Later a leaf spring was attached to the serpentine. When the lever was squeezed, the serpentine tilted towards the priming pan and when the lever was released, the serpentine returned to its home position.

In later versions, other types of 'trigger' such as ring-shaped triggers or short and straight levers, were linked to the firing rod. This latter improvement was the actual predecessor of the current trigger system.

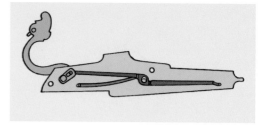

## The matchlock with a firing button

Around 1500 the 'trigger' was replaced by a firing button. This innovation would play a major role in later developments. The lock plate had a button to which a pin was connected that ran through the lock plate. The serpentine in this system was spring loaded as well, but its action was exactly the other way around compared with the system above.

The serpentine had to be pulled back manually, after which its base engaged with the firing button pin and was held by it. When the button was pushed, the pin moved inwards to release the base of the serpentine. The spring force would make the serpentine pivot forwards, towards the priming pan. This was the first single-action system. The figures in the drawing below refer to the following elements:

1. serpentine spring,
2. firing pin,
3. firing button.

*Matchlock with firing button: 1. serpentine spring, 2. firing pin, 3. firing button.*

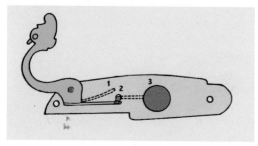

## The matchlock with a lidded priming pan

It must have been quite difficult to fire these early firearms in bad weather. A strong gust of wind could blow the fine-grained gunpowder out of the priming pan and ignition was virtually impossible when it was raining. This situation was improved by the year 1550 when a flat, horizontally hinged lid was mounted onto the priming pan. To fire the gun the lid had to be slid off the priming pan so that the match could reach the priming powder. This may seem quite laborious nowadays, but for our early ancestors it was a great improvement.

## The wheel-lock

Although it was possible to keep the gunpowder dry by 1550, the glowing match was still problematic. A shower of rain could easily extinguish it and for military purposes it was a disadvantage that a musketeer in hiding would be betrayed by the light of the glowing match. Therefore around 1550 the

*Matchlock with a hinged priming pan lid*

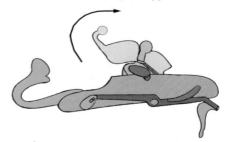

*Drawing of a wheel-lock*

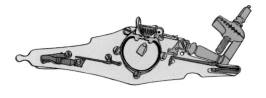

*Drawing of the inside of the complicated wheel-lock system*

matchlock was modified. The actual match was removed and replaced by a cock, into which a piece of mineral could be clamped between two jaws. The lock had a serrated wheel that could be rotated by spring pressure, provided that the spring had been

*Top view of the wheel of a wheel-lock*

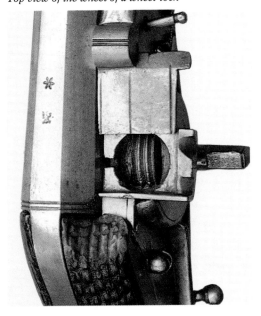

spanned or wound. A winding key was used for this purpose. Once the spring was wound it could be locked. Next the cock was tilted backwards and locked. When the trigger was pressed, the cock moved forwards. At the same time the spring was released and the serrated wheel started to turn around and scraped along the piece of mineral in the jaws. This produced a shower of sparks that fell into the priming pan, provided that everything worked the way it should. This mechanism, which could be compared to a modern cigarette lighter, was a lot more complex than the matchlock and more expensive to manufacture. In the early days of this new lock system, it was not uncommon for firearms to have two lock systems. Not everybody was equally keen on the new developments and, due to all the handwork involved, the manufacture of a wheel-lock was quite costly. Also, at that time there was no high-grade steel available, as a result of which the mechanism would wear significantly with frequent use. For that reason the simple matchlock was used in good weather and the wheel-lock system in less favourable conditions. The weapon displayed below has both a wheel-lock and a matchlock. As indicated before, there were serious disadvantages connected to the wheel-lock. First of all, it was very expensive to manufacture and secondly, the complicated system was easily affected by dirt and wet powder residue. As a result the wheel-lock was replaced by the flintlock by approximately 1547.

*Gun with a combined matchlock and wheel-lock*

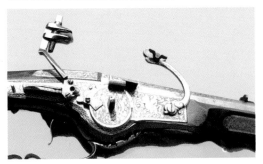

## The Flintlock

The name flintlock refers to the use of a piece of flint in the cock jaws. This flint hit an iron plate, the 'steel', to create a spark that was designed to fall into the priming pan. The flintlock went through various stages of development as well.

## The snaphaunce lock

There are many stories about the origins of the name 'snaphaunce'. One of them is that it comes from the Dutch *snaphaan* that was supposed to mean chicken thief. At that time the wheel-lock was far too expensive for poachers, whereas the matchlock with its glowing and smouldering match was too risky.

They therefore developed their own flint system which did not have these setbacks. However, a more likely explanation for the name of this lock is that the shape and the movement of the steel hitting the flint resembled the head of a pecking (in old

*Drawing of a Dutch snaphaunce lock*

Dutch 'snapping') bird. The first snaphaunce lock was introduced around 1547, although it is not certain in which country or by whom it was developed.

The Netherlands had a fast growing weapons industry at that time and the Dutch snaphaunce lock was very popular in those days. But some Scandinavian countries, Germany, England, Spain and Italy had their own snaphaunce locks as well. Basically the system consists of a cock with two jaws into which a piece of flint is clamped.

To fire the weapon the cock must be tilted backwards by hand, where it locks.

*Flintlock made by Giovan Beretta, c. 1750 (photograph by Beretta)*

*Drawing of a Dutch snaphaunce lock combined with a matchlock*

*Spanish Miquelet lock*

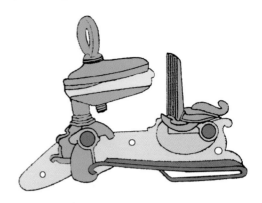

Opposite the cock a second arm had been mounted on the lock plate to which a ribbed steel was mounted. As soon as the trigger was pressed, the steel – the 'snaphaunce' – would move back, until it was straight above the priming pan. Almost at the same time the cock was swung forwards and the flint in the cock jaws struck the steel to create a spark that fell into the priming pan. The primer then ignited the main powder charge in the barrel via the small flash hole.The snaphaunce lock was popular in many countries. The picture below shows a Scandinavian snaphaunce lock with its typical, slender cock.

plate has been abandoned and the steel plate has been mounted vertically onto a cover plate over the priming pan. This was an important step into the right direction. The powder stayed dry and could not be blown away by the wind, because the priming pan was closed off by a lid. After the cock had been pulled back by hand, the trigger could be pulled. The cock then struck against the steel. The impact caused the steel and the pan lid to tilt forward and allow the spark to fall into the priming pan.

*Drawing of a Scandinavian snaphaunce lock*

## The English flintlock

The English lock was developed around 1620. On the outside it does not seem to be very different from the Miquelet lock. Internally however there is a great differ-

*Italian flintlock (photograph by Benelli)*

## The Miquelet lock

The Miquelet lock was first developed around 1580 and was used in Mediterranean countries. The Spanish Miquelet lock has a typical austere design. The Italian Miquelet lock on the other hand is decorated abundantly with angels, etc. As the photographs show, the separate arm with the steel striker

20

ence, as it worked with a so-called tumbler. This was a lever system that was mounted between the trigger and the cock. This lever helped the trigger to release the cock, as a result of which the trigger pressure could be kept relatively low. This principle basically worked as follows: when the cock was tensioned, the tumbler engaged with a lug in the base or tail of the cock. The tumbler

*Flintlock of a Brown Bess musket*

was hooked into the trigger or into its extension, the trigger lever. As soon as the trigger was pushed, the spring pressure would cause the tumbler to make one rotation. This would release the cock which could strike forwards.

## The French lock

The English lock was only made until c. 1650. The French lock was developed in France in 1625. This lock was not only better than the English lock, but its manufacture was a lot cheaper as well, and gunsmiths in many countries were quick to adopt the French lock.

The French flintlock owed its popularity primarily to its firing system with its improved tumbler which had two notches. The first was a safety notch. If the cock was pulled backwards and released halfway, the first deep

21

*French flintlock*

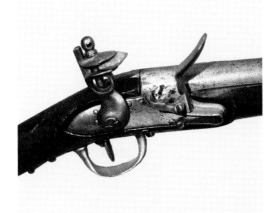

*French flintlock*

notch on the tumbler engaged with the tail of the cock. This put the weapon in its 'half-cock' safety position from where it could not be fired by pulling the trigger. If the cock was tilted all the way back, the second tumbler notch would engage with the tail of the cock. This notch was less deep and could be released by means of the trigger to fire the charge.

## The box-lock

The first flinted box-lock was produced around 1750 and was mainly used in pistols. The lock-work was no longer

*English box-lock of a Twigg double-barrelled pistol*

mounted to a lock plate, but packed into a brass or iron casing. A good example of this is the English Twigg double-barrelled flint-lock pistol from 1780. No catches or springs can be seen on the outside: everything has been housed neatly inside the casing.

## The percussion lock

A next step in the development of firearms was the invention of fulminating powder. This invention was claimed by several people. A predecessor of fulminating powder, the so-called mercury fulminate, is supposed to have been invented by the German chemist Johann Kunckel around 1700. The invention of fulminating powder by Nicolas Lemery was announced in France in 1712. This dangerous substance initially reacted far too explosively and was considered unsuitable for use in light firearms.

It was not until 1799 that Edward Howard, an Englishman, managed to control this explosive mixture. Strangely enough his purpose was not to find a good ignition agent, but to find a substitute for gunpowder. Around 1801, Alexander John Forsyth, a cleric from Aberdeenshire, discovered that fulminates could be used very effectively to ignite gunpowder. Forsyth patented his 'scent-bottle' lock in 1807. The sobriquet arose from the resemblance of the lock to

*English scent-bottle percussion lock*

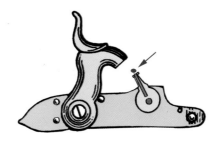

the cosmetic phials of the day. This percussion lock contained a priming-powder magazine that rotated through 180 degrees when the hammer was pulled back to half-cock and allowed a tiny amount of mercuric fulminate to enter the flash-hole channel. Other English gunmakers such as Joseph Egg and Westley Richards developed similar systems, but they were all faced with the difficulty of how to house the priming powder and to release it in an effective way so that not all of it would ignite in one blow. One of the systems that was developed was to press a small amount of fulminate into a pill or pellet that was held together by gum arabic.

*Drawing of a priming tube lock*

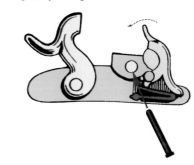

*The priming tube lock*

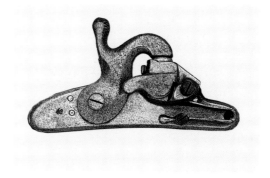

This type of ignition was also called the pill-primer lock. The pill could be placed in the head of the cock or in a hollow tube on the barrel. Joseph Manton from London was a famous gunmaker who produced guns using priming pills. An alternative to this principle was disc-priming, where the pellet was pressed into a small disc. The English rifle makers Thomas Cartmell and Samuel Nock and William Westely Richards applied this ignition system until 1810.

Another system was the priming tube where the priming powder was housed in a thin brass tube that was slid into the side of the priming pan. Joseph Manton obtained a patent to this principle in 1818. Other gunmakers that used this system were Giuseppe Colsole from Milan in Italy and the renowned English rifle maker Charles

Lancaster. An interesting variation on these types of ignition system is the tape system which is still used in toy guns today. Around 1850, this was an accepted system that was used for army rifles. Grains of fulminate were pressed into a ribbon that was rolled up and stored in a housing which could be opened and closed by means of a hinged lid. Eventually all these systems were replaced by the development of the percussion cap in combination with a thin pillar, the nipple.

The nipple was screwed into the rear of the barrel. The nipple had a tapered shape and a percussion cap could be clamped on top of the nipple. This cap was a brass thimble filled with fulminate. When the trigger was pulled, the hammer would strike on the cap to ignite the fulminate with a bright flash. The priming flash travelled through the channel in the nipple and ignited the main charge in the barrel.

This system dates from 1822 and was used for a number of years until the self-contained cartridge was introduced. The first gunmaker who patented the eventual shape of the percussion cap as it is still used, was the American Joshua Shaw.

## Needle fire

Developments in the field of firearms and ammunition have taken place continuously. In 1814 Dreyse, a German, was already experimenting with cartridges. In 1841, the Prussian army tested the Dreyse

*Nipple of a percussion lock. The priming channel is indicated by the red dotted line*

*Cross-section of a black powder percussion revolver. The nipples are indicated by the red arrow*

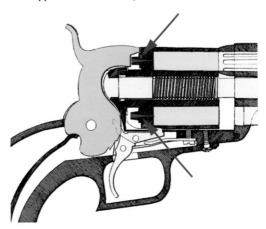

*Drawing of a needle-fire cartridge. The primer is located in the centre of the cartridge as indicated by the red arrow*

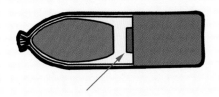

needle-fire rifle and immediately ordered 60,000 rifles of this type. This rifle had a breech-loading system with bolt action that could be loaded with paper cartridges fast enough to allow a trained marksman to shoot 5–6 shots per minute.

This was a significant military advantage at that time. The needle-fire cartridge consisted of a paper case with the powder charge, the primer and the bullet inside. The pin, shaped like a long needle, pierced the paper cartridge bottom until it reached roughly halfway where it struck some fulminate, causing the cartridge to ignite.

## Rim fire

A next step forward was the rim-fire system which was developed by the Frenchman Louis Nicolas Auguste Flobert around 1845. This invention really was the logical

*Flobert type rim-fire cartridge (Remington)*

consequence of the brass percussion cap. Flobert extended the cap to create a real cartridge, onto which he placed a bullet point. The priming fulminate remained in the case, where it was cast into a protruding rim, hence the name rim fire. This formed the basis for our modern, current-day ammunition. In fact the rim-fire cartridge itself is still used today in many varieties.

## Pin fire

At about the same time a pin-fire cartridge was developed by another Frenchmen, Eugene Gabriel Lefaucheux of Paris. These cartridges, based on an invention by Lefaucheux's father Casimir, were patented in 1850.

The cartridge consisted of a copper case which contained the powder charge and the bullet. A little piece of fulminate was fitted inside the base of the case. A small steel pin protruded from the bottom cover of the case. The hammer struck the end of the pin, driving it into the case where it hit the fulminate which ignited the powder charge.

Lefaucheux and many other European gunsmiths developed weapons for this system. The calibre of the cartridges ranged from 2 to 15 mm and there were even pin-

*Double-barrelled pin-fire rifle with the circular openings for the detonation pins clearly showing*

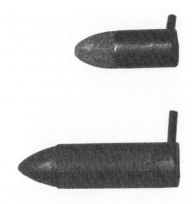

fire shot cartridges. A small circular opening for the pin-fire pin was normally made at the end of the breech.

## Centre fire

All the developments discussed above finally led to the current centre-fire system that was introduced around 1866. The centre-fire cartridge consists of a brass case with the percussion cap in its base, and the powder charge and bullet point crimped into the case. The percussion cap consists of a small brass cup, clamped into the centre of the base of the case, hence the name centre fire. The percussion cap contains a layer of fulminate, with a so-called anvil over it.

When the firing pin strikes the percussion cap, the cap is dented and pressed against the anvil, causing the fulminate to ignite with a bright flame. The above cross section of a percussion cap shows:
1. cartridge base,
2. percussion cap,
3. fulminate,
4. anvil,
5. powder charge in the case.

The flame then strikes through the bottom of the case, causing the powder charge in the case to ignite. In principle there are two types of centre-fire systems: the Berdan primer system with two or more primer vents and the Boxer system with only one central primer vent. Both systems are still used nowadays, but the Boxer principle is by far the most popular.

The letters in the cross section of a case below are:
A. case,
B. case base,
C. percussion cap opening,
D. primer vent.

The development of the centre-fire system has led to hundreds of different calibres, from the .17 Remington to the .700 Nitro Express. The first centre-fire cartridge was the .44 Henry, produced by Winchester for the Henry rifles.

*Cross-section of a percussion cap (Remington). 1. cartridge base, 2. percussion cap, 3. fulminate, 4. anvil, 5. powder charge*

*Cross-section of a case base: A. case, B. case base, C. percussion cap opening, D. primer vent*

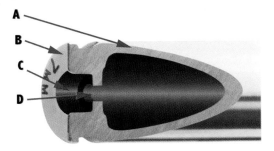

# Safety devices

*Drawing of a pivoting priming pan lid*

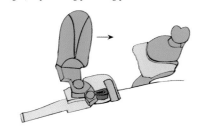

The first users of firearms quickly discovered that a loaded weapon could be dangerous.

A shot could be fired unintentionally, which could hit the shooter himself or a bystander. Therefore through the ages gun designers have used their skills to devise and further develop safety devices.

## The priming pan slide

The most evident way of making a firearm safe is to close off the ignition system, so that sparks cannot reach the powder charge. This was already applied with the earliest wheel-lock guns. The simplest method was to fit a horizontally sliding lid onto the priming pan.

To fire a shot, the lid had to be slid away by hand to allow the flint to reach the serrated wheel. In later models the opening of the lid was connected to the tensioning of the cock; when the cock was pulled back by the shooter, the priming pan lid mechanically moved sideways. Another advantage of this system was that it kept the priming powder dry.

*Drawing of a sliding priming pan lid on a wheel-lock gun*

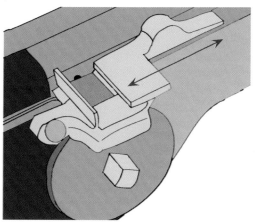

## The priming pan lid

The pivoting priming pan lids of flintlock guns were derived from this system. The priming pan lid now also served as the steel plate which was struck by the piece of flint to create a spark. The shooter could make his weapon safe by twisting the vertical steel plate a quarter turn by hand. This prevented the cock with the flint from reaching it. As it was now not possible to strike a spark, the weapon could not be fired.

## The pivoting pan

The next step was the pivoting pan. In this system the steel plate also served as the pan lid.

The priming pan itself was housed in a kind of cylinder with a wheel that could be rotated by hand. To make the weapon safe, the shooter would rotate the wheel to pivot the powder pan opening away. This would prevent sparks from falling into the priming powder unintentionally.

*Drawing of a pivoting priming pan*

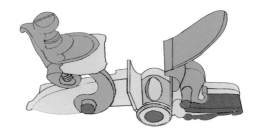

## The sear

The predecessor of modern systems is the sliding sear that was developed by the English gunsmith Bond. In this system the shooter first had to pull back the cock to tension it. It could then be blocked by a sliding sear on the lock plate, just behind

*Safety sear on a 4-barrelled Twigg pistol. The blue arrow indicates the rotary knob to operate the priming pans for the lower two barrels*

the cock. To fire the gun, the shooter first had to pull the sear back to release the cock. Another example of a sliding sear is shown on the English Twigg pistol. Here both priming pan lids can be opened independently of each other.

They are locked by a sear on the neck of the stock. When one cock (or both) was pulled to half-cock position it was blocked by the sear that engaged with a notch in the tail of the cock.

## Half-cock

The half-cock safety is the most widely used safety system for firearms. Two notches are cut into the tail of the cock or the hammer.

The first (largest) notch is large and deep. As soon as the hammer is in half-cock the tumbler connecting the trigger and the hammer engages with the first notch. The hammer has now been locked. Due to the size of the notch, the hammer is held tight

*Hammer in half-cock*

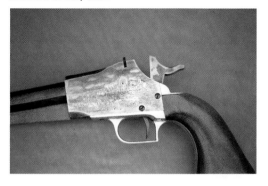

*The same weapon but now fully cocked*

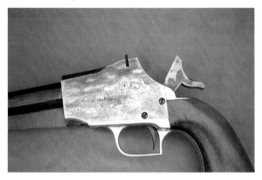

*Drawing of a hammer with a hammer base and the half-cock and firing notches*

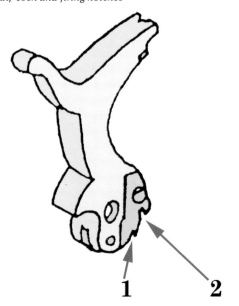

and it cannot be released by the trigger, so that the gun can be fired. To do this, first the shooter has to fully cock the hammer. This causes the tumbler to slide out of the first safety position and to engage with the second, smaller notch, the firing position.

As this notch is smaller and less deep, the trigger is capable of lifting the tumbler from this notch. The safety position notch is indicated by the number 2 in the drawing below. The number 1 indicates the firing position.

## The grip safety device

The large-scale application of the grip safety system in pistols started at the beginning of the 20th century. Examples of pistols with this safety system are the Colt 1911 pistol and the more recent Heckler & Koch P7.

However this system had actually already been devised as early as 1700 by an Austrian gunsmith. The Maurer rifle is a good example of this. A safety pin is fitted in the spring-loaded trigger bracket. If the trigger bracket is not pushed properly, the hammer remains disconnected from the trigger.

*Example of a grip safety device*

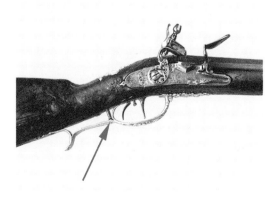

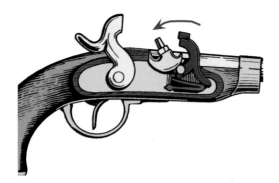

## The nipple safety

Even in the percussion era it was important that a gun could be made safe. One of the first systems resembles the principle used during the flint period, i.e. making it impossible for the primer to be ignited. The simplest way of doing this is by preventing an ignition spark being produced. In order to ensure this, an extra safety arm was fitted to the lock plate. On this arm an extra cap was mounted that would fall over the

percussion cap. If the hammer did strike forward, the percussion cap was sufficiently safeguarded so that it could not be hit by the head of the hammer.

A similar system is where a long safety arm extends well beyond the nipple to serve as a kind of half-cock lock. An added benefit is that the percussion cap is also retained by the safety arm. For example, during a very physical horseback ride the cap will be kept in place.
The horseman only needs to fully cock the hammer and swivel away the safety arm to fire the weapon.

## The hammer-locking sear

Gunsmiths invented various systems to make it safe to carry a loaded firearm. Many of those systems were intended to lock the hammer in some way or other so that it could not reach the percussion cap. However it should be possible to fire the weapon in a matter of seconds. For target

*Lock plate with a nipple safety*

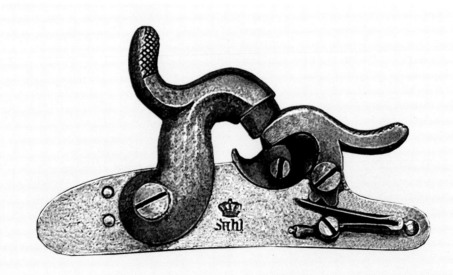

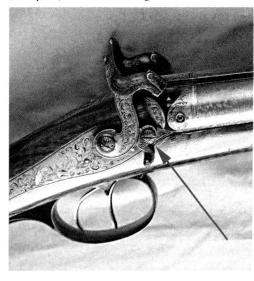

*Drawing of an engaged safety hook*

shooting or when duelling, it was not so important that the weapon could be fired quickly, but for military use and for hunting it was of vital importance. To achieve this a sear was mounted on the lock plate. Mostly this was operated by hand to lock the hammer in half-cock so that the loaded weapon could be carried safely. In later versions, a knob was sometimes mounted onto the safety sear for easier handling. This would make the sear look like a kind of crank.

For military weapons that had to be handled in rough conditions, a sturdier safety system was used to lock the hammer. The sear could then look like a kind of hook. When the gun was in half-cock the safety hook was slid forward and the hammer was released slightly so that the hook could engage with a notch in the base of the hammer. To undo the safety, the shooter

*Example of a hammer-locking sear*

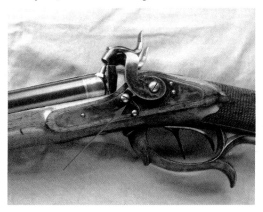

first had to pull the hammer all the way back after which he pulled the safety hook back to release the hammer. An unusual system, especially for revolvers, is shown in the picture below.

A large hook has been mounted onto the frame of the revolver. If the hook is pressed down, it will hook into the cylinder chamber to prevent the cylinder from being rotated.

The weapon has now been locked effectively. By pressing the arm up, the hook will fall down, thus releasing the cylinder. A much more sophisticated system is found on the Webley–Fosbery revolver. A large rotating sear that locks the trigger is

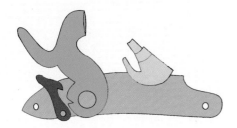

*Drawing of a safety hook that is dis-engaged*

located on the left-hand side of the frame just behind the trigger and above the grip plate.

*Safety hook to lock a revolver cylinder*

*Safety sear on the frame of a Webley–Fosbery revolver*

# Breech-loading or 'action' systems

When a firearm is fired, the powder charge is ignited to create a high force that will drive the bullet out of the barrel. This force is called the gas pressure. Due to the chemical reaction that is created when the powder is burnt, the gas pressure inside the gun can become very high. This pressure should escape from the gun through the muzzle.

However the force of the reaction that drives the bullet through the barrel also acts in a reverse direction, towards the rear of the barrel and towards the shooter. This is no problem with single-shot firearms where the barrel is closed at the rear, but for repeating weapons and for breech-loading weapons it is important that the action is sealed properly and safely. In the course of time, many breech-loading systems were developed for firearms. They are discussed below.

## *Breaking barrels*

Barrels that break open are mainly used on shotguns and large-calibre double-barrelled rifles. In the past this system was occasionally used for pistols or revolvers as well. The barrel of the weapon is hinged and can be broken open to open the breech. Mostly special catches or hooks are fitted to the barrel. They engage with openings in the breech section. A sliding or rotating catch lever is used to open and close the breech. A good, yet simple, example of this is shown in the picture below.

In this single-barrelled pin-fire rifle the catch is located below the barrel. When the breech is closed, the catch lever neatly covers the trigger guard. A barrel hook is fitted at the end of the barrel. This hook

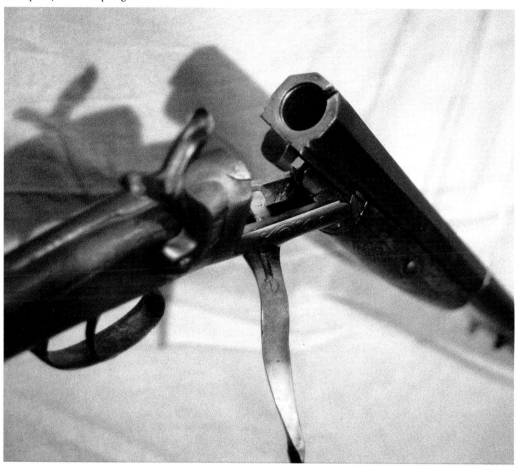

can be caught by a large catch attached to the catch lever. If the catch lever is turned, the pin secures the barrel to seal the breech. This is visible in the Förster double-barrelled rifle. A similar system, but then with the catch lever on top of the neck of the stock is seen in the Nowotny double-barrelled rifle in the picture below. The barrel hook below the barrel is just visible here. The German gunmaker Johann

*Catch lever around the trigger guard*

*Double-barrelled rifle with barrel hook lock*

*Dreyse hunting rifle with barrels that swing sideways*

*Dreyse hunting rifle with barrels that swing sideways*

*Webley revolver with open extractor star plate*

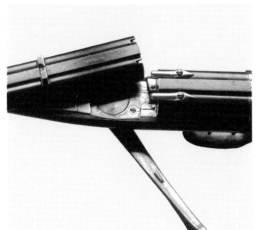

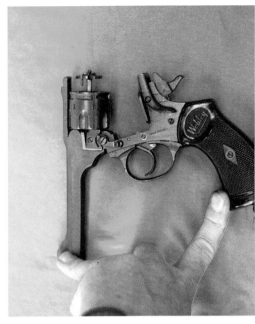

Nikolaus Dreyse invented a clever variation to the break-open barrels for his needle-fire rifles. In the Dreyse hunting rifle the barrel, when opened, does not fold forwards, but swivels sideways. A completely different example is the top-break system of the Webley revolver.

On top of the frame, at the notched sight, there is a catch lever that engages with an extended barrel strip. The barrel section and the cylinder turn around a hinge pin on the frame, in front of the trigger guard. When the barrel is completely opened, a rod pushes the extractor star plate out of the cylinder, forcing the cases or cartridges out of the cylinder.

## Rotating-bolt action

A wonderful example of the inventiveness of gunmakers is displayed by the rotating action Werndl rifle from 1867. Here the barrel is sealed by a cylinder, one-third of which has been removed.
If the bolt is opened, the chamber in the barrel can be reached to load the cartridge or eject the spent case. After this the shooter closes the bolt again and the rifle is locked.

*Break-open action on a Webley revolver*

*Rotating bolt of the Werndl M1867 rifle*

*Detail of the Chassepot rifle with bolt-action*

## The bolt lever

In early bolt-action rifles the breach was only sealed by the bolt lever itself. In the picture above you see that the bolt lever is raised straight up. This weapon is now unlocked.

The shooter can now slide a cartridge into the chamber. He then pushes the lever forward and finally turns it a quarter turn. The lever then locks behind the recess in the tailpiece to lock the weapon.

## The lug bolt

With later versions of bolt-action rifles, the rifle was not only locked by the bolt lever, but also by one or more lugs on the bolt itself. These lugs were at the front or at the back of the bolt.

When the weapon was closed the lugs would engage in matching recesses in the tailpiece to lock the breech. This is

*Lug bolt-action on a Steyr M1886 army rifle*

a very reliable locking system that can resist a very high gas pressure. This principle is still applied in modern bolt-action rifles.

## The folding bolt

The folding bolt on the Montigny needle-fire rifle is a classic display of ingeniousness. In this weapon a large and heavy bolt, sunk into the neck of the stock, can be folded up.

This will cause the bolt block to slide back and open the barrel chambers. The picture shows a double bolt block made for a double-barrelled rifle.

## Rolling-block action

By the mid-19th century, gunmakers had already devised an intricate system to seal the breech. This consisted of a steel section that could be rotated. The round disc was fitted with a lever to allow the rolling block to be swivelled away.

The round disc had a hollow duct for the firing pin. Remington was one of the companies to apply this system on a large scale. Other gunmakers used it as well, whether under a licence or not. Another example of the rolling-block action can be

*The folding bolt of the Montigny needle-fire rifle*

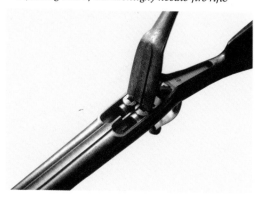

seen on the beautiful double-barrelled Bartel shotgun in the picture below. Here the shotgun is open and ready for loading or unloading.

## *Tip-up action*

The tip-up system was devised specifically for handguns. It dates from the time when the swinging cylinder was not commonly used yet.

Actually tip-up action is the opposite of top-break action. Here the barrel does not

*Rolling-block action on the Bartel double-barrelled shotgun*

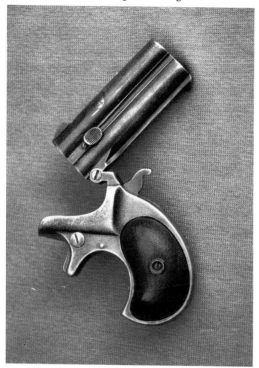

# Trapdoor action

Trapdoor or swing-up block actions stem from the time when muzzle-loading percussion rifles were changed into breech loaders.

Even in those days people were thrifty and governments found it a shame to throw away perfectly good military rifles, but they did not want to lag behind on technical developments. Various gunmakers devised different systems for this conversion, which all boil down to the same principle. Basically the conversion was done as follows. First the rear part of the percussion barrel was sawn off and a hinge element was fitted to the barrel. Then a solid steel block was mounted to the hinge. To load the rifle, this block had to be swung upwards.

After loading, the block was swung down to seal the breech. In some cases a latch was fitted on the block to stop the sealing block from opening spontaneously as a result of the high gas pressure. Three such systems are shown below. The first one is from the Austrian gunmaker Wanzl, the next is the Tersen system and the last one is Baranow.

fold down, but it tips up. There was a pivot in front of the cylinder or on top of the frame with a latch located at the bottom of the frame.

By pushing or pulling the latch the barrel block was released and could be swung upwards.

*Wanzl rifle trapdoor action*

*Smith & Wesson tip-up action*

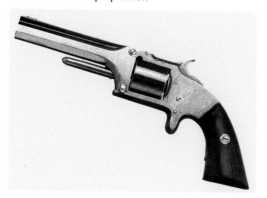

*Tersen system trapdoor action*

*Pin-fire pepperbox with swinging cylinder*

*Baranow trapdoor action*

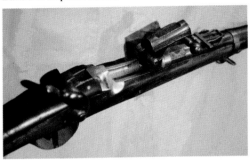

A good example of another type of trapdoor is shown in the picture below. This was not connected with the conversion from muzzle loading to breech loading. For the many types of Flobert cartridge rifles a breech-loading system had to be devised as well.

This did not have to be very heavy, since the gas pressure of these cartridges was relatively low. First the hammer had to be pulled back, after which the sealing block was swung up.

*Trapdoor action on a Flobert rifle*

## The swinging cylinder

It took a long time before gunmakers were ready to provide revolvers with a reliable system to allow the cylinder to be swung out of the frame. This was why the Colt single-action Army and other comparable models dominated the market for so long. However, as early as the mid-19th century there were several gunsmiths who constructed revolvers with swinging cylinders.

An example of this is the little Lefaucheux pin-fire revolver from 1850.

Below the frame, in front of the trigger, there is a pushbutton. If this button is pushed, the cylinder can be pushed forward and then swung aside. Other models only allowed the cylinder to be moved forwards to provide easy access to the chambers. Another example is the Italian Guerriero pin-fire revolver, which shows more resemblance to modern-day revolvers.

A remarkable feature of this weapon is the lid at the rear of the cylinder. This also served as a transport system to rotate the cylinder.

## Falling-block action

The falling-block system is operated by an enlarged trigger guard that serves as a lever. These levers could be folded down or, in certain weapons, forwards.

This action causes a solid block to slide

*Details of the Guerriero needle-fire revolver*

*Falling-block action of the Comblain rifle*

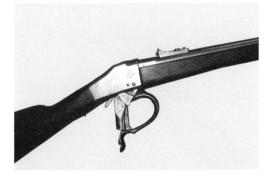

*Falling-block action of the Spencer carbine*

down along guides to clear the barrel and the chamber. As soon as the trigger guard is returned to its initial position, the sealing block moves up again to seal the chamber. The falling-block mechanism was initially used only in single-shot rifles. A second example of this is shown below. This is a sporting rifle with Martini action. The falling block does not slide completely down, but is hinged at the front. The pivot can be seen immediately behind the aperture sight.

The falling-block action was also used in the Spencer carbine. Here the falling block was hinged at the front of the trigger guard lever, as can be seen clearly from the picture in the right top corner. The falling-block system is combined with an automatic cartridge supply system. Every time the trigger guard is operated and returned, one cartridge is fed from the tubular magazine in the stock. With the Winchester lever-action carbine, the falling-block action is combined with a kind of 'cartridge lift'. With every reloading cycle, a new cartridge is fed from the tubular magazine below the barrel.

When the lever/trigger guard is folded back, the cartridge lift slides up to align the cartridge to the barrel. If the lever is pushed all the way back, the falling-block action finally moves forward to push the cartridge into the chamber. The cartridge lift has been marked with a red arrow in the illustration below.

*Winchester falling-block action with cartridge lift*

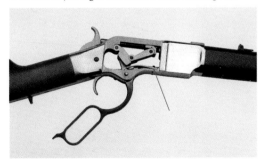

*Flobert rifle with Martini falling-block action*

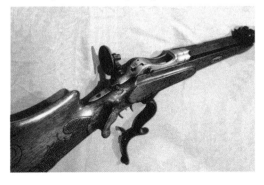

## Folding bolt action

Folding bolt actions come from a time when muzzle-loading rifles were converted to breech loaders and when a solution had to be found to safely seal the breech. Such a system is shown on the French Manceaux

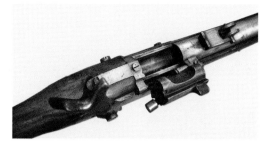

rifle from 1862. The ignition has remained unchanged, i.e. percussion, but the weapon can be reloaded faster and more effectively though the breech opening. Remarkable is its folding bolt action which also locks the sealing block.

Paper cartridges were already used for this rifle to avoid laborious reloading with loose components. A second example of the lateral folding bolt action is the Snider system. This was used to convert percussion rifles to centre-fire weapons. The rear end of the old percussion barrel was sawn off and the bolding bolt was attached to the tailpiece, using a large hinge. To fire a shot the shooter had to move the bolt sideways, slide a cartridge into the chamber and then move the bolt back. The picture shows how the firing pin runs through the sealing block. In the period from 1867 to 1870 the Dutch army had all its percussion rifles converted to the centre-fire system.

The Snider system was also used for this conversion, although in a slightly changed form. Characteristic here is the large cap at the back of the firing pin.

*Snider folding bolt*

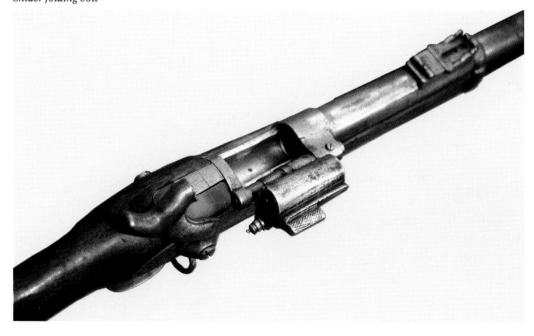

# Loading systems

## Muzzle loaders

Until roughly the 19th century all firearms had to be loaded manually through their muzzles. Such weapons are called muzzle loaders. First an amount of gunpowder was poured into the barrel from a powder flask after which the powder was rammed down using a ramrod. Then the bullet, sometimes wound in some cloth, was rammed down onto the powder using the same ramrod. The weapon was held in a vertical position for this purpose. Finally the shooter had to hold the weapon horizontally to put some fine priming powder into the priming pan before the weapon could be fired. In the flintlock period the first attempts at developing multi-shot weapons were undertaken.

The two- and four-barrelled pistols by the English gunsmith Twigg are examples of such attempts. It was not until the advent of the percussion lock that five- and six-shot

*French muzzle-loading pistol*

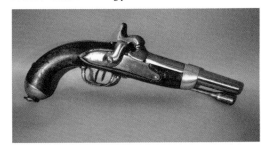

*English pepperbox*

revolvers were created at a large scale. These revolvers were also front loaders. They were either loaded by their muzzles, e.g. pepperboxes, or through the front of

*Colt percussion revolver with a ram below its barrel*

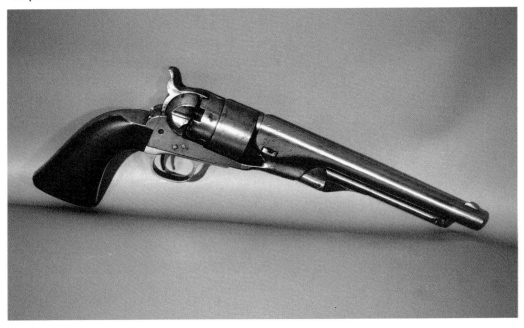

*Marlin tip-up revolver*

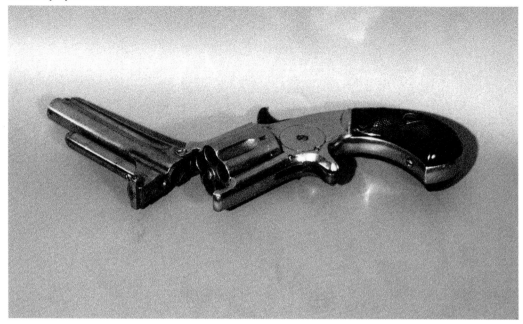

the cylinder. Percussion revolvers were mostly fitted with a ram below the barrel which could be undone and folded down to allow the rod to ram the bullet down in the cylinder. This method was not only used on handguns, but on rifles and carbines as well.

The ramrod for such long weapons was mostly housed in the front of the stock, below the barrel.

## The single-shot breech-loader

The first single-shot breech-loading rifles were built around 1850. They were often converted percussion muzzle-loaders.

An example of this is the 1867 Werndl rifle, where the rear barrel section of a percussion rifle was sawn off and replaced by a tailpiece with a loading gate, mostly a rotating or folding bolt.

A good example of a folding bolt is shown in the Baranow rifle in the lower picture. The cartridges had to be loaded separately, one by one, as follows: open the bolt, slide

one cartridge into the chamber, close the bolt, fire the cartridge, open the bolt, remove the spent case, etc.

*Werndl single-shot rifle with rotating bolt*

*Baranow single-shot rifle with folding bolt*

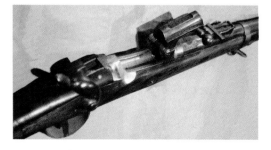

## 'Break-open' weapons

A major improvement in the loading speed was made possible with the introduction of firearms which broke open. The barrel could be folded up (tip-up system) or down to make the cylinder easily accessible. When the barrel of the Webley revolver displayed above was opened, the spent cases were ejected as well.

## The loading gate

A development that occurred almost simultaneously with this was the development of the single-action revolver with a fixed cylinder which could not be swung out of the gun. The cylinder chambers had to be loaded with cartridges via the loading gate one by one. The spent cases were similarly unloaded one by one. On most of these guns, a spring-loaded rod was fitted to eject the cases from the cylinder chambers. Sometimes the hammer had to be pulled to half-cock, or fully cocked, to allow the cylinder to be rotated from chamber to chamber by hand.

In later models the loading gate was connected to the firing mechanism for safety purposes, so that the weapon could not be fired when the loading gate was open. The manner of opening the loading gate could also differ in that sometimes it was swung sideways, or sometimes it was pulled back.

*Loading gate of a single-action revolver*

*Revolver with a loading gate that folds backwards*

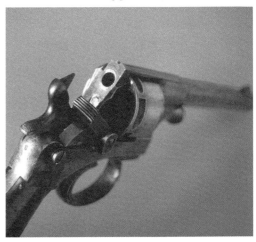

## The magazine

The development of the magazine did not get fully underway until 1870. The first type of magazine was housed in the stock, usually in front of the trigger guard. To load the magazine, a lever had to be pulled back to operate the bolt action.

A number of cartridges could then be pressed into the magazine through the bolt opening. Every time the lever was operated a new cartridge was taken from the maga-zine and fed into the breech. Magazines differed but each could hold only a limited number of cartridges. The cut-away picture below of the Mauser G98 rifle clearly shows the magazine.

The cartridge positioning and lifting plate is marked 1, the magazine spring is marked 2.

*Internal magazine of a Mauser G98 (1. cartridge positioning and lifting plate; 2. magazine spring)*

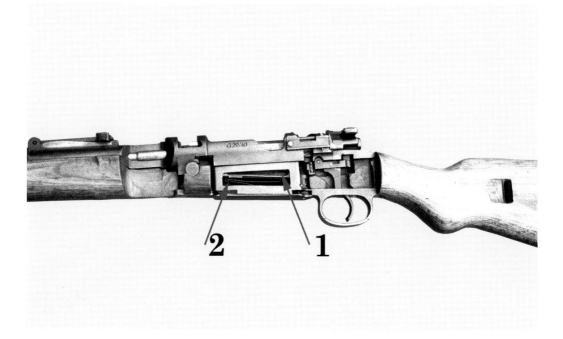

*Marlin lever-action carbine with a tubular magazine below the barrel*

At the top of the magazine there is a plate that holds the cartridges in position horizontally.

The magazine spring acts on this plate to raise the cartridges. An example of a fixed-type magazine with a large cartridge capacity is the steel magazine for the Beaumont–Vitali rifle. This magazine could be removed from the rifle for maintenance.

It was loaded through the bolt opening using clips. The spring steel clip held five cartridges that could be pushed into the magazine in one action. The strange bulge on the side of the magazine contained the magazine spring.

Another type of internal magazine is the so-called tubular magazine that was normally fitted below the barrel. As the name indi-

*Detail of the Marlin with the loading gate*

*Detail of a Winchester Hotchkiss rifle. The red arrow indicates the cartridge positioning element.*

cates, the cartridges were loaded into a tube. They were positioned nose to base. Dependent on the type and brand of gun the tubular magazine could be loaded from the bottom or through a gate on the side of the weapon.

The magazine spring pushed the cartridges backwards or forwards. The tubular magazine was mainly used for so-called lever-action repeating rifles. Every time the lever was operated, a cartridge was supplied from the tubular magazine and pushed into the breech by means of a cartridge lift or other system.

Another type of tubular magazine was housed in the stock. Here the coiled magazine spring supplied the cartridges from the rear of the magazine. The cartridges were now held in position by a round iron cap or stop as indicated by the red arrow in the photograph on page 46. As soon as the lever was pulled back, a new cartridge was pushed forward into the bolt opening. When the bolt was pushed forwards, the new cartridge was fed straight into the breech. A similar system was used for the Spencer carbine. This used a falling block that could be moved down by the lever/trigger guard. The Spencer carbine also contained the tubular magazine inside the stock.

## The swing-out cylinder

A revolver with a cylinder that could swing or fold out was extremely handy for the shooter. When the cylinder was swung out of the frame, it could be loaded and unloaded very easily. This system was introduced in the second half of the 19th century.

The cylinder was fitted to the frame by means of a sturdy hinge, the cylinder arm. This system is still used for modern revolvers.

*Guerriero pin-fire revolver with open cylinder*

# Sighting systems

Modern firearms are often fitted with intricate aiming devices such as the micrometre sight, or optically and electronically amplified telescopic sights.

Although technology was less advanced, the sighting systems used on antique firearms were often quite sophisticated for that time.

## The notched sight

Handguns, such as pistols and revolvers, were normally fitted with a fixed notch at the rear of the weapon. This was a small raised lip on the frame, in which the gunsmith made a V- or U-shaped notch. A vertical pin, the bead, was then fixed at the

*Fixed notch sight and bead of a German pin-fire revolver from 1870*

*Height-adjustable notch sight on a Remington carbine*

front of the barrel. If a firearm is aimed at the appropriate range with the notch and bead in line, the bullet should hit the target. At the time however, sights were not yet adjustable.

Therefore the only way in which they could be adapted to improve the sight picture was by raising or lowering the bead, or making the notch deeper by filing it out.

## The adjustable notched sight

A major improvement was the introduction of the adjustable notched sight. This was mainly used for rifles and carbines. The effective range of these firearms was longer, which brought its own difficulties. The trajectory of the bullet is always curved in some way; and is never 100% straight. The earliest types of firearm required some aiming experience.

To have some chance that a bullet would land somewhere near a far away target, the shooter had to compensate by aiming high above the target. Later a loose notched leaf was developed that could be slid up and down in the sight base to accommodate various ranges. A later step was to fit the sight base with lines indicating the approximate range to the target in feet.

*Adjustable notched sight on a Dutch Snider rifle*

*Folding sight with four notched leaves for various ranges*

*Adjustable notched sight on a Belgian Remington carbine*

certain range. To aim at a target, e.g. at 100 ft, the rifleman had to select the appropriate notched leaf. The graduations used on antique rifles to indicate these ranges differed from country to country. The British foot compared to metric 30.48 cm, the Antwerp foot was somewhat shorter, 28.7 cm, whereas the Amsterdam foot was only 28.31 cm.

## The bead

The bead is an element of the sighting system. It is used in combination with a notched leaf or with a fixed notched sight. Many shotguns have no notches, but use the strip between the two barrels for aiming.
If the rifleman just sees the small bead, he has aimed the rifle correctly. There has always been great variation in the sizes and

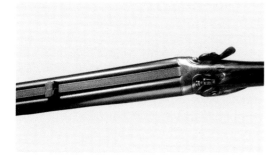

*Folding sight on a British double-barrelled rifle*

*Simple bead, combined with barrel band*

## The folding sight

Folding sights were mainly used for high-calibre, double-barrelled hunting rifles. To minimise any problems with protruding parts, the folding notched sight leaves were integrated in the strip between the two barrels.
The number of notched leaves could vary from two to six. Every leaf represented a

shapes of beads and it sometimes formed part of the barrel band. The problem with a bead that was attached to the barrel was that it was difficult to replace. For that reason gunsmiths in the mid-19th century started producing firearms with loose beads, as illustrated by the below photograph of a pin-fire revolver with a pointed bead on a high bead mount.

This was also the time when new types of bead were developed. Thus the Webley revolver had a bead with a square rear plate that was riveted to the barrel so that it could be replaced more easily. This allowed

*Pointed bead of a pin-fire revolver*

*Square bead of a Webley revolver*

for a more careful adjustment of the revolver by fitting a higher or lower bead plate.

*Simple graduated sight of the Gras rifle*

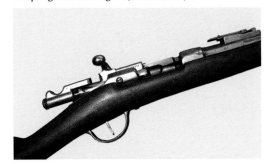

## The graduated sight

The graduated sight was the next step in the development of firearms. It was mainly used on military weapons. The range could be adjusted very precisely. The notched leaf could be slid up and down along a graduated ladder to change the point of impact of the bullet.

Early graduated sights were only height adjustable, but later sights also allowed lateral adjustment. A graduated sight is a very accurate sighting instrument that is still used on modern firearms as well. Most graduated sights were hinged at the front

*Graduated sight of the Chassepot rifle*

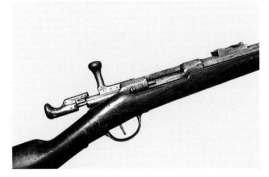

*Graduated sight of the Comblain rifle*

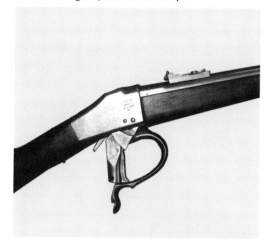

*Aperture sight*

of the sight base, but the English Snider rifle was hinged at its rear. It is not clear why this was done, but presumably it would allow the rifleman to adjust this type of graduated sight faster and more accurately.

## The aperture sight

The aperture sight is an extremely accurate precision instrument, but it is highly vulnerable because it protrudes high above the weapon. This was no problem for the sporting rifles produced by the end of the 19th

*Graduated sight of a British rifle with Snider conversion*

*Aperture sight of a Flobert rifle with Martini action*

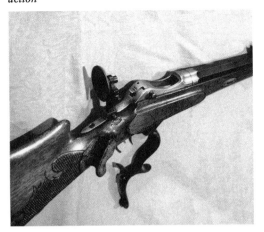

*Aperture sight on a Winchester carbine*

century, but it was virtually useless on hunting rifles and military weapons. A solution to this problem was found by developing folding aperture sights which were folded up before aiming the weapon and which were folded down to transport the firearm.

A beautiful example is the folding aperture sight on the double-barrelled Plaschil pinfire rifle which can be folded safely into the neck of the stock. Another example is the aperture sight that was used on Winchester long-range rifles.

## Telescopic sight

The first real telescopic sights were developed around 1860. They consisted of a long brass tube that was mounted onto the barrel by a number of rings. The front and rear openings of the tube had lenses to allow a rudimentary form of magnification.

The telescopic sights shown were popular with snipers during the American Civil War and with buffalo hunters as they allowed them to shoot at targets at great distances. Some marksmen of that time were famous for their accuracy with targets out to 1000 yards.

*Aperture sight of a hunting rifle*

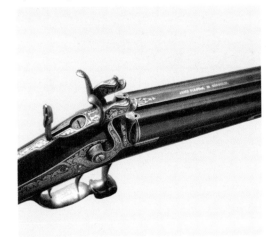

*Telescopic sights from 1860*

# Ammunition

Initially firearms were mainly loaded with rocks or bronze balls. In c. 1450 these were replaced by lead balls that were cast to match the inside barrel diameter. In those days all barrels were smooth instead of rifled and their reach and accuracy were not impressive. When loading, first the gunpowder was poured into the barrel through the muzzle, after which a felt wad was inserted to seal the charge. Then the soft, lead bullet was inserted and rammed down in the barrel. As a result of the ramming action the bullet was deformed a little to take on the exact inner diameter of the barrel, so that the gas pressure caused by the gunpowder being detonated could not escape around the lead bullet. Since it took a lot of time to load a firearm, the effectiveness of military firearms was quite low. Around 1540, a faster gun-loading method was discovered. The gunpowder and the lead bullet were housed together in a paper case: the so-called paper cartridge,

although as yet this contained no ignition agent. Sometimes glue or shellac was applied to the paper cartridges to protect them from moisture and in later types of cartridge the paper was sometimes replaced by linen.

When the gun was loaded, the rear of the paper cartridge was torn loose, so that a fixed quantity of gunpowder was deposited in the barrel. Then a ramrod was used to ram down the rest of the cartridge, paper and all. Finally a few grains of priming powder were put in the priming pan and the weapon was ready to be fired. The paper cartridge would be used for a long time, even after the introduction of the percussion system around 1800. The

*Paper cartridge: 1. paper case, 2. black powder charge, 3. lead bullet, 4. ropes for sealing*

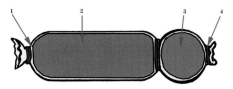

*Round lead bullets (photograph courtesy of Remington)*

percussion cap is a soft brass case filled with a primer. The percussion cap was placed on a nipple at the rear end of the barrel. After the trigger was pulled, the cock struck forward to detonate the primer with a heavy blow. Percussion caps are still used for percussion guns, nowadays. The invention of the primer or 'fulminate' used in these caps is ascribed to the Scottish clergyman, Alexander Forsyth from Belhelvie in Aberdeenshire.

The cap itself is supposed to be the result of the combined developments of several gunsmiths. In 1816, a number of British gunsmiths, including Joseph Egg, Joseph Manton and James Purdey, introduced different percussion weapons with corresponding percussion caps of their own making. Two years later the French gunmakers Deboubert and Prélat invented similar systems, while Joshua Shaw patented the percussion cap in his own name in America. Johann Niklaus von

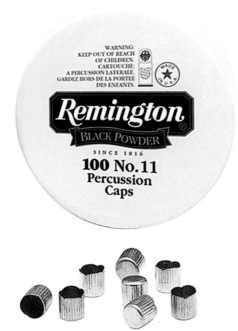

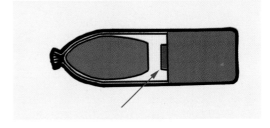

Dreyse of Sommerda in Germany was working on an improved version of the percussion cap in 1814, using a priming fulminate developed by a Frenchman, Bertholet. Together with his partner Carl Collenbusch he founded the Dreyse & Collenbusch Zündhütchenfabrik in 1817.

In those days the production of percussion caps was quite a costly matter and for that reason the German Army asked Dreyse to look into ways of reusing spent percussion caps. His first attempts seemed successful, but the reused caps caused too many problems, making the effective use of firearms difficult. Dreyse then decided to place a loose amount of priming fulminate in the centre of a cartridge so that the expensive brass cup was no longer necessary. This resulted in one of the first self-contained cartridges: the Dreyse needle-fire cartridge. Then in 1828 he introduced his first needle-fire rifle.

This was a muzzle-loading rifle which he converted into a real breech-loader in 1836. In 1840, this rifle was introduced by the Prussian Army as the 'Ordonnanzgewehr'. The drawing above shows a Dreyse needle-fire cartridge with the priming pellet indicated by a red arrow.

At that time it was a problem to effectively seal the barrel and control the gas pressure of the ignited powder so that it could be used effectively to propel the bullet. Any gas pressure leakage resulted in a decreased effective bullet range. Many experiments were carried out using expanding bullets. In most systems a hollow space was

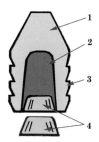

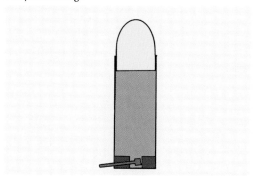

provided in the rear of the bullet into which a wedge-shaped piece of iron was clamped. The gas pressure would drive this wedge into the bullet which then expanded. A similar principle was invented by the French Army officer Henry Gustave Delvigne in 1826 and further developed by his colleague, Charles Claude Etienne Minié in 1847. One of the improvements made by Minié was the use of grooves in the side of the bullet to create a better gas seal.

The name Casimir Lefaucheux is closely related with the pin-fire cartridge which he patented in 1836. This was a self-contained cartridge with a brass case. A small pin protruded from the side of the case at the bottom. The priming fulminate inside the case was ignited by striking this pin with the hammer. However, Lefaucheux was not the first gunsmith to use this system. In 1829, another Frenchman, Pottet, had already developed a similar cartridge with a pin located centrally in the bottom of the case.

A fellow countryman, Le Page, received a patent on a similar ignition system in 1832. However, Lefaucheux was the most successful and he built a great number of revolvers and shotguns in various calibres for his pin-fire cartridges. In 1854, the well-known Horace Smith and Daniel B. Wesson founded the Volcanic Repeating Arms Company in New Haven, Connecticut. They produced the Volcanic

pistol that fired a novel cartridge after experimenting with a type of self-contained cartridge which required no case. The black powder and the primer were packed together in the hollow bullet head. When they needed money to invest in a new factory for rim-fire revolvers in 1855 they sold their factory and the patent to Oliver Winchester.

Louis Nicole Auguste Flobert, a gunsmith from Paris, developed the first rim-fire cartridge in 1848 as an improved version of an 1846 patent of Houllier, a fellow countryman. The name rim-fire refers to the location of the priming fulminate in the brass case: inside the rim at the bottom of the case. In fact the first Flobert cartridges were no more than an extended percussion cap with a round bullet clamped on top. The introduction of his cartridge at the

Volcanic cartridge: 1. cork disk, 2. seat for the cork disk, 3. seat for the priming pellet, 4. priming pellet, 5. powder charge, 6. bullet body

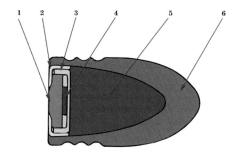

Great Exhibition in London in 1851 was a great success, so much so that Smith and Wesson patented this cartridge for the American continent in 1854. After this they bought the patent for a revolver with drilled-through cylinder chambers owned by Rollin White in 1855. Their monopoly made it impossible for competing American gun factories to make revolvers with drilled-through cylinders until 1872. The .22 Short cartridge was developed in the United States on the basis of the 6-mm Flobert cartridge. In 1857, Smith and Wesson introduced the first revolver for this calibre, appropriately named the 'First Model'. This revolver was intended for target shooting, but it was also considered a serious self-defence weapon. Originally the cartridge had a 1.9-g bullet and a 0.26-g black powder charge.

It was not until 1927 that the Remington Company introduced a non-corrosive primer composition. Up until then the priming fulminate in all cartridges consisted of mercury, potassium chlorate and sulphuric antimony and barrels were seriously affected by the sulphuric and chlorine compounds. Strictly speaking the .22 Long cartridge can be seen as a kind of transition phase from the .22 Short to the .22 LR. This calibre was introduced in 1871. The .22 Long cartridge originally had a 1.9-g lead bullet and a 0.32-g black powder charge. The popularity of the .22 Long decreased after the introduction of the .22 LR cartridge in 1887. The .22 LR

*Overview of well-known Flobert cartridges. From the left to the right: 6-mm Flobert, .22-Short, .22-Long, .22-L.R. (Long Rifle)*

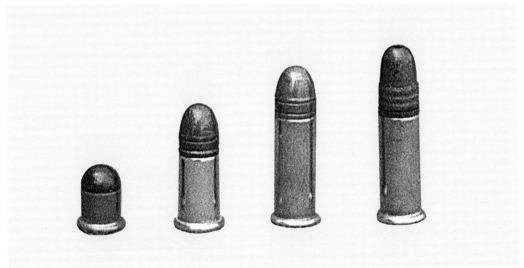

*Cup-priming cartridge: 1. case, 2. bullet, 3. powder charge, 4. priming fulminate*

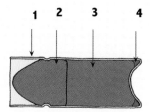

*Teat cartridge: 1. case, 2. bullet, 3. black powder charge, 4. priming fulminate*

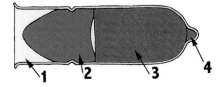

*Cut-away drawing of a case: A. case, B. case base, C. percussion cap opening, D. Boxer primer vent (photograph courtesy of Remington)*

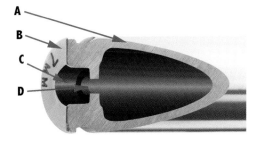

*Percussion cap of a shot cartridge (photograph courtesy of Remington)*

cartridge is said to have been developed by the American J. Stevens Arms and Tool Company in 1887. This cartridge originally had a 2.6-g bullet with 0.32 g of black powder to propel it. The monopoly enjoyed by Smith and Wesson forced other manufacturers to look for ways of evading the patent rights. One such attempt led to the cup-priming system. This was also a type of rim-fire cartridge, but then used in a revolver which did not have drilled-through cylinder chambers. The inventors, William C. Ellis and John N. White, patented this principle in 1859 and 1863. The cup-priming cartridge was loaded from the front of the cylinder chambers. Small slots had been cut into the rear of the cylinder chambers.

The tip of the hammer could strike through these slots to hit the rim of the cartridge. Another example from this time was the Teat cartridge, patented by David Williams in 1864. This cartridge was made for a revolver produced by the Moore's Patent Fire Arms Company. When developing this revolver Moore not only had to consider the Smith and Wesson patent, but he had to take the patent rights to the cup-priming system into account as well. This cartridge was also loaded from the front of the cylinder chambers. Small openings had been made into the rear of the cylinder chambers so that the tip of the hammer could strike through these openings. The priming fulminate had been placed centrally on the round interior base of the cartridge case. The first real centre-fire cartridges were

*Drawing of a case base with a percussion cap: 1. case base, 2. percussion cap, 3. primer composition, 4. anvil, 5. black powder charge (photograph courtesy of Remington)*

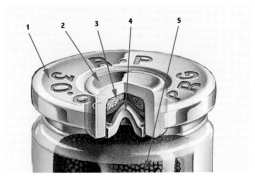

made around 1860. Initially they were filled with a black powder charge, but after 1892 black powder was replaced by smokeless or nitro-propellants. The centre-fire cartridge has a hole in the centre of the case base. A loose percussion cap was fitted into this hole. The cartridge bottom over which the percussion cap fits has one or more priming vents to ignite the powder charge. In 1866, Hiram Berdan, a general in the American Army, developed the centre-fire ignition system for metal cartridges together with A.C. Hobbs of the Union Metallic Company. Typical of the Berdan system are the two or three vents over the percussion cap. In Great Britain, Col. Edward Mounier Boxer was granted a patent to the Boxer ignition system in 1866. This system only used one central vent. Boxer ignition has been the most popular system for many years now.

# Miniature firearms

Miniature firearms were already collected as early as the 19th century. Often they were exact replicas of existing weapons that could be fired really. Famous examples are the miniature Colt revolvers and many flint-lock and pin-fire guns. These weapons could even be worn on a watch chain, and sometimes ladies from the upper classes would wear them as earrings. The more exclusive firearms were mostly made as complete sets, in a beautiful wooden case, with a powder flask and even little tools to make bullets, etc.

Many of these weapons were made and sold as commercial merchandise. They were also made by apprentices to qualify for the gunsmiths' guilds. Renowned names in this field are the Egg family and Joseph

*Vachon Peavy Knife & Pistol set*

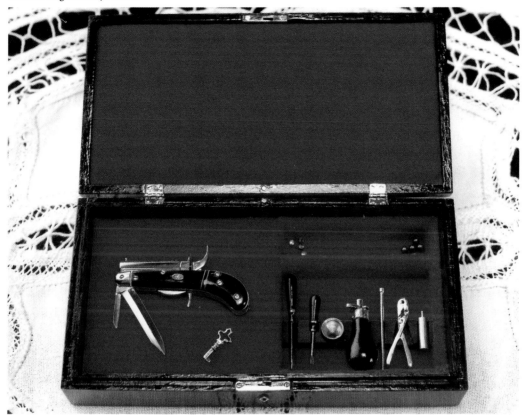

Childs of London. Major collections of miniature firearms can be found in museums such as the Hermitage in St Petersburg, the Metropolitan in New York and the Victoria and Albert Museum in London. Prices for these miniatures can be quite high, especially if the sets are complete. Miniature firearms are still produced today, e.g. by the Canadian knife and gunsmith Yvon Vachon. Some examples of his products are described on these pages.

## *Yvon Vachon peavy knife and pistol set*

The miniature stiletto with integrated percussion pistol. The total length is only 1–1/8" (28.6 mm). The blade has been made of ATS-34 steel. The ramrod is housed in the buffalo horn handle. The bolsters, screws and hammer are 14-carat gold.

The Chacahvante wood case contains: the powder flask, a bullet mould, screwdrivers, a small powder funnel and a powder dispenser.

## *Yvon Vachon English knife pistol*

A combination of a stiletto and a percussion pistol with a length of 1–3/8" (34.9 mm). The larger blade is the stiletto, the smaller one is a regular folding blade. Both have been made of ATS-34 steel. The screws, the safety catch and the hammer are 10-carat gold.

The handle has been made of African Blackwood. It has a compartment for stor-

*Vachon Percussion Cutlass Pistol*

ing the bullets. The case is ebony. It has a stainless steel lock with two 10-carat gold keys.

### Yvon Vachon percussion cutlass pistol

The total length of this miniature dagger and percussion pistol is 3.75" (95.3 mm). The blade has been made of ATS-34 steel. The screws are 10-carat gold. The handle and sheath are made of snake wood, as is the case that houses the entire set.

*Vachon sword with flintlock pistol*

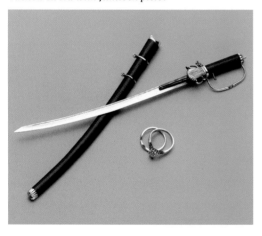

### Yvon Vachon reproduction of the Unwin and Rodgers percussion knife pistol of 1845

Miniature of an original knife pistol produced by Unwin and Rodgers in 1845. The scale of the reproduction is 1:4, its length is 1.63" (41.3 mm).

The handle is buffalo horn and has a hidden compartment to store the bullets. All screws and pins are 10-carat gold. The entire set is housed in a snake wood case.

*Vachon–Unwin and Rodgers Percussion Knife Pistol 1845*

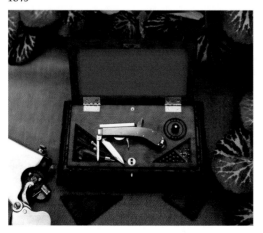

### Vachon sword with flintlock pistol

A miniature sword with a miniature flintlock pistol in its handle. The total length is 6.75" (171.5 mm). The handle and the sheath are acacia wood. The decorations are 10-carat gold.

The miniature is supplied complete with all components, such as flints, powder flask, bullet mould, screwdrivers, powder funnel, bullets and a powder charger, housed in a mahogany case.

# Exploded views

The expression 'exploded view' refers to two-dimensional drawings of all components in a machine or device, such as a firearm. In this encyclopedia of antique firearms we are using some specific expressions which may not be clear to the reader. These drawings will help you quickly find the names of the components. Most firearms work according to a common system and these exploded views will make it easier to understand their operation.Not all the names for all tiny pins, screws and springs in the drawings are indicated. We have limited ourselves to the main components.

Exploded view of a Colt Baby Dragoon

percussion revolver with a so-called 'open frame', so without an upper strip over the cylinder joining the barrel and the hammer sections.

1. barrel
2. bead
3. frame
4. cylinder
4a. nipple
5. cylinder axis pin
6. trigger
7. cylinder stop
8. hammer
9. lever
10. trigger spring
11. hammer spring
12. trigger guard with sub-frame
12a. back of grip
13. grip

*Exploded view of a Colt Baby Dragoon*

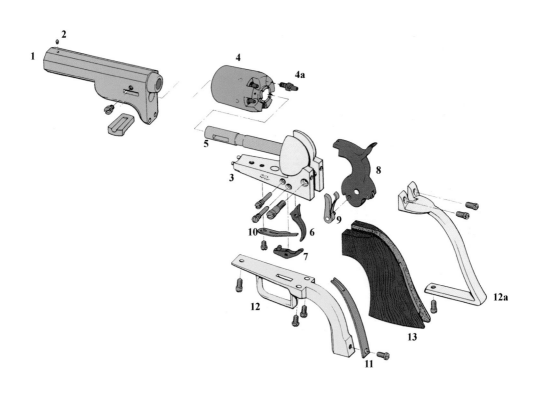

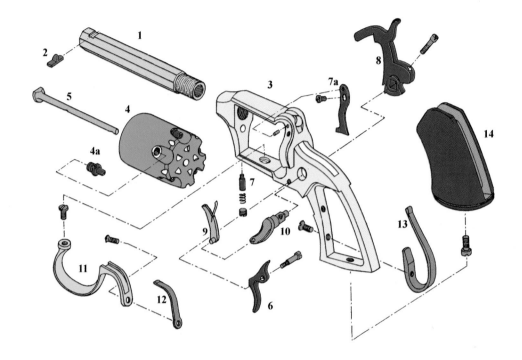

Exploded view of a Remington percussion revolver with a closed frame, so with a strip over the cylinder.

1. barrel
2. bead
3. frame
4. cylinder
4a. nipple
5. cylinder axis pin
6. trigger
7. cylinder stop catch
7a. cylinder stop catch spring
8. hammer
9. lever
10. hammer pin
11. trigger guard
12. trigger spring
13. hammer spring
14. grip

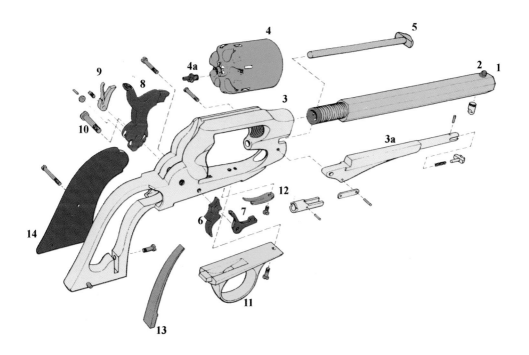

Exploded view of a Remington New Army percussion revolver with a closed frame and a loading lever below the barrel to load the (round) bullets into the cylinder chambers from the front.

1. barrel
2. bead
3. frame
3a. loading lever
4. cylinder
4a nipple
5. cylinder axis pin
6. trigger
7. cylinder stop catch
8. hammer
9. lever
10. hammer pin
11. trigger guard
12. trigger spring
13. hammer spring
14. grip plate

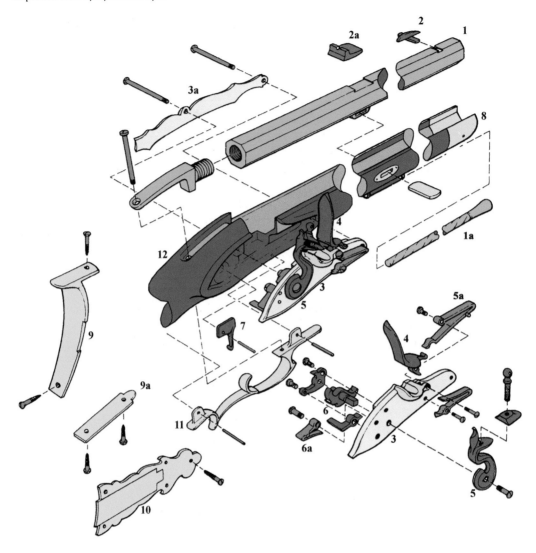

The following list gives the names of the various parts shown in the exploded view of a flintlock rifle displayed above.

1. barrel
1a. ramrod
2. bead
3. lock plate
3a. left lock plate
4. steel plate
5. cock
5a. cock spring
6. tumbler
6a. tumbler spring
7. trigger
8. barrel band
9. stock plate
9a. stock bedplate
10. patch box
11. trigger guard
12. stock

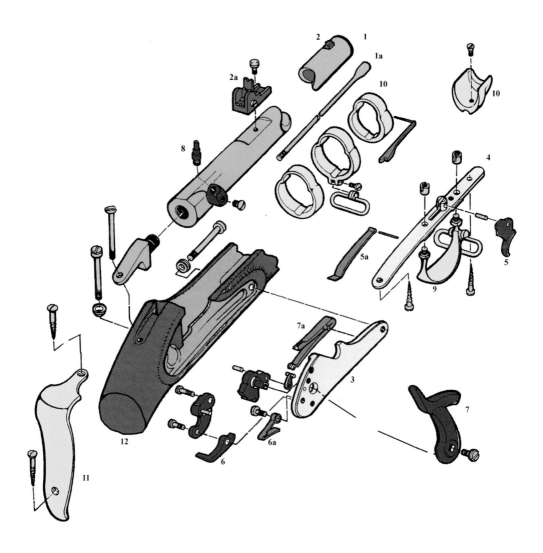

Exploded view of a Springfield Model 1861 percussion rifle

1. barrel
1a. ramrod
2. bead
2a. sight
3. lock plate
4. trigger guard plate
5. trigger
5a. trigger spring
6. tumbler
6a. tumbler spring
7. hammer
7a. hammer spring
8. nipple
9. trigger guard
10. barrel bands
11. stock plate
12. stock

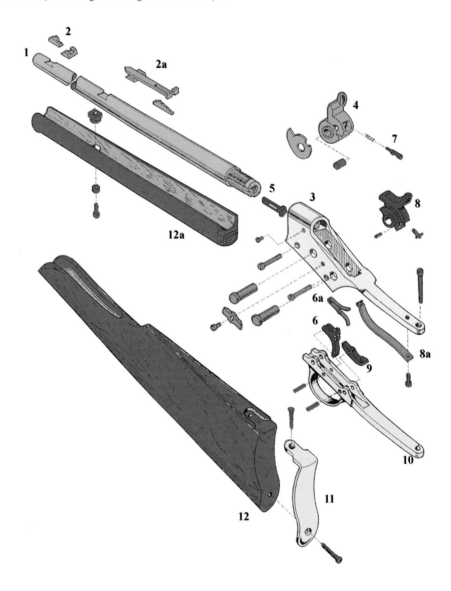

Exploded view of a Remington rolling block action rifle

| | |
|---|---|
| 1. barrel | 6a. trigger spring |
| 2. bead | 7. firing pin |
| 2a. sight | 8. hammer |
| 3. frame | 8a. hammer spring |
| 4. bolt | 9. tumbler |
| 5. cartridge ejector | 10. trigger guard |
| 6. trigger | 11. stock plate |
| | 12. stock |
| | 12a. forward grip |

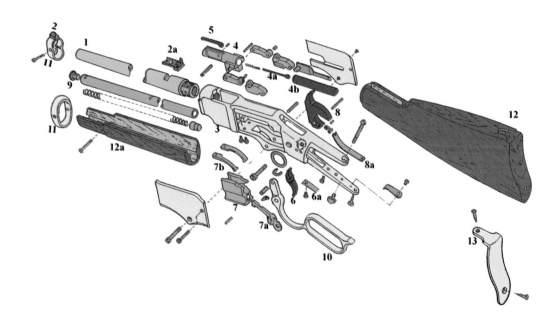

Exploded view of a Winchester Model 1866 repeating lever-action rifle

1 barrel
2. bead
2a. sight
3. frame
4. bolt (with the green coloured parts of the falling block action on both sides)
4a. firing pin
4b. firing pin block
5. cartridge ejector
6. triggerr
6a. trigger spring
7. cartridge lift
7a. cartridge lift rod
8. hammer
8a. hammer spring
9. tubular magazine
10. trigger guard (also lever for repeating action)
11. barrel band
12. stock
12a. forward grip
13. stock plate

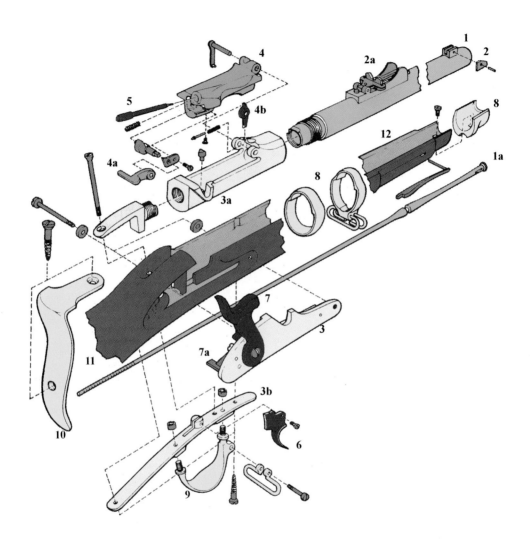

Exploded view of a Springfield Model 1873
Trapdoor (folding bolt) rifle

1. barrel
1a. cleaning rod
2. bead
2a. sight
3. lock plate
3a. tailpiece
4. bolt

4a. bolt lever
5. firing pin
6. trigger
7. hammer
8. barrel band
9. trigger guard
10. stock plate
11. stock
12. forward grip

*Exploded view of a Mauser K98 bolt-action rifle*

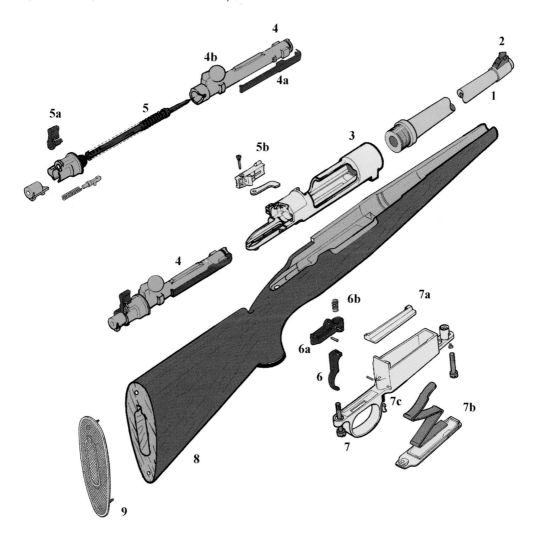

Exploded view of a Mauser K98 bolt-action rifle

1   barrel
2.  bead
3.  tailpiece
4.  bolt
4a. cartridge extractor
4b. bolt lever
5.  firing pin
5a. butterfly safety catch

5b. bolt stop
6.  trigger
6a. tumbler
6b. tumbler spring
7.  trigger guard with magazine housing
7a. (cartridge magazine) loader
7b. magazine spring with magazine lid
7c. magazine lid catch
8.  stock
9.  stock plate

*Bartl double-barrelled hunting rifle, c. 1880*

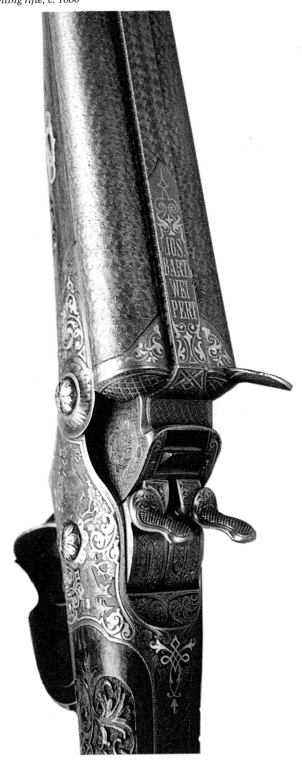

# 1 Austrian firearms from 1710 to 1898

## Maurer flintlock rifle, c. 1710

**TECHNICAL SPECIFICATIONS**

| | |
|---|---|
| Calibre | : 15.2 mm (.60") |
| Cartridge capacity | : single-shot |
| Operation | : single-action |
| Firing system | : flintlock |
| Breach-loading | : N/A |
| Length | : 120 cm (47.2") |
| Barrel length | : 76.2 cm (30") |
| Weight | : 3.9 kg (8.6 lb) |
| Sight | : folding sight |
| Safety | : half-cock and grip safety |
| Stock | : walnut |

*Specific details*: An elaborately decorated flintlock rifle, made around 1710 by the Austrian gunsmith Elias Maurer from Vienna. This rifle has a folding sight for various ranges. The rifle has an adjustable trigger and an accelerator (front 'trigger'). Highly unusual for those days is the extra safety in the rear end of the extended trigger guard.

When this is squeezed the trigger lock is released. For this reason the round end of the trigger guard, just behind the trigger, is not fixed to the lock plate. There are only

*Maurer flintlock rifle c. 1710*

*Safety system on Maurer rifle*

few examples of similar safety systems from that time.

## Austrian Cavalry pistol, conversion 1844

**TECHNICAL SPECIFICATIONS**

| | |
|---|---|
| Calibre | : 16.9 mm (.66") |
| Cartridge capacity | : single-shot |
| Operation | : single-action |
| Firing system | : priming tube lock |
| Breach-loading | : N/A |
| Length | : 420 mm (16.5") |
| Barrel length | : 215 mm (8.5") |
| Weight | : 1550 g (54.7 oz) |
| Sight | : bead only |
| Safety | : half-cock |
| Grip | : nut |

Specific details: The Augustin-type conversion system was used to convert Austrian flintlock pistols to the priming tube lock system for percussion firearms.

This system was invented by several people including Augustin and Console. The weapon was loaded via the muzzle with a

*Austrian Cavalry pistol, conversion 1844*

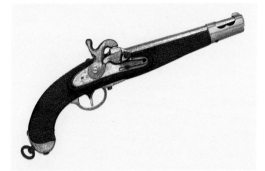

*Siegel rifle owned by Emperor Franz-Joseph.*

paper cartridge. Before sliding the cartridge into the barrel, the paper around the cartridge had to be torn to make the powder easily accessible for the flash from the priming tube.

The priming tube section could be folded up to allow the priming tube to be installed in the ignition system. The first weapons that were converted to the Augustin system were the Austrian infantry rifles around 1840, followed by the handguns. The first new army rifles that incorporated this system were manufactured in 1842. In 1854 the Austrian Army changed over to the percussion system with the percussion cap.

*Details of double-barrelled Siegel rifle*

## Double-barrelled Siegel rifle owned by Emperor Franz-Joseph, c. 1850

**TECHNICAL SPECIFICATIONS**

| | |
|---|---|
| Calibre | : 11.4 mm (.450") |
| Cartridge capacity | : double-barrelled, single-shot |
| Operation | : single-action |
| Firing system | : percussion |
| Breach-loading | : N/A |
| Length | : 120.5 cm (47.4") |
| Barrel length | : 73.6 cm (29") |
| Weight | : 3.6 kg (7.9 lb) |
| Sight | : folding sight |
| Safety | : half-cock |
| Stock | : walnut |

*Specific details*: A double-barrelled rifle, made by Johann Siegel of Salzburg around

1850. Emperor Ferdinand I ruled over Austria-Hungary until 1848, when he abdi-

*Details of double-barrelled Siegel rifle*

cated in favour of his nephew Franz-Joseph. The gun in the picture belonged to the Emperor Franz-Joseph. The cover of the patchbox in the stock is exquisitely engraved.

## Set of Mang percussion pistols, c. 1855

**TECHNICAL SPECIFICATIONS**

| | |
|---|---|
| Calibre | : 13.2 mm (.52") |
| Cartridge capacity | : single-shot |
| Operation | : single-action |
| Firing system | : percussion |
| Breach-loading | : N/A |
| Length | : 420 mm (16.5") |
| Barrel length | : 260 mm (10.2") |
| Weight | : 1100 g (38.8 oz) |
| Sight | : keepsight |
| Safety | : half-cock |
| Grip | : walnut |

*Specific details*: A pistol set made by the Austrian gunsmith Martin Mang in the period 1850/1855. Both target-shooting pistols and duelling pistols were built in those days.

## Wanzl Model 1854/67 conversion

**TECHNICAL SPECIFICATIONS**

| | |
|---|---|
| Kaliber | : 13.7 mm (.54") |
| Cartridge capacity | : single-shot |
| Operation | : single-action |
| Firing system | : rim-fire |
| Breach-loading | : folding bolt |
| Length | : 132,7 cm (52.25") |
| Barrel length | : 87.6 cm (34.5") |
| Weight | : 5.6 kg (12.3 lb) |
| Sight | : graduated sight |
| Safety | : half-cock hammer |
| Stock | : walnut |

*Specific details*: In 1867, the Emperor Franz-Joseph I decided that the existing percussion army rifles should be converted into breech-loaders. The Austrian War Department selected the Wanzl system, developed by the Viennese gunsmith Wanzl. He had improved the Swiss Amsler-Millbank system, with a bolt that could be opened by folding it forwards to allow the cartridge to be loaded into the breech. Application of the Wanzl conversion was only a temporary solution, as the Werndl rifle was already selected as the army rifle in 1867 as well.

*Wanzl Model 1854/67 conversion*

*Set of Mang percussion pistols, c. 1855*

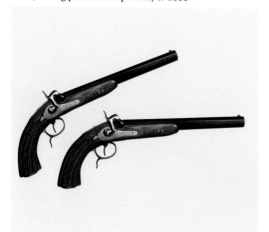

*Werndl rifle Model 1867*

rifle with its rotating bolt action together with his Czech partner Karel Holub. Werndl had owned a gun factory, the Öster-reichische Waffenfabrik Gesellschaft, in Steyr since 1864. In 1868, Werndl also made a cavalry carbine with a 56-cm (22") long barrel. This rifle initially fired a straight-cased 11.4 mm cartridge. The calibre was changed to 11.15 x 58R in 1877 and the rifles that had already been produced were modified. The new calibre had a bottle-neck case.

## Werndl rifle Model 1867

### TECHNICAL SPECIFICATIONS

| | |
|---|---|
| Kaliber | : 11.4 mm (.45"), later 11.15 x 58R |
| Cartridge capacity | : single-shot |
| Operation | : single-action |
| Firing system | : centre-fire |
| Breach-loading | : rotating bolt |
| Length | : 128 cm (50.4") |
| Barrel length | : 84.3 cm (33.2") |
| Weight | : 4.5 kg (9.9 lb) |
| Sight | : graduated sight |
| Safety | : half-cock hammer |
| Stock | : walnut |

*Specific details*: This was introduced by the Austrian Army in 1867 and used until approximately 1886. Werndl designed this

*Details of the Werndl M1867 rifle*

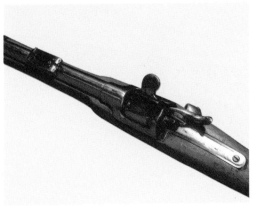

## Plaschil pin-fire shotgun, c. 1870

### TECHNICAL SPECIFICATIONS

| | |
|---|---|
| Calibre | : 12 |
| Cartridge capacity | : double-barrelled, single-shot |
| Operation | : single-action |
| Firing system | : pin-fire |
| Breach-loading | : barrel lock action |
| Length | : 118 cm (46.5") |
| Barrel length | : 76 cm (30") |
| Weight | : 2.9 kg (6.4 lb) |
| Sight | : bead |
| Safety | : half-cock hammer |
| Stock | : walnut |

*Specific details*: A 19th century double-barrelled shotgun by Josef Plaschil from Napagedl in the Austrian-Hungarian Empire. The gun was built for calibre 12

*Plaschil pin-fire shotgun, c. 1870*

revolver thinking it was a good way to win the King's favour.

pin-fire shot cartridges. An interesting feature is the folding sight in the neck of the stock.

## Gasser Montenegro revolver, c. 1875

**TECHNICAL SPECIFICATIONS**

| | |
|---|---|
| Calibre | : 10.7 mm (.42") |
| Cartridge capacity | : 5-shot |
| Operation | : single-action |
| Firing system | : centre-fire |
| Breach-loading | : N/A |
| Length | : 264 mm (10.4") |
| Barrel length | : 135 mm (5.3") |
| Weight | : 940 g (33 oz) |
| Sight | : fixed notch through upper bridge, bead |
| Safety | : half-cock hammer |
| Grip | : walnut |

*Specific details*: An Austrian revolver made by the Gasser company. This factory made several different revolvers for various customers including the Austrian-Hungarian Army in the period from 1862 to 1890.

The word Montenegro is a collective name for these types of weapon and had no brand name. Nicolas, the King of Montenegro, is said to have had a major financial interest in the Gasser plant. In fact many influential people bought such a

## Steyr Guedes–Castro M1885 rifle

**TECHNICAL SPECIFICATIONS**

| | |
|---|---|
| Calibre | : 8 X 60 mmR |
| Cartridge capacity | : single-shot |
| Operation | : single-action |
| Firing system | : centre-fire |
| Breach-loading | : falling block action (modified Martini-Henry action) |
| Length | : 1217 cm (47.9") |
| Barrel length | : 84.5 cm (33.25") |
| Weight | : 4.1 kg (9 lb) |
| Sight | : adjustable graduated sight |
| Safety | : safety sear immediately behind the trigger |
| Stock | : walnut |

*Specific details*: This was designed by Luis Guedes Dias, an officer in the Portuguese Army, in the period 1882/1884. This rifle was initially made in an 11-mm calibre, but this was changed as a result of the intro-

*Steyr Guedes-Castro M1885 rifle (photograph: F. Vink)*

duction of smokeless powder for French army guns in 1885. The Austrian Steyr factory built some 40,000 Guedes rifles for the Portuguese Army in 1885 and 1886. This weapon was already being replaced by the Kropatschek rifle with an 8-shot tubular magazine below its barrel in March 1886. As a result a large share of the rifles that were ordered, were never bought by the Portuguese government. In 1895 some 2700 of these rifles were sold to Transvaal in South Africa, followed by another 5000 in 1897. The Orange Free State bought another 3500 Steyr Guedes rifles in 1898. These rifles played an important role in the second Boer War against Great Britain from 1899 to 1902. Strangely enough the sale of these rifles was transacted after mediation by the British firm of Alfred Field & Company of Birmingham.

## Steyr M1886 rifle

**TECHNICAL SPECIFICATIONS**

| | |
|---|---|
| Calibre | : 8 x 50R mm |
| Cartridge capacity | : 5-shot |
| Operation | : single-action |
| Firing system | : centre-fire |
| Breach-loading | : bolt action with breech-sealing lugs |
| Length | : 128 cm (50.38") |
| Barrel length | : 76.5 cm (30.1") |
| Weight | : 4.4 kg (9.7 lb) |
| Sight | : graduated sight |
| Safety | : catch on rear of bolt |
| Stock | : wooden stock and forward grip |

*Steyr M1886 rifle*

*Specific details*: Josef Wendl founded the company Josef und Franz Wendl & Comp. in Steyr together with his brother Franz in 1864. Two years later he tried to convince the Austrian War Department that his Werndl–Holub breech-loading rifle should be issued to the entire Austrian Army. After extensive testing by the Army they commissioned the manufacture of 100,000 Model 1867 rifles by Wendl. The factory in Steyr was enlarged and a subsidiary was opened up in Budapest. Due to these investments the company ran into financial difficulties. Werndl decided to strengthen the company by issuing shares and changed it into the Österreichische Waffenfabriks-Gesellschaft ('OWG') with Vienna as its registered office. In 1873, the Royal Prussian Army commissioned Werndl to manufacture no less than 500,000 Mauser Model 1871 rifles. After that Werndl was flooded with orders from the French, Persian, Rumanian, Greek, Chinese and Chilean governments. Production of a new breech-loading rifle with a 5-cartridge magazine with Mannlicher action started in 1885. The company immediately received an order for 87,000 of these rifles. Josef Werndl died of pneumonia in 1899. The company was continued by a four-man committee until 1896 when its management was taken over by Otto Schönauer.

## Steyr M1895 rifle

**TECHNICAL SPECIFICATIONS**

| | |
|---|---|
| Calibre | : 8 x 56R mm |
| Cartridge capacity | : 5-shot |
| Operation | : single-action |
| Firing system | : centre-fire |
| Breach-loading | : bolt action with breech-sealing lugs |
| Length | : 127 cm (50") |
| Barrel length | : 76.5 cm (30.1") |
| Weight | : 3.8 kg (8.3 lb) |
| Sight | : graduated sight |
| Safety | : catch on rear of bolt |
| Stock | : wooden stock and forward grip |

*Steyr M1895 rifle*

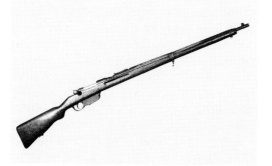

*Steyr M1895/96 carbine with extended bayonet*

*Specific details*: In 1892, the M1886 was found to have been outdated in comparison to the arms used in other European countries and the Austrian government decided to look for a replacement. This was found in the M1895 rifle that was introduced with the Austrian-Hungarian Army in 1895. This rifle had a bolt that was pulled back in a straight line, without the need to rotate it. The Bulgarian Army started using this weapon in 1897. The magazine was loaded with a cartridge clip that fell out of the bottom of the magazine after the last shot was fired. This is not really a rare weapon as more than 3.5 million of these rifles were made.

## Steyr M1895/96 carbine

**TECHNICAL SPECIFICATIONS**
Calibre          : 8 x 56R mm
Cartridge capacity : 5-shot
Operation        : single-action

*Steyr M1895/96 carbine*

| Firing system | : centre-fire |
| Breach-loading | : bolt action with breech-sealing lugs |
| Length | : 100.3 cm (39.5") |
| Barrel length | : 49.9 cm (19.65") |
| Weight | : 3.4 kg (7.5 lb) |
| Sight | : graduated sight |
| Safety | : catch on rear of bolt |
| Stock | : wooden stock and forward grip |

*Specific details*: This was derived from the M1895 rifle and designed as a short rifle with two versions. The first one is an M1895 cavalry carbine without a bayonet and with a 19.7" (50-cm) barrel. The second version was the M1895 Repetier-Stützen which also had a 19.7" (50-cm) barrel, plus a folding bayonet.

## Rast & Gasser Ordonnanz Revolver Model 1998

**TECHNICAL SPECIFICATIONS**
Calibre          : 8 mm Rast & Gasser
Cartridge capacity : 8-shot
Operation        : double-action
Firing system    : centre-fire
Breach-loading   : N/A
Length           : 225 mm (8.9")
Barrel length    : 115 mm (4.5")
Weight           : 915 g (32.3 oz)
Sight            : fixed
Safety           : hammer locked when loading gate is open
Grip             : nut

*Specific details*: This was produced by Rast & Gasser of Vienna. This weapon was introduced into the Austrian Army in 1898. When the loading gate on the right-hand side of the frame is opened the hammer is locked by means of the Abadie safety system.

A special feature of this revolver is the trigger guard that can be folded downwards after which the entire left-side plate can be swung back to perform maintenance on the interior components. Over 180,000 of these revolvers were manufactured for the armies of Austria and Italy.

# 2 Belgian firearms from 1780 to 1895

Belgium
Belgien
België
Belgique

Belgian Cadet musket 1780

## Belgian Cadet musket 1780

### TECHNICAL SPECIFICATIONS

| | |
|---|---|
| Calibre | : 15 mm (.59") |
| Cartridge capacity | : single-shot muzzle-loader |
| Operation | : single-action |
| Firing system | : flintlock |
| Breach-loading | : N/A |
| Length | : 115.2 cm (45.4") |
| Barrel length | : 81.3 cm (32") |
| Weight | : 4.2 kg (9.3 lb) |
| Sight | : bead |
| Safety | : half-cock |
| Stock | : walnut |

*Specific details*: This was produced as a training rifle for the French Army from c. 1780 to 1822. This musket was probably derived from the French Velite Infantry M1777 rifle. A large number of these rifles were made in Belgium in workshops around Liège.

## Liège percussion pocket pistol, c. 1795

### TECHNICAL SPECIFICATIONS

| | |
|---|---|
| Calibre | : 10.2 mm (.400") |
| Cartridge capacity | : single-shot |
| Operation | : single-action |
| Firing system | : percussion |
| Breach-loading | : N/A |
| Length | : 178 mm (7") |
| Barrel length | : 63.5 mm (2.5") |
| Weight | : 250 g (8.8 oz) |
| Sight | : none |
| Safety | : sliding sear behind the hammer |
| Grip | : walnut, mother of pearl or ivory |

*Specific details*: This was produced in Liège, Belgium from c. 1790 to 1800. This weapon was intended as a pocket or travelling pistol for self-defence. An interesting feature of this pistol is the barrel that can be unscrewed for breech loading. Such pistols are often engraved. When the hammer is cocked a folding trigger springs out of the bottom of the frame. The French gunsmiths Boutet and Le Page also made many of

Liège percussion pocket pistol, c. 1795

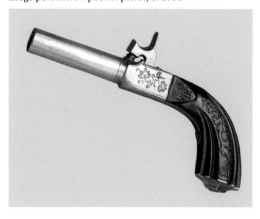

Set of Liège percussion pocket pistols

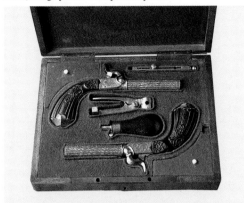

Set of Liège percussion pocket pistols

Details of Tersen 1848 rifle with open bolt

Details of Tersen 1848 rifle

these pistols, mostly as a full set in a gift case. A similar set of pocket pistols is shown above.

## Belgian Tersen 1848 rifle

**TECHNICAL SPECIFICATIONS**

| | |
|---|---|
| Calibre | : 11 mm (.43") |
| Cartridge capacity | : single-shot |
| Operation | : single-action |
| Firing system | : centre-fire |
| Breach-loading | : hinged block |
| Length | : 128 cm (50.4") |
| Barrel length | : 85 cm (33.5") |
| Weight | : 4.3 kg (9.5 lb) |
| Sight | : graduated sight |
| Safety | : half-cock hammer |
| Stock | : walnut |

*Specific details*: A percussion rifle that was converted by fitting a hinged block or trap-

door action. The firing pin extends through the hinged block. This rifle was used by the Belgian Army until 1881. The large bolt lever can be rotated a quarter turn, after which the action block can be folded up and forwards.

The Belgian Army also used the Albini–Brändlin rifle as well as the Tersen M1848. Both models were replaced by the Comblain rifle in 1881.

Belgian Tersen 1848 rifle

Lefaucheux-type pin-fire revolver, c. 1850

## Lefaucheux-type pin-fire revolver, c. 1850

*Lefaucheux-type pin-fire revolver, c. 1851*

**TECHNICAL SPECIFICATIONS**

| | |
|---|---|
| Calibre | : 7, 9 or 12 mm (.28, .35 or .47") |
| Cartridge capacity | : 5–8 barrels |
| Operation | : single- of double-action |
| Firing system | : pin-fire |
| Breach-loading | : N/A |
| Length | : varied |
| Barrel length | : varied |
| Weight | : varied |
| Sight | : none |
| Safety | : none |
| Grip | : varied |

*Lefaucheux-type pin-fire revolver, c. 1851*

*Specific details*: This has been produced since 1850, by gunsmiths such as Decortis, Deprez, Francotte and Hainfux of Liège, Devisme of Paris and Hill & Son of Sheffield in Great Britain. Most of these revolvers had folding triggers. A pin or catch is often mounted at the front to allow the barrel section to be swung sideways or slid forward to load the barrels. This type of weapon was intended as a pocket or travelling revolver for self-defence.

## Lefaucheux-type pin-fire revolver, c. 1851

**TECHNICAL SPECIFICATIONS**

| | |
|---|---|
| Calibre | : 11 mm (.43") pin-fire |
| Cartridge capacity | : 6-shot |
| Operation | : single-action |
| Firing system | : pin-fire |
| Breach-loading | : N/A |
| Length | : 280 mm (11") |
| Barrel length | : 127 mm (5") |
| Weight | : 960 g (33.9 oz) |
| Sight | : bead (notch in head of hammer) |
| Safety | : half-cock hammer |
| Grip | : walnut |

Specific details: Lefaucheux-type pin-fire revolver from the period 1851 to 1865 was made by various Belgian gunsmiths in the Liège area where large-scale production of pin-fire weapons, mainly based on the design by the French engineer Lefaucheux, was carried out at that time. At the Great Exhibition in London in 1851, Lefaucheux created a great impression by the introduction of the pin-fire cartridge and various pin-fire guns. This type of gun was copied in large numbers in virtually all European countries, sometimes under a licence. Pin-fire revolvers were made in calibres ranging from 6 to 15 mm and from 5 to 24 shots. Their collectors' value is not very high, but the pin-fire system makes them interesting items.

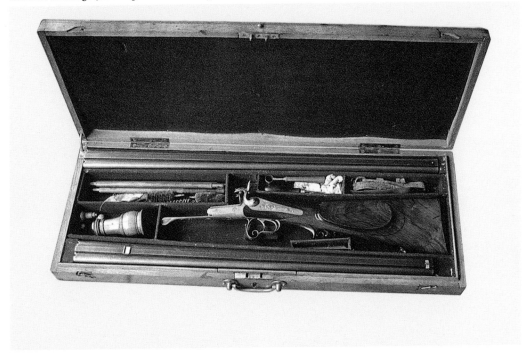

## Ahrendt hunting rifle/shotgun with exchangeable barrels, c. 1860

**TECHNICAL SPECIFICATIONS**

| | |
|---|---|
| Calibre | : 12 |
| Cartridge capacity | : double-barrelled, |
| Operation | : single-action |
| Firing system | : pin-fire |
| Breach-loading | : N/A |
| Length | : 127 cm (50") |
| Barrel length | : shot: 71 cm (28"); bullet: 65 cm (26") |
| Weight | : approx. 3.6 kg (7.9 lb) |
| Sight | : folding sight (bullet barrel) |
| Safety | : half-cock hammer |
| Stock | : walnut |

*Specific details*: A hunting rifle set with double rifle barrels and double shot barrels, made by the Belgian rifle-maker Ahrendt of Liège around 1860.
The rifle barrels had a folding sight for various ranges. The shot barrels were only fitted with a bead sight.

## Montigny double-barrelled needle-fire shotgun, c. 1860

**TECHNICAL SPECIFICATIONS**

| | |
|---|---|
| Calibre | : 15.2 mm (.60") |
| Cartridge capacity | : double-barrelled, single-shot |
| Operation | : single-action |
| Firing system | : needle-fire |
| Breach-loading | : large bolt on system frame |
| Length | : 120 cm (47.2") |
| Barrel length | : 70 cm (27.6") |
| Weight | : approx. 3.8 kg (8.4 lb)) |
| Sight | : folding sight |
| Safety | : none |
| Stock | : walnut |

*Specific details*: A very special needle-fire hunting rifle for paper cartridges made by the Belgian rifle-maker Montigny of Liège. Together with Fafchamps, a captain in the Belgian Army, in 1865 he developed a multi-barrelled automatic rifle that could be loaded very quickly using a large slide-shaped magazine. The construction of the

*Montigny double-barrelled needle-fire shotgun, c. 1860*

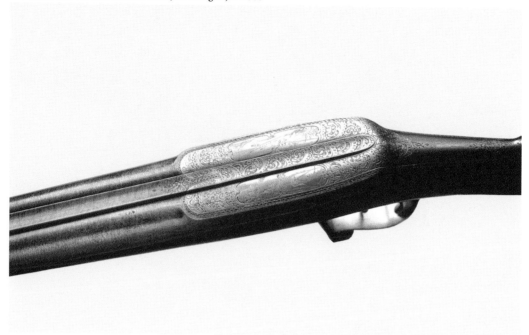

needle-fire rifle shown is very special construction, since it has no protruding elements.

## Belgian pin-fire revolver, c. 1865

**TECHNICAL SPECIFICATIONS**

Calibre : 9 mm pin-fire (.35")
Cartridge capacity : 7-shot
Operation : double-action

*Montigny double-barrelled needle-fire shotgun with open bolt*

| | |
|---|---|
| Firing system | : pin-fire |
| Breach-loading | : N/A |
| Length | : 270 mm (10.6") |
| Barrel length | : 150 mm (5.9") |
| Weight | : 960 g (33.9 oz) |
| Sight | : notch in head of hammer |
| Safety | : half-cock hammer |
| Grip | : walnut |

*Specific details*: This is a typical Lefaucheux-type pin-fire revolver. The folding trigger is not particularly special, as this was used on many of these pin-fire revolvers. More interesting is the folding bayonet with heart-shaped tip below the barrel. Its pivot is mounted in a dovetail slot. This was probably a travelling revolver. If seven shots were not sufficient, attackers could be warded off with the bayonet. Unfortunately the make of this special weapon is unknown, but Liège marks betray Belgian origins. The special construction makes this weapon truly unique and highly interesting to the collectors of pin-fire weapons.

*Belgian pin-fire revolver, c. 1865*

*Details of Belgian Albini-Brändlin 1868 rifle*

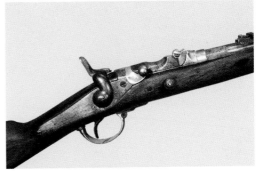

## Belgian Albini-Brändlin 1868 rifle

**TECHNICAL SPECIFICATIONS**

| | |
|---|---|
| Calibre | : 11 x 50R Albini M67/72 |
| Cartridge capacity | : single-shot |
| Operation | : single-action |
| Firing system | : centre-fire |
| Breach-loading | : hinged block |
| Length | : 134 cm (52.8") |
| Barrel length | : 85 cm (33.5") |
| Weight | : 4.5 kg (9.9 lb) |
| Sight | : graduated sight |
| Safety | : half-cock hammer |
| Stock | : walnut |

*Belgian Albini-Brändlin 1868 rifle*

*Belgian pocket revolver c. 1880*

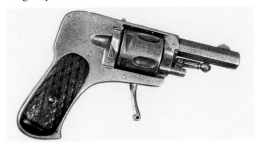

Specific details: This has a hinged block action according to a patent owned by the Italian Navy officer Augusto Albini, which was used to convert a large number of muzzle-loading rifles. In cooperation with the Belgian engineer Brändlin the original system was improved considerably. The rifle was used by military units in Bavaria and Württenberg in Germany, in Belgium and in several British colonies.

The Albini-Brändlin rifle was used by the Belgian Army simultaneously with the Tersen M1848 until both rifles were replaced by the Comblain rifle in 1881. This bolt action was also used to convert Russian percussion rifles into Baranow Model 1869 rifles that were being built in St Petersburg.

## Belgian pocket revolver, c. 1880

**TECHNICAL SPECIFICATIONS**

| | |
|---|---|
| Calibre | : .320 revolver (8 mm) |
| Cartridge capacity | : 5 cartridges |
| Operation | : only double-action |
| Firing system | : centre-fire |
| Breach-loading | : N/A |
| Length | : 160 mm (6.3") |
| Barrel length | : 50 mm (1.97") |
| Weight | : 510 g (18 oz.) |
| Sight | : small fixed notch, large bead |
| Safety | : rotating sear on left-hand side of frame |
| Grip | : ebonite or walnut |

Specific details: A small pocket revolver with an internal hammer, enclosed by the frame. The trigger can be folded forwards. This weapon was made by Manufacture Liegoise d'Armes à Feu, a gun factory in Liège. After 1900 these revolvers were also made in 6.35 mm (.25 ACP) and 7.65 mm (.32 ACP) pistol calibres.

## Belgian Comblain 1881 rifle

### TECHNICAL SPECIFICATIONS

| | |
|---|---|
| Calibre | : 11 x 52R Comblain M71 |
| Cartridge capacity | : single-shot |
| Operation | : single-action |
| Firing system | : centre-fire |
| Breach-loading | : falling block action |
| Length | : 128 cm (50.4") |
| Barrel length | : 88 cm (34.6") |
| Weight | : 4.3 kg (9.5 lb) |
| Sight | : graduated sight |
| Safety | : half-cock hammer |
| Stock | : walnut |

Specific details: The Comblain rifle dates from 1871, but it was not taken into use by the Belgian army until 1881. When the action is opened, the block falls down to allow easy access to the breech. This rifle has an unusual trigger as can be seen in the photographs of the rifle details.
Outside Belgium this rifle was also used in several South American countries such as Brazil. There are several versions of this rifle: with or without an external hammer, and with a continuous or three-quarter forward grip.

## Belgian Salon Pistol, c. 1885

### TECHNICAL SPECIFICATIONS

| | |
|---|---|
| Calibre | : 6 mm Flobert |
| Cartridge capacity | : single-shot |
| Operation | : single-action |
| Firing system | : rim-fire |
| Breach-loading | : none, but breech sealed by sealing plate |

Belgian Comblain 1881 rifle

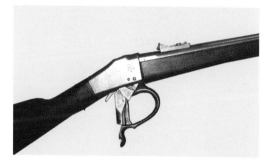

Details of Belgian Comblain 1881 rifle

Details of Belgian Comblain 1881 rifle

Belgian Salon Pistol, c. 1885

| | |
|---|---|
| Length | : 290 mm (11.4") |
| Barrel length | : 152 mm (6") |
| Weight | : 1080 g (38 oz) |
| Sight | : fixed notch, bead |
| Safety | : none |
| Grip | : walnut |

*Specific details*: A gallery pistol for indoor target shooting, made by an unknown gunsmith of Liège.
The weapon is of simple construction, but it is beautifully finished.

## Warnant Flobert rifle, c. 1885

**TECHNICAL SPECIFICATIONS**

| | |
|---|---|
| Calibre | : 6 mm Flobert rim-fire |
| Cartridge capacity | : single-shot |
| Operation | : single-action |
| Firing system | : rim-fire |
| Breach-loading | : Warnant hinged action |
| Length | : 110 cm (43.3") |
| Barrel length | : 56 cm (22") |
| Weight | : 3.2 kg (7.1 lb) |
| Sight | : adjustable aperture sight |
| Safety | : none |
| Stock | : walnut |

*Specific details*: A special sporting rifle for the small-calibre Flobert rim-fire cartridge. The forward trigger acts as an accelerator so that the rifle can be fired with little pressure on the rear trigger. This type of gun

*Detail of Warnant Flobert rifle, c. 1885*

was the ancestor of the modern small-calibre match rifle, but it is still used itself. It has a heavy octagonal barrel and an exquisitely shaped trigger guard, which was typical for this type of rifle.
Warnant of the Belgian town of Charette near Liège was a well-known designer of guns, who registered many patents in his own name.

## Belgian Velo-Dog revolver, c. 1885

**TECHNICAL SPECIFICATIONS**

| | |
|---|---|
| Calibre | : .320 revolver (8 mm) |
| Cartridge capacity | : 5 cartridges |
| Operation | : single-action |
| Firing system | : centre-fire |
| Breach-loading | : N/A |
| Length | : 155 mm (6.1") |

*Belgian Velo-Dog revolver, c. 1885*

*Warnant Flobert rifle, c. 1885*

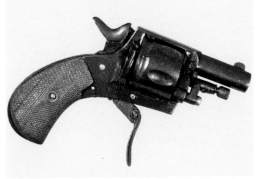

| | |
|---|---|
| Barrel length | : 51 mm (2") |
| Weight | : 420 g (14.8 oz.) |
| Sight | : bead |
| Safety | : none |
| Grip | : walnut |

*Specific details*: A small Velo-Dog type pocket revolver, made by Leopold Ancion-Marx of Liège. The folding trigger can be folded forwards.

When the hammer is cocked in the single-action position, the trigger springs down. At that time stray dogs were a nuisance to cyclists and pedestrians and so it was quite useful to have a small pocket revolver at hand.

Galand of Paris even developed a special centre-fire cartridge for these weapons in 1894: the 5.5 mm Velo Dog.

## Flobert rifle, c. 1885

**TECHNICAL SPECIFICATIONS**

| | |
|---|---|
| Calibre | : 6 mm Flobert rim-fire |
| Cartridge capacity | : single-shot |
| Operation | : single-action |
| Firing system | : rim-fire |
| Breach-loading | : none |
| Length | : 110 cm (43.3") |
| Barrel length | : 56 cm (22") |
| Weight | : 2.9 kg (6.4 lb) |
| Sight | : adjustable notched sight |
| Safety | : none |
| Stock | : walnut |

*Specific details*: A sporting rifle for the small-calibre Flobert rim-fire cartridge, but of simpler construction than the Warnant rifle. This rifle has no falling block action. The double-winged breech seal only serves as a cartridge extractor.

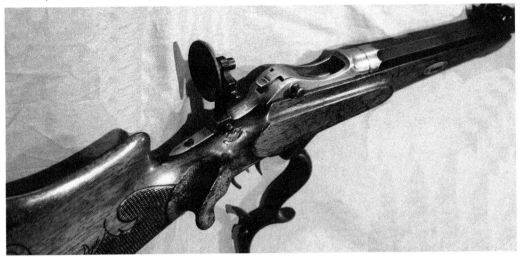

## Flobert rifle with Martini action, c. 1885

**TECHNICAL SPECIFICATIONS**

| | |
|---|---|
| Calibre | : .22 LR (Long Rifle) |
| Cartridge capacity | : single-shot |
| Operation | : single-action |
| Firing system | : rim-fire |
| Breach-loading | : Martini falling block |
| Length | : 110 cm (43.3") |
| Barrel length | : 56 cm (22") |
| Weight | : 3.2 kg (7.1 lb) |
| Sight | : adjustable aperture sight |
| Safety | : none |
| Stock | : walnut |

*Specific details*: Another special sporting rifle for the small-calibre Flobert rim-fire cartridge. Here a Martini-type action has been used.

When the trigger guard is pivoted down, the falling block is lowered so that the breech can be loaded. The rifle has double triggers, the foremost of which serves as an accelerator.

This gun has a heavy octagonal barrel and an exquisitely shaped trigger guard, as was usual for this type of rifle.

## Belgian pocket revolver, c. 1895

**TECHNICAL SPECIFICATIONS**

| | |
|---|---|
| Calibre | : .320 revolver (8 mm) |
| Cartridge capacity | : 5 cartridges |
| Operation | : double-action |
| Firing system | : centre-fire |
| Breach-loading | : N/A |
| Length | : 180 mm (7.1") |
| Barrel length | : 77 mm (3.03") |
| Weight | : 510 g (18 oz.) |
| Sight | : bead |
| Safety | : sear on left-hand side of frame |
| Grip | : walnut |

*Specific details*: A pocket revolver made by Leopold Ancion-Marx of Liège. At that time it was not uncommon to provide pocket revolvers with safety sears. This habit was abandoned after 1900.

*Belgian pocket revolver, c. 1895*

# 3 Swiss firearms from 1842 to 1889

## Swiss Army pistol, c. 1842

**TECHNICAL SPECIFICATIONS**

| | |
|---|---|
| Calibre | : 17.5 mm (.69") |
| Cartridge capacity | : single-shot |
| Operation | : single-action |
| Firing system | : percussion |
| Breach-loading | : N/A |
| Length | : 360 mm (14.2") |
| Barrel length | : 210 mm (8.3") |
| Weight | : 1300 g (45.9 oz) |
| Sight | : bead only |
| Safety | : half-cock hammer |
| Grip | : walnut |

*Specific details*: A pistol for the Swiss military, produced by several gunsmiths in Liège in Belgium, including Auguste Francotte & Cie. This weapon strongly resembles the French army pistol which was taken into use by the French army in the same year.

The Francotte company was established in 1810 and was the market leader in Liège from 1850 to approximately 1900. Francotte produced pistols, military rifles, hunting guns and sporting rifles. In addition the company produced a number of weapons under license, in close collaboration with many other gunsmiths in the Liège area.

## Vetterli rifle Model 1869

**TECHNICAL SPECIFICATIONS**

| | |
|---|---|
| Calibre | : 10,4 x 38R (see Specific details) |
| Cartridge capacity | : 12 cartridges (tubular magazine) |
| Operation | : single-action |
| Firing system | : centre-fire |
| Breach-loading | : bolt action with breech-sealing lugs |
| Length | : 132 cm (51.95") |
| Barrel length | : 84 cm (33.1") |
| Weight | : 4.7 kg (10.27 lb) |
| Sight | : quadrant sight |
| Safety | : sear on right-hand side of tailpiece |
| Stock | : walnut |

*Specific details*: This was designed by the Swiss Friedrich Vetterli, who was employed by the Schweizerische Industrie Gesellschaft, currently known as SIG. The weapon was used as a repeating rifle with a tubular magazine under the M1869 barrel

*Swiss Army pistol, c. 1842*

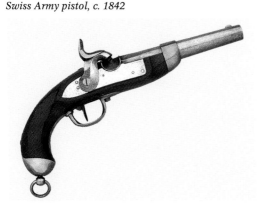

*Vetterli rifle Model 1869*

in a 10.4 x 38R calibre by the Swiss army and as a single-shot M1870 rifle in a 10.35 x 47R calibre with carbine versions in a 10.47 x 35R calibre by the Italians. This weapon was produced by many Swiss gun manufacturers, such as SIG (59,000 from 1869 to 1874) and the Eidgenössische Waffenfabrik Bern (14,000 from 1875 to 1878).

The Italian single-shot version was mainly produced by Beretta. In 1887 this rifle was modified with the integration of a Vitali magazine, comparable to the Dutch Beaumont–Vitali rifle.

The rifle in the photograph is the Swiss M1871 Stutzen with a Thury trigger group comprising two triggers. This weapon was intended for use by snipers and had a trigger accelerator.

## Schmidt Ordonnanz revolver Model 1882

### TECHNICAL SPECIFICATIONS

| | |
|---|---|
| Calibre | : 7.5 mm (.30") |
| Cartridge capacity | : 6-shot |
| Operation | : double-action |
| Firing system | : centre-fire |
| Breach-loading | : N/A |
| Length | : 235 mm (9.25") |
| Barrel length | : 130 mm (5.1") |

| | |
|---|---|
| Weight | : 750 g (26.5 oz) |
| Sight | : fixed |
| Safety | : hammer lock when loading gate is open |
| Grip | : ebonite grip plates, later version with walnut grip |

*Specific details*: A total of 37,000 of these military revolvers were produced by the Swiss National Armoury in Bern and by the Neuhausen (SIG) gun factory from 1882 to 1932.

The weapon was designed by the Swiss officer R. Schmidt, who was the Director of the National Armoury at that time. In 1882, the revolver was officially selected as an army weapon to succeed Model 1878. The M1882 has a loading gate on the right-hand side of the frame.

When this is opened, the hammer is locked (Abadie safety system). This revolver was initially intended only for Swiss Army officers. After 1890 the M1882 was also issued to several other military units such as the artillery, the cavalry and the Grenzwacht (frontier guards). The Neuhausen gun factory, later to be called SIG, also produced this revolver for the civilian market.

The 7.5 Army revolver cartridge was used by the Swiss from 1882 to 1903. Until 1887 the cartridge had a lead bullet which was later replaced by a copper-clad bullet point.

## Schmidt–Rubin rifle Model 1889

**TECHNICAL SPECIFICATIONS**

| | |
|---|---|
| Calibre | : 7.5 x 53.5 mm |
| Cartridge capacity | : holder for 12 cartridges |
| Operation | : single-action |
| Firing system | : centre-fire |
| Breach-loading | : rotating action with two lugs at the rear end of the bolt |
| Length | : 130.2 cm (51.25") |
| Barrel length | : 78 cm (30.7") |
| Weight | : 4.85 kg (10.7 lb) |
| Sight | : graduated sight |

*Schmidt–Rubin rifle Model 1889*

| | |
|---|---|
| Safety | : clamping ring on rear end of bolt that has to be rotated a quarter turn |
| Stock | : walnut |

*Specific details*: This rifle was designed by the Swiss colonel and weapons expert Rudolf Schmidt, who was also the Director of the National Armoury at that time. The first Schmidt–Rubin rifles were issued to the Swiss army in 1889. A total of 212,000 of these rifles were produced in the period from 1889 to 1897. Colonel Eduard Rubin, who worked for the Thuner ammunition works, was responsible for the special 7.5 x 53.5 and 7.5 x 55 mm calibres. The bolt action of the Model 1889 Schmidt–Rubin rifle was unusual for its time: it was pulled back straight, instead of a rotation with bolt lugs. There was a tensioner that caused a rotating bolt to turn inside a bolt housing. As a result the bolt lugs at the rear end of the bolt engaged with opening in the tailpiece. In the later version of this rifle, the Model 1911, they were moved to the front of the bolt housing.

*Details of the Schmidt–Rubin M 1889 rifle*

*Case with travelling pistols by William Bond, c. 1820*

# 4 German firearms from 1650 to 1898

*Stifter wheel-lock rifle, c. 1650*

*Details of Stifter wheel-lock rifle*

## Stifter wheel-lock rifle, c. 1650

**TECHNICAL SPECIFICATIONS**

| | |
|---|---|
| Calibre | : 14 mm (.55") |
| Cartridge capacity | : single-shot, muzzle-loader |
| Operation | : single-action |
| Firing system | : wheel-lock and flint |
| Breach-loading | : N/A |
| Length | : 104 cm (41") |
| Barrel length | : 71 cm (28") |
| Weight | : 3,4 kg (7.5 lb) |
| Sight | : none |
| Safety | : pushbutton catch on right lock plate |
| Stock | : walnut |

*Specific details*: The wheel-lock rifle was made by the German gunsmith Stifter around 1650. This rifle displays the typical straight stock of those days with a butt plate protruding from the bottom. Unusual for this time is the accelerator in front of the trigger.

The ivory strip on the right-hand side of the stock shows a hunting scene. The lock plate has an engraving of the siege of a city, complete with cannons. The left-hand side of the stock has another hunting scene, cut from an ivory plate.

*Details of Stifter wheel-lock rifle*

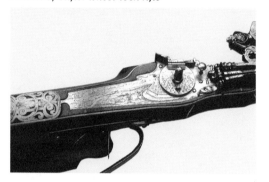

## Wideman shotgun, c. 1720

**TECHNICAL SPECIFICATIONS**

| | |
|---|---|
| Calibre | : 18 |
| Cartridge capacity | : single-shot |
| Operation | : single-action |
| Firing system | : flintlock |
| Breach-loading | : N/A |
| Length | : 125 cm (49.25") |
| Barrel length | : 81.3 cm (32") |
| Weight | : 3.3 kg (7.3 lb) |
| Sight | : bead |
| Safety | : half-cock |
| Stock | : walnut |

*Wideman shotgun, c. 1720*

*Kirchberger flintlock rifle, c. 1720*

*Detail of Wideman shotgun*

*Details of Kirchberger flintlock rifle*

*Detail of Wideman shotgun*

*Details of Kirchberger flintlock rifle*

*Specific details*: A single-barrel flintlock shotgun, made by the German gunsmith Peer Widemann around 1720. The weapon is decorated with beautiful ornaments and engravings. The barrel, close to the lock mechanism, shows Diana, the goddess of hunting. The rear side of the lock plate is decorated with the engraved head of a faun: a woodland god.

## *Kirchberger flintlock rifle, c. 1720*

**TECHNICAL SPECIFICATIONS**

| | |
|---|---|
| Calibre | : 15.2 mm (.60") |
| Cartridge capacity | : single-shot, muzzle-loader |
| Operation | : single-action |
| Firing system | : flintlock |
| Breach-loading | : N/A |
| Length | : 120 cm (47.2") |

| | |
|---|---|
| Barrel length | : 76 cm (30") |
| Weight | : 3.5 kg (7.7 lb) |
| Sight | : notched sight and bead |
| Safety | : half-cock |
| Stock | : walnut |

*Specific details*: A flintlock hunting rifle, made around 1720 by Kirchberger, a gunsmith from Carlsbad. The rifle is beautifully decorated with gold-plating on the lock plate, trigger guard and the stock. The trigger is adjustable and fitted with an accelerator, a system that became popular at the beginning of the 18th century. The breech of the octagonal barrel has gold-inlaid figures.

## *Poltz flintlock pistols, c. 1725*

**TECHNICAL SPECIFICATIONS**

| | |
|---|---|
| Calibre | : 14 mm (.55") |
| Cartridge capacity | : single-shot |
| Operation | : single-action |
| Firing system | : flintlock |
| Breach-loading | : N/A |
| Length | : 490 mm (19.3") |
| Barrel length | : 300 mm (11.8") |
| Weight | : 1100 g (38.8 oz) |
| Sight | : bead |
| Safety | : half-cock |
| Grip | : walnut |

*Poltz flintlock pistols, c. 1725*

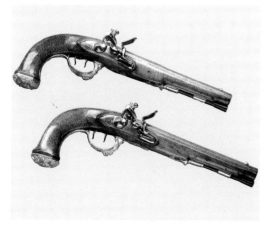

*Specific details*: A set of pistols made around 1725 by the German gunsmith Poltz of Carlsbad. The weapons are of the same type as cavalry pistols, but more abundantly decorated and fitted with damask steel barrels.

This set was probably made for duelling, as they are slightly too large to serve as travelling pistols. Carlsbad was an important arms-producing centre in those days.

## *Amberg wall rifle 1833*

**TECHNICAL SPECIFICATIONS**

| | |
|---|---|
| Calibre | : 12 |
| Cartridge capacity | : single-shot |
| Operation | : single-action |
| Firing system | : percussion |
| Breach-loading | : N/A |
| Length | : 120 cm (47.2") |
| Barrel length | : 70 cm (27.6") |
| Weight | : 6.5 kg (14.3 lb) |
| Sight | : adjustable |
| Safety | : half-cock hammer |
| Stock | : walnut |

*Specific details*: From 1820 to 1840, the German arms factory Amberg mainly produced rifles and carbines for the Prussian army, such as the Model 1826 Cuirasser carbine.
They also manufactured the so-called wall rifles, large calibre rifles which were used to defend fortifications. The combination of the heavy, thick barrel and the adjustable 'graduated' sight allowed great accuracy at long ranges.
Unfortunately this also made the rifle so heavy that it could only be used in a stationary position. Amberg made some 630 of these rifles. The example in the photograph has serial number 31.

*Amberg wall rifle, 1833*

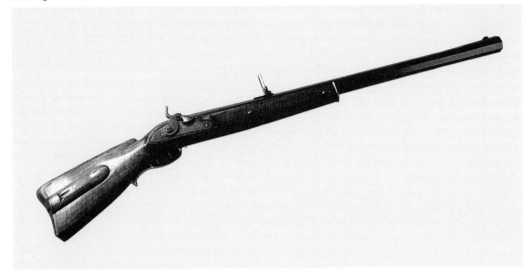

*Potsdam infantry rifle, Model 1840*

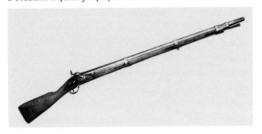

*Details of Potsdam infantry rifle, Model 1840*

## Potsdam infantry rifle Model 1840

### TECHNICAL SPECIFICATIONS

| | |
|---|---|
| Calibre | : 17.5 mm (.69") |
| Cartridge capacity | : single-shot, muzzle-loader |
| Operation | : single-action |
| Firing system | : percussion |
| Breach-loading | : N/A |
| Length | : 148 cm (58.3") |
| Barrel length | : 109 cm (43") |
| Weight | : 4.5 kg (9.9 lb) |
| Sight | : bead |
| Safety | : half-cock |
| Grip | : walnut |

*Specific details*: A German infantry rifle, made by the Potsdam rifle factory in 1812. Following the trend in other European countries this flintlock rifle was converted into a percussion system around 1840. A percussion nipple with a base has been mounted at the place where the priming pan used to be. This can be clearly seen in the detailed photographs.

*Details of Potsdam infantry rifle, Model 1840*

*German military pistol, c. 1848*

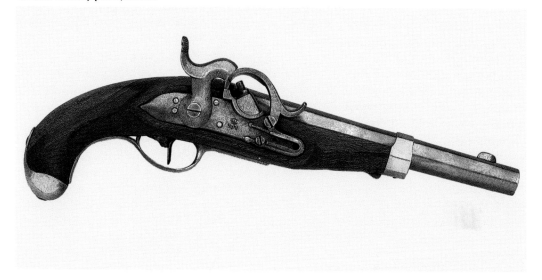

## German military pistol, c. 1848

**TECHNICAL SPECIFICATIONS**

| | |
|---|---|
| Calibre | : 17.5 mm (.69") |
| Cartridge capacity | : single-shot |
| Operation | : single-action |
| Firing system | : percussion |
| Breach-loading | : N/A |
| Length | : 395 mm (15.6") |
| Barrel length | : 240 mm (9.5") |
| Weight | : 1300 g (45.9 oz) |
| Sight | : fixed |
| Safety | : folding guard over nipple |
| Grip | : walnut |

*German cavalry pistol, c. 1850*

*Specific details*: A German military pistol that was converted from flintlock to percussion ignition between 1845 and 1849. The nipple safety is a typical Saxon feature, which was often used by gunsmiths in Suhl, as with the conversion of French flintlock cavalry pistols that had originally been built in Italy and that were captured by the Germans in the war of 1813–1815.

Such pistols were converted to the percussion system in Suhl around 1845 and were used by German military units until 1870.

## German cavalry pistol, c. 1850

**TECHNICAL SPECIFICATIONS**

| | |
|---|---|
| Calibre | : 15.2 mm (.60") |
| Cartridge capacity | : single-shot |
| Operation | : single-action |
| Firing system | : percussion |
| Breach-loading | : N/A |
| Length | : 380 mm (15") |
| Barrel length | : 230 mm (9.1") |
| Weight | : 1400 g (49.4 oz) |
| Sight | : fixed notch and bead |
| Safety | : folding guard over nipple |
| Stock | : walnut |

*Specific details*: A military pistol for the Prussian cavalry during the period 1850–1855. These pistols were made in Suhl in large numbers and are not very expensive.

The German town of Suhl was home to a great number of gunsmiths, including famous names such as Bader, Baumgarten, Bornmüller, Haenel, Sauer, Simson and Spangenberg. The spring-loaded safety guard can be folded over the nipple manually to prevent the hammer from reaching the percussion cap.

Most weapons that were made for the mounted troops were fitted with lanyard rings to catch the weapon if it slipped from the riders hand.

## German military pistol, c. 1850

**TECHNICAL SPECIFICATIONS**

| | |
|---|---|
| Calibre | : 14 mm (.55") |
| Cartridge capacity | : single-shot, muzzle-loader |
| Operation | : single-action |
| Firing system | : percussion |
| Breach-loading | : N/A |
| Length | : 450 mm (17.7") |
| Barrel length | : 220 mm (8.7") |
| Weight | : 1300 g (45.9 oz) |
| Sight | : bead |
| Safety | : half-cock hammer |
| Grip | : walnut |

*Specific details*: This was made as a mili-

tary pistol in Hannover around 1850. A separate stock could be fitted to the rear of the pistol so that it could be used as a small carbine.

The brass grip cap and the brass ring at the front of the barrel indicate that this particular pistol was intended for the navy.

## Ulrich pistol set, c. 1855

**TECHNICAL SPECIFICATIONS**

| | |
|---|---|
| Calibre | : 13.7 mm (.54") |
| Cartridge capacity | : single-shot |
| Operation | : single-action |
| Firing system | : percussion |
| Breach-loading | : N/A |
| Length | : 375 mm (14.8") |
| Barrel length | : 230 mm (9.1") |
| Weight | : 1050 g (37 oz) |
| Sight | : bead |
| Safety | : half-cock hammer |
| Grip | : walnut |

*Specific details*: A complete pistol set in wooden case, made by the German gunsmith Friedrich Ulrich of Stuttgart around 1855.

The exquisitely etched barrels are a very interesting feature. In addition to pistols, Ulrich also made beautiful hunting rifles, complete with handsome wooden cases.

*German military pistol, c. 1850*

*Ulrich pistol set, c. 1855*

## *Infantry Model 1857*

### TECHNICAL SPECIFICATIONS

| | |
|---|---|
| Calibre | : 13.7 mm (.54") |
| Cartridge capacity | : single-shot, muzzle-loader |
| Operation | : single-action |
| Firing system | : percussion |
| Breach-loading | : N/A |
| Length | : 138 cm (54.3") |
| Barrel length | : 100 cm (39.4") |
| Weight | : 4.3 kg (9.5 lb) |
| Sight | : simple graduated sight |
| Safety | : half-cock hammer |
| Stock | : walnut |

*Specific details*: One of the factories to make this rifle was the Württembergische Gewehrfabrik which was later taken over by Gebr. Mauser & Co. The sight was adjusted in steps from 200 to 1000 steps. One step equalled 2.75 Württembergische feet.

Such sight adjustment was customary in those days. There are no exact figures as to how many of these rifles were produced. The German Mauser company markets an excellent replica of this rifle.

## *Ulrich rifle, c. 1859*

### TECHNICAL SPECIFICATIONS

| | |
|---|---|
| Calibre | : 15.7 mm (.62") |
| Cartridge capacity | : single-shot |
| Operation | : single-action |
| Firing system | : percussion |
| Breach-loading | : N/A |
| Length | : 120 cm (47.2") |
| Barrel length | : 76 cm (30") |
| Weight | : 4.4 kg (9.7 lb) |
| Sight | : folding sight en bead |
| Safety | : half-cock hammer with folding safety catch |
| Stock | : walnut |

*Ulrich rifle, c. 1859*

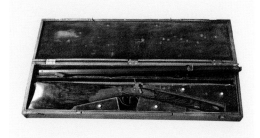

*Specific details*: A rifle in wooden case, produced by the German gunsmith Friedrich Ulrich of Stuttgart around 1859/1860. The large rifle with its heavy barrel was probably intended for hunting big game. The notch sight has folding leaves for various ranges. This type of rifle in its original case is much sought after as a collector's item.

## Hellmann double-barrelled percussion rifle, c. 1860

**TECHNICAL SPECIFICATIONS**

| | |
|---|---|
| Calibre | : 15 mm (.59") |
| Cartridge capacity | : double-barrelled, single-shot |
| Operation | : single-action |
| Firing system | : percussion |
| Breach-loading | : N/A |
| Length | : 118 cm (46.5") |
| Barrel length | : 73.6 cm (29") |
| Weight | : 4.8 kg (10.6 lb) |
| Sight | : bead |
| Safety | : half-cock hammer with extra safety device |
| Stock | : walnut |

*Specific details*: A double-barrelled percussion rifle, made by Hellmann, a rifle maker of Heilbrunn on the River Neckar, around 1860. Heilbrunn or Heilbronn is in the current federal state of Baden-Württemberg. In the 8th century Heilbrunn was initially called Villa Helibruna. It was

Dreyse needle-fire rifle model 1868

awarded privileges as a city in 1281 and it became a Reichsstadt (Imperial city) in 1371. Small-scaled gun production began here in the 17th century. This mainly involved the production of hunting arms as exemplified by the weapon shown. The carved wooden trigger guard is a beautiful display of craftsmanship.

## Dreyse needle-fire rifle Model 1868

**TECHNICAL SPECIFICATIONS**

| | |
|---|---|
| Calibre | : 15.43 mm paper cartridge |
| Cartridge capacity | : single-shot |
| Operation | : single-action |
| Firing system | : needle-fire |
| Breach-loading | : bolt lever |
| Length | : 135 cm (53") |
| Barrel length | : 89 cm (35") |
| Weight | : 4.1 kg (9 lb) |
| Sight | : folding sight with notched leaves for various ranges |
| Safety | : see Specific details |
| Stock | : walnut |

Hellmann double-barrelled percussion rifle, c. 1860

Details of Hellmann double-barrelled percussion rifle

*Specific details*: A needle-fire rifle designed by Johann Niklaus von Dreyse (1787–1867) of Sommerda. It was the German Emperor who was responsible for this needle-fire rifle being issued to the Prussian Army in 1840.

This rifle was loaded by means of a paper cartridge, in which the bullet, the powder and the priming fulminate were housed together. After the rifle was opened the paper cartridge had to be inserted into the breech after which the firing pin needle was tensioned by hand. The rifle had no other safety devices. The percussion cap was more or less in the centre of the cartridge. A long, thin needle struck through the paper cartridge and the powder charged to ignite the percussion cap. Around 1870 the needle-fire rifle became disused after the introduction of the centre-fire cartridge with a brass case.

*Drawing of needle-fire cartridge*

*German pin-fire revolver, c. 1870*

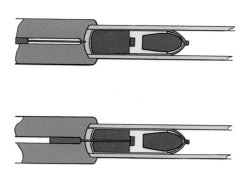

## German pin-fire revolver, c. 1870

**TECHNICAL SPECIFICATIONS**

| | |
|---|---|
| Calibre | : 9 mm pin-fire |
| Cartridge capacity | : 5-shot |
| Operation | : single-action |
| Firing system | : pin-fire |
| Breach-loading | : N/A |
| Length | : 245 mm (9.7") |
| Barrel length | : 152 mm (6") |
| Weight | : 590 g (21 oz) |
| Sight | : fixed |
| Safety | : half-cock hammer |
| Grip | : walnut |

*Specific details*: German pin-fire revolver with an integral barrel and upper bridge was made by an unknown maker, probably of Suhl. Several of these improved pin-fire revolvers were made around 1870. Similar types were made by Renault in Liège, Belgium and by Verney-Carron of St Etienne in France. At that time the various manufacturers were trying to interest the national armies of several European countries in this type of robust revolver with its closed frame.

## Double-barrelled Dreyse needle-fire rifle 1870

**TECHNICAL SPECIFICATIONS**

| | |
|---|---|
| Calibre | : 15.24 mm (.60") |
| Cartridge capacity | : single-shot, double-barrelled, |
| Operation | : single-action |
| Firing system | : needle-fire |
| Breach-loading | : catch below forward grip |
| Length | : 145 cm (57") |
| Barrel length | : 88.9 cm (35") |
| Weight | : 4.4 kg (9.7 lb) |
| Sight | : fixed keepsight |
| Safety | : tensioning lever at rear end of bolt |
| Stock | : walnut |

*Specific details*: Johann Niklaus von Dreyse (1787–1867) of Sommerda in Germany was a well-known engineer who

*Double-barrelled Dreyse needle-fire rifle 1870*

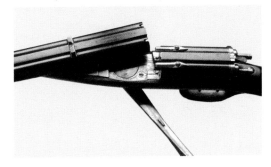

*Details of double-barrelled Dreyse needle-fire rifle*

*Details of Dreyse needle-fire rifle*

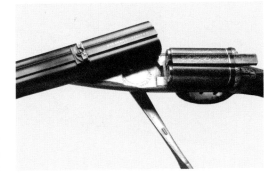

*Details of Dreyse needle-fire rifle*

invented the Dreyse needle-fire rifle that was introduced as the standard rifle for the Prussian Army in 1840. In addition to military arms, his factory also produced a large variety of needle-fire pistols and needle-fire hunting weapons. After Dreyse's death in 1867 the company was continued by his son Franz. The weapon shown is from that period.

After Franz's death in 1894 his cousin Nikolaus von Dreyse took over the company. In 1901 it merged with the Rheinische Metallwaren- und Maschienenfabrik of Düsseldorf. Under the inspiring management of Nikolaus von Dreyse, in particular, the von Dreyse gun factory became recognised for splendidly finished and decorated needle-fire rifles. A good example is shown in the bottom right photograph on the previous page. Note the horn trigger guard. Several von Dreyse triplet needle-fire shotguns also stem from this period.

## Mauser infantry Model 1871

**TECHNICAL SPECIFICATIONS**

| | |
|---|---|
| Calibre | : 11.15 x 60R |
| Cartridge capacity | : single-shot |
| Operation | : single-action |
| Firing system | : centre-fire |
| Breach-loading | : bolt lever in tailpiece |
| Length | : 99.4 cm (39.15"); rifle: 134.5 cm (52.95") |
| Barrel length | : carbine: 50.5 cm (19.9"); rifle: 85.5 cm (33.65") |
| Weight | : 3.4 kg (7.54 lb); rifle: 4.5 kg (10.1 lb) |
| Sight | : graduated sight |
| Safety | : none |
| Stock | : walnut |

*Specific details*: This military rifle was issued to the German Army in 1872. It was produced by the Königliche Gewehrfabrik Spandau (1872–1884), the Österreichische Waffenfabrik Gesellschaft of Steyr (1873–1878), Mauser & Co in Oberndorf (1873–1884), and the Produktions Genossenschaft in Suhl (1876–1882). A small order of some 6000 rifles was also commissioned to the National Arms and Ammunitions Company Ltd of Birmingham (UK) in the period from 1876 to 1878. Various versions were made on the basis of this rifle, such as the M1871 Jägerbuchse with a total length of 124 cm (48.8") and a barrel length of 75 cm (29.5") and the M1871 carbine with a total length of 99.4 cm (39.15") and a barrel length of 50.5 cm (19.9").

A new type of M71 with a tubular magazine for 8 cartridges, the M71/84, was developed in 1882, which was followed by the Model M87 with a 9.5 mm calibre for the Turkish Army in 1887. The carbine version was made from 1876 to 1885 with a total output of well over 150,000. The differences with the rifle model are not only its length, but also its curved bolt lever and the stock that continues all the way up to the muzzle. The weapon in the photograph is the M1871 carbine.

## Mauser zigzag revolver Model 1878

**TECHNICAL SPECIFICATIONS**

| | |
|---|---|
| Calibre | : 7.6, 9 or 10.6 mm |
| Cartridge capacity | : 6-shot |
| Operation | : double-action |
| Firing system | : centre-fire |
| Breach-loading | : lever at front of trigger guard |
| Length | : 298 mm (11.7") |
| Barrel length | : 80 mm (3.2") |
| Weight | : 1150 g (40.6 oz) |
| Sight | : fixed |
| Safety | : safety lug for cylinder, also bolt locking lug |
| Grip | : ebonite |

*Specific details*: This was developed by Peter Paul Mauser in 1878. When the hammer is cocked a guide lug, set in the frame, slides through the zigzag grooves to rotate a cylinder chamber in position. When the shot was fired, the lug returned to its original position for the next round. An

*Mauser Zigzag revolver Model 1878*

unusual feature is the firing or hammer spring, a coiled spring fitted in the frame between the cylinder and the trigger. By pulling forwards the ring catch set near the front of the trigger guard, the barrel was broken upwards, so that the cylinder could be loaded or unloaded.

The model shown is a civilian version, without a lanyard ring at the bottom of the grip. Mauser also made a Zigzag Model 2 revolver with a closed frame.
This weapon is not a 'top-break', but can be loaded via a loading gate on the right-hand side, behind the cylinder. Typical of this second Model is its round barrel with the flared muzzle.

## Dreyse Reichsrevolver 1879

[photo number: D-18]

**TECHNICAL SPECIFICATIONS**

| | |
|---|---|
| Calibre | : 10.6 mm |
| Cartridge capacity | : 6-shot |
| Operation | : single-action |
| Firing system | : centre-fire |
| Breach-loading | : N/A |
| Length | : 340 mm (13.4") |
| Barrel length | : 180 mm (7.1") |
| Weight | : 1320 g (46.6 oz) |
| Sight | : fixed |
| Safety | : sear on left-hand side of frame |
| Grip | : walnut |

*Dreyse Reichsrevolver 1879*

*Cöster double-barrelled rifle, c. 1880*

*Details of Cöster double-barrelled rifle*

*Specific details*: This was designed and produced by Friedrich von Dreyse of Sommerda. Other manufacturers were Haenel, Gebr. Mauser, Sauer & Sohn and Schilling. A typical military revolver with a big rim around the breech and a sear, which was unusual for revolvers.

It was taken into use by the German army in 1879. In 1883 this revolver was replaced by the Reichsrevolver M1883 with a 117-mm long barrel in the same calibre. The main differences are the shorter barrel, the slightly different frame shape and the round grip.

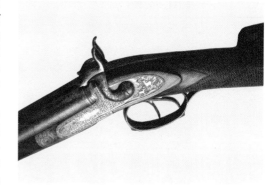

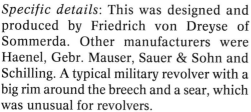

*Details of Cöster double-barrelled rifle*

## Cöster double-barrelled rifle, c. 1880

**TECHNICAL SPECIFICATIONS**

| | |
|---|---|
| Calibre | : unknown |
| Cartridge capacity | : double-barrelled, single-shot |
| Operation | : single-action |
| Firing system | : pin-fire |
| Breach-loading | : barrel lugs with catch below forward grip |
| Length | : 123 cm (48.4") |
| Barrel length | : 71 cm (28") |
| Weight | : 4.1 kg (9 lb) |
| Sight | : bead |
| Safety | : half-cock hammer |
| Stock | : walnut |

*Specific details*: A double-barrelled rifle, made by the gunsmith J.A. Cöster of

Hanau, Germany, in around 1880. The calibre is not exactly known. Presumably Cöster supplied his own calibre pin-fire bullet cartridges along with the rifle. The weapon is beautifully finished, engraved and inlaid with golden roes and deer on both lock plates.

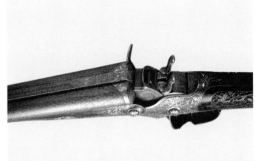

## Förster double-barrelled rifle, c. 1880

**TECHNICAL SPECIFICATIONS**

| | |
|---|---|
| Calibre | : .400 Nitro for black powder |
| Cartridge capacity | : single-shot, double-barrelled, |
| Operation | : single-action |
| Firing system | : centre-fire |
| Breach-loading | : barrel lugs with catch below trigger guard |
| Length | : 110 cm (43.3") |
| Barrel length | : 68.6 cm (27") |
| Weight | : 4.4 kg (9.7 lb) |
| Sight | : folding sight for various ranges |
| Safety | : half-cock hammer |
| Stock | : walnut |

*Specific details*: A double-barrelled rifle with external hammers, made by the Förster, a gunsmith of Suhl, by around 1880. The rifle has side locks, i.e. the firing mechanism is mounted to the inside of the lock plates and can be removed completely. The trigger pressure for the double triggers, one for each barrel, can be adjusted per

*Details of Förster double-barrelled rifle*

trigger. The .400 Nitro calibre was developed by Kynoch by the end of the 19th century and was widely used in British double-barrelled hunting rifles, as made by Purdey and others. This type of weapon was commonly used to hunt big game in India and Africa.

## Double-barrelled Bartl hunting rifle, c. 1880

**TECHNICAL SPECIFICATIONS**

| | |
|---|---|
| Calibre | : 9.3 x 72R |
| Cartridge capacity | : double-barrelled, single-shot |
| Operation | : single-action |
| Firing system | : centre-fire |
| Breach-loading | : Remington rolling block |
| Length | : 123 cm (48.4") |
| Barrel length | : 68 cm (26.8") |
| Weight | : 3.4 kg (7.5 lb) |
| Sight | : folding sight |
| Safety | : half-cock |
| Stock | : walnut |

*Specific details*: A double-barrelled rifle with Remington rolling-block action. The rifle and its stock are beautifully engraved. Joseph Bartl of Weipert, Germany, made this rifle around 1880. Weipert was a well-known firearms-producing centre. Another well-known gunsmith from Weipert was Gustav Fükert who manufactured similar weapons.

*Mauser infantry rifle Model 1871/84*

*Mauser navy rifle Model 1871/84*

# Mauser infantry rifle Model 1871/84

**TECHNICAL SPECIFICATIONS**

| | |
|---|---|
| Calibre | : 11.15 x 60R |
| Cartridge capacity | : tubular magazine for 8 cartridges |
| Operation | : single-action |
| Firing system | : centre-fire |
| Breach-loading | : by bolt lever in tailpiece |
| Length | : 129.7 cm (51.1") |
| Barrel length | : 80 cm (31.5") |
| Weight | : 4.6 kg (10.2 lb) |
| Sight | : graduated sight |
| Safety | : none |
| Stock | : walnut |

*Specific details*: This was built by the national German firearms factories in Danzig, Erfurth and Spandau from 1885 to 1889, by the Royal Arms Factory in Amberg from 1886 to 1890, and by Mauser from 1885 to 1887. Over 950,000 of these rifles were manufactured in total. On the outside

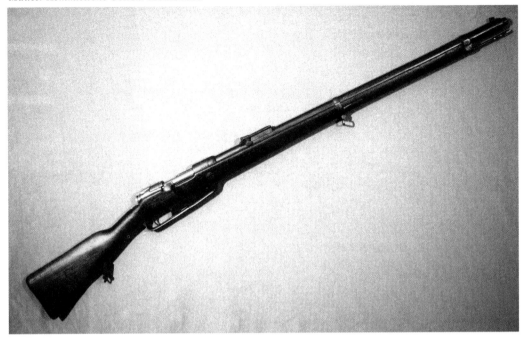

this rifle strongly resembles the Model 1871 rifle, but in the M1871/84 an 8-cartridge tubular magazine has been fitted below the barrel. They are fed into the breech by means of a cartridge lift, controlled by the bolt action. This rifle also exists in a navy version with two barrel bands, as shown on the previous page.

## Mauser Kommissions Gewehr Model 1888

### TECHNICAL SPECIFICATIONS

| | |
|---|---|
| Calibre | : 8 x 57 I (318" bullet point) |
| Cartridge capacity | : 5 cartridges (internal magazine) |
| Operation | : bolt action |
| Firing system | : centre-fire |
| Breach-loading | : 2-lug action |
| Length | : 124 cm (48.9") |
| Barrel length | : 74 cm (29.1") |
| Weight | : 3.9 kg (8.6 lb) |
| Sight | : graduated sight |
| Safety | : safetyscatch on rear of bolt |
| Stock | : nut |

*Specific details*: In 1888 Mauser produced the Gewehr 88, or Kommissions Gewehr, for the German Army in 7.92-mm calibre. Senior officers were not satisfied with the M1871 rifle. The new rifle has a blued barrel and tailpiece and no wooden hand protection. A metal protective tube runs from the tailpiece to the muzzle. The magazine takes a 5-cartridge Mannlicher clip. In 1889 the Belgian Army decided to switch over to a Mauser rifle in the 7.65-mm calibre, produced under a licence by the FN factories. The Spanish Army also wanted this weapon, but in the 7-mm caliber (7x57 mm). It proved to be such an exceptional weapon for its time that it caused the Americans serious problems during the Spanish–American War of 1898. The American army decided to have a similar rifle developed by the Springfield Armory, the Springfield M1903. However, this rifle appeared to be so identical to the Mauser design that the American government was forced to pay a compensation of $200,000 to Mauser for violation of their patent.

## Borchardt pistol Model 1893

### TECHNICAL SPECIFICATIONS

| | |
|---|---|
| Calibre | : 7.65 Borchardt |
| Cartridge capacity | : 8 cartridges |
| Operation | : single-action |
| Firing system | : centre-fire |
| Breach-loading | : toggle bolt |
| Length | : 350 mm (13.8") |
| Barrel length | : 190 mm(7.5") |
| Weight | : 1275 g (45 oz) |
| Sight | : fixed |
| Safety | : sear on left-hand side of frame above grip plate |
| Grip | : walnut |

*Specific details*: This was one of the very first semi-automatic pistols. Designed by Hugo Borchardt, who was born in Germany but emigrated with his parents to Connecticut in his teens. He was employed by various arms companies, including the Pioneer Breechloading Arms Company and the Winchester Repeating Arms Company. Around 1876 he designed a revolver for Winchester. This weapon did not go into production because Colt saw it as a rival. Borchardt left in disillusion and joined the Sharps Rifle Company. In 1880 he became unemployed when Sharps went into liquidation. After that he designed the Borchardt pistol. Since he could not find any American factory that wanted to produce his design, he went back to Europe. In 1891 he was employed by the German company Ludwig Loewe & Co in Berlin, who were interested in producing this pistol. An interesting detail is that Borchardt's assistant was called George Luger. In 1896 the weapons producing activities of Loewe, including the Borchardt pistols, were continued by Deutsche Waffen- und Munitionsfabriken (DWM) of Berlin. Their telegram address was Parabellum–Berlin. This is how the 1908 Luger pistol got its nickname. Some 3100 Borchardt pistols were produced in total. The collector's value of this weapon is quite high.

*Borchardt pistol Model 1893*

*Bergmann pistol Model 1897 (No. 5)*

*Mauser Gewehr 98*

## Bergmann pistol Model 1897 (No. 5)

### TECHNICAL SPECIFICATIONS

| | |
|---|---|
| Calibre | : 7.8 mm Bergmann |
| Cartridge capacity | : 5-shot |
| Operation | : single-action |
| Firing system | : centre-fire |
| Breach-loading | : falling-block type action |

*Cut-away view of the Mauser G98*

| | |
|---|---|
| Length | : 268 mm (10.6") |
| Barrel length | : 112 mm (4.4") |
| Weight | : 980 g (34.6 oz) |
| Sight | : fixed |
| Safety | : rotating lug on left-hand side of frame |
| Grip | : ebonite |

*Specific details*: A semi-automatic pistol, designed by Luis Schmeisser and produced by the Theodor Bergmann arms factory of Suhl in Germany. The extension No. 5 after the model name refers to the fact that Bergmanm produced four other semi-automatic pistol models before this one. Only about one thousand M1897s were made because no European army was interested in buying them.

In addition Bergmann built another 450 of these revolvers as carbines with a separate stock. The pistol has a rather high collector's value.

## Mauser Gewehr 98

**TECHNICAL SPECIFICATIONS**

| | |
|---|---|
| Calibre | : 8 x 57 IS |
| Cartridge capacity | : 5 cartridges |
| Operation | : bolt action |
| Firing system | : centre-fire |
| Breach-loading | : 2-lug action |

| | |
|---|---|
| Length | : 125 cm (49.2") |
| Barrel length | : 74 cm (29.1") |
| Weight | : 4.1 kg (9 lb) |
| Sight | : graduated sight (400–2000 m) |
| Safety | : safetyscatch on rear of bolt |
| Stock | : nut |

Specific details: In 1898 the German Army decided to introduce the Model 1898 rifle developed by Mauser as the Gewehr 98 in the 7.92-mm Mauser calibre. Shortened versions were named Kar-98a in 1904, Kar-98b (after World War I) and Kar-98K in 1935.

In total more than 200 different versions have been produced, apart from the many hunting rifle varieties in several calibres from .22 Long Rifle to 9.3 x 57 mm. The military versions are marked 'GEW. 98', followed by the name of the manufacturer, since many G98s were not made by Mauser, but by other manufacturers who had been licensed by Mauser. In the Second Boer War (1899–1902) many South African Boers bought these rifles to fight the British.

The photograph shows a special limited edition to commemorate the 100th anniversary of the Mauser 98 system. A series of 1998 of these limited edition rifles will be built in total.

# 5 French firearms from 1715 to 1892

*Aubton flintlock pocket pistol, c. 1715*

## Aubton flintlock pocket pistol, c. 1715

**TECHNICAL SPECIFICATIONS**

Calibre : 19 mm (.75")
Cartridge capacity : single-shot, muzzle-loader
Operation : single-action
Firing system : flintlock
Breach-loading : N/A
Length : 210 mm (8.25")
Barrel length : 81 mm (3.2")
Weight : 540 g (19 oz)
Sight : none
Safety : half-cock
Grip : walnut

*Specific details*: Travelling by coach was not always safe in the 18th and 19th centuries with the roads often being frequented by highwaymen. For that reason travellers often took compact pocket revolvers with them. However sets of identical pocket pistols are only rarely found. These sets were often quite luxuriously made and stored in a special case, complete with all accessories, such as a bullet mould, maintenance tools and extra flints. The set of flintlock pocket pistols in the photograph was made by the French gunsmith Aubton of Nantes around 1715. The ramrod stored in the barrel has an ivory ram.

## French Chobert duelling pistol, c. 1770

**TECHNICAL SPECIFICATIONS**

Calibre : 12.7–15.7 mm (.500–.62")
Cartridge capacity : single-shot, muzzle-loader
Operation : single-action
Firing system : flintlock
Breach-loading : N/A
Length : 370 mm (14.5")
Barrel length : 203 mm (8")
Weight : 910 g (32 oz)
Sight : none
Safety : half-cock
Grip : walnut

Specific details: It was a set of simple duelling pistols during the period 1770–1790, made in France by the French

*French Chobert duelling pistol, c. 1770*

gunsmith Chobert of Paris. The barrels are semi-octagonal and semicircular. The priming pan lid with a spring that is located outside the lock plate also serves as the anvil for the flint. As usual in those days, the muzzle is flared outward somewhat. More luxurious pistols sometimes had an extra safety catch on the rear of the cock tail.

After pulling the cock back into the single-action position it could be locked with a sliding sear. These types of pistols are special in that they mostly come in identical pairs, housed in a beautiful leather or wooden case, together with the loading accessories. The history of duelling weapons dates back to our earliest recorded history. Until the introduction of handguns, it was customary to settle an offence by the sword. From the 16th century onwards pistols were increasingly used for this. At the French court under King Louis XIV there were so many duels that the King made duels illegal by Royal Decree in 1679. In other countries it was considered vulgar to use a firearm to defend one's honour.

In order to settle a dispute as fairly as possible, both opponents should be given an equal chance and that is why both pistols had to be identical. Rules were even drawn up for this, as in the British Code of Duelling of 1829. This laid down that the minimum distance between both duellists should be 25 ft and that they could only fire after they had been instructed to do so by their second or seconds. The code of honour held that no multi-shot pistols could be used for duelling. One of the most famous people who fell victim to the practice of duelling was the Russian poet Alexander Pushkin.

He was killed in a duel by Baron d'Anthès, the adopted son of the Dutch ambassador, Baron van Heeckeren, in St Petersburg in 1837. Duelling pistols come in all types: from very simple versions to exquisitely engraved and gold-inlaid pistols, reflecting the owner's financial position. Famous producers of duelling pistols were: Clarke, Dickson, Henshall, Mills, Manton, Mortimer, Parker, Richards and Wogdon & Barton from Great Britain and Boutet, Gastinne & Renette and Verney from France. Some famous German names in this field are Bramhoffer, Schenk and Ulbricht.

These weapons were not only used to kill an opponent, but also for target shooting, a highly respected sport for a gentleman of means.

## French Army rifle Model 1777

**TECHNICAL SPECIFICATIONS**

| | |
|---|---|
| Calibre | : 17.5 mm (.69") |
| Cartridge capacity | : single-shot, muzzle-loader |
| Operation | : single-action |
| Firing system | : flintlock |
| Breach-loading | : N/A |
| Length | : 152 cm (59.8") |
| Barrel length | : 102 cm (40.2") |
| Weight | : 4.6 kg (10.1 lb) |
| Sight | : bead |
| Safety | : half-cock |
| Stock | : walnut |

*Specific details*: France was the first country to introduce the flintlock rifle in 1717 as

*French Army rifle Model 1777*

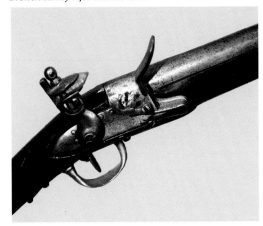

the standard army rifle. This rifle was derived from the 1717 model. In 1776, a number of modifications were implemented. They included a slanted bronze priming pan and a diagonally drilled touchhole.

A shorter version was available for the French cavalry, the M1777 carbine with a 76-cm (30") barrel length. This rifle was very modern for its time and was copied by lots of manufacturers from Liège in Belgium such as Ancion, Beuret, Francotte, Gulikers, Malherebe, Petry, Tanner and Tilken.

## Thonon double-barrelled flintlock shotgun, c. 1780

### TECHNICAL SPECIFICATIONS

| | |
|---|---|
| Calibre | : 26 |
| Cartridge capacity | : double-barrelled, |
| Operation | : single-action |
| Firing system | : flintlock |
| Breach-loading | : N/A |
| Length | : 123 cm (48.4") |
| Barrel length | : 81 cm (32") |
| Weight | : 3.4 kg (7.5 lb) |
| Sight | : fixed notch and bead |
| Safety | : half-cock |
| Stock | : walnut |

*Thonon double-barrelled flintlock shotgun, c. 1780*

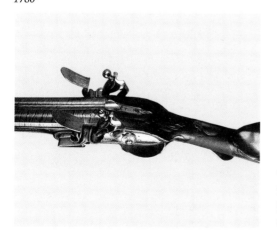

*Detail of Thonon double-barrelled flintlock shotgun*

*French army pistol, c. 1804*

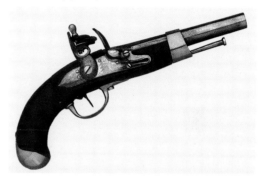

*Specific details*: It was made by the French gunsmith Thonon of Paris. The weapon is beautifully decorated with gold-inlaid medallions. Both barrels were made of damask steel and the forward grip has been inlaid with a golden thread.

## French army pistol, c. 1804

### TECHNICAL SPECIFICATIONS

| | |
|---|---|
| Calibre | : 17 mm (.67") |
| Cartridge capacity | : single-shot |
| Operation | : single-action |
| Firing system | : flintlockslot |
| Breach-loading | : N/A |
| Length | : 350 mm (13.8") |
| Barrel length | : 200 mm (7.9") |
| Weight | : 1220 g (43 oz) |
| Sight | : none |
| Safety | : half-cock |
| Grip | : walnut |

*Specific details*: A cavalry pistol from the time of Napoleon's army. This type of pistol was made in Saint Etienne and was extensively copied in many places, including Liège in Belgium. The weapon in this photograph shows no French test marks and probably comes from Liège.

*Mas Model 1822-T40*

## Boutet flintlock pistol 1815

**TECHNICAL SPECIFICATIONS**

| | |
|---|---|
| Calibre | : 14.7 mm (.58") |
| Cartridge capacity | : single-shot |
| Operation | : single-action |
| Firing system | : flintlock |
| Breach-loading | : N/A |
| Length | : 330 mm (13") |
| Barrel length | : 178 mm (7") |
| Weight | : 950 g (33.5 oz) |
| Sight | : bead |
| Safety | : half-cock |
| Grip | : walnut |

*Specific details*: French gunsmith and goldsmith Nicolas Noel Boutet (1761-1833) worked in a guild's workshop in Versailles. A favourite of the Emperor Napoleon, for whom he made a number of specially decorated firearms. In his workshop he mainly employed craftsmen from Liège in Belgium. Next to beautiful duelling pistols and hunting weapons, Boutet also produced military firearms.

*Boutet flintlock pistol, 1815*

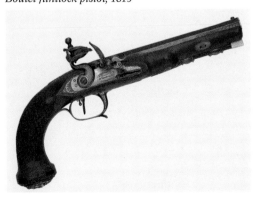

## Mas Model 1822-T40

**TECHNICAL SPECIFICATIONS**

| | |
|---|---|
| Calibre | : 18 mm (.71") |
| Cartridge capacity | : single-shot, muzzle-loader |
| Operation | : single-action |
| Firing system | : percussion |
| Breach-loading | : N/A |
| Length | : 147 cm (58") |
| Barrel length | : 108 cm (42.5") |
| Weight | : 4.2 kg (9.3 lb) |
| Sight | : bead |
| Safety | : half-cock hammer |
| Stock | : walnut |

*Specific details*: The French Model 1822-Infantry flintlock rifle was converted into a percussion rifle using a system devised by the French Army Captain Arcellin. As this was started in 1840 the extension T40 (Transformé) was added to the model name. The rifle in the photograph comes from Saint Etienne. It bears the production date 1827 and must have been converted into a percussion rifle after 1840. This model also

*Detail of Mas Model 1822-T40*

comes in a cavalry version with a 60-cm (23.5") barrel. Both models were extensively copied by gunmakers from Liège in Belgium such as Ancion, Falise and Francotte.

## Le Page duelling pistol, c. 1830

**TECHNICAL SPECIFICATIONS**

| | |
|---|---|
| Calibre | : 13.2 mm (.52") |
| Cartridge capacity | : single-shot |
| Operation | : single-action |
| Firing system | : percussion |
| Breach-loading | : N/A |
| Length | : 410 mm (16.1") |
| Barrel length | : 250 mm (9.8") |
| Weight | : 940 g (33.2 oz) |
| Sight | : notched sight |
| Safety | : half-cock hammer |
| Grip | : walnut |

*Specific details*: Le Page was a famous name in the 19th century firearms industry. The Le Page family owned gun factories in Paris and in Liège, Belgium and Bastin. Le Page was even the royal gunsmith to the French King Louis XVI. He was granted the patent to a pin-fire cartridge in 1832 and to a rim-fire cartridge in 1837. The weapon in the photograph is intended for target shooting and has a trigger accelerator: the lever in front of the actual trigger. Several companies, including Pedersoli, make excellent replicas of this type of pistol.

*Le Page duelling pistol, c. 1830*

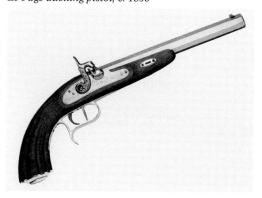

*French duelling pistol, c. 1835*

## French duelling pistol, c. 1835

**TECHNICAL SPECIFICATIONS**

| | |
|---|---|
| Calibre | : 12.7 mm (.500") |
| Cartridge capacity | : single-shot |
| Operation | : single-action |
| Firing system | : percussion |
| Breach-loading | : N/A |
| Length | : 229 mm (9") |
| Barrel length | : 102 mm (4") |
| Weight | : 1050 g (37 oz) |
| Sight | : bead |
| Safety | : half-cock hammer |
| Grip | : walnut |

*Specific details*: A set of simple duelling pistols; the weighted knob under the grip balances the weapon. The heavy octagonal barrels were made of damask steel. Both pistols were part of a set with a bullet mould, screwdriver, pump rod, powder flask, wooden loading hammers and a box for the percussion caps.

*Detailed photograph of Le Page shotgun with safety sear (arrow)*

# Le Page shotgun, c. 1840

**TECHNICAL SPECIFICATIONS**

| | |
|---|---|
| Calibre | : 13 |
| Cartridge capacity | : double-barrelled, single-shot |
| Operation | : single-action |
| Firing system | : percussion |
| Breach-loading | : N/A |
| Length | : 122 cm (48") |
| Barrel length | : 78.7 cm (31") |
| Weight | : 3.1 kg (6.8 lb) |
| Sight | : bead |
| Safety | : half-cock hammer with sear |
| Stock | : walnut |

*Specific details*: Double-barrelled shotgun by French gunsmith and engineer Bastin Le Page of Paris. Le Page owed his fame to his duelling pistols. He also supplied firearms to the French King Louis XVI and to the Emperor Napoleon I. As early as 1832, he obtained a patent to a type of pin-fire cartridge with a brass bottom cover and a paper case. In 1837, he was granted a patent to a rim-fire cartridge.

# Mas Navy pistol, c. 1840

**TECHNICAL SPECIFICATIONS**

| | |
|---|---|
| Calibre | : 17.8 mm (.700") |
| Cartridge capacity | : single-shot, muzzle-loader |
| Operation | : single-action |
| Firing system | : percussion |
| Breach-loading | : N/A |
| Length | : 330 mm (13") |
| Barrel length | : 157 mm (6.2") |
| Weight | : 940 g (33.2 oz) |
| Sight | : none |
| Safety | : half-cock hammer |
| Grip | : nut |

*Mas Navy pistol, c. 1840*

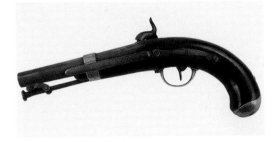

Specific details: It was produced as a self-defence weapon for the navy by MAS (St. Etienne) and MAC (Chatellerault) from c. 1840 to 1842. As was customary for that time, a hinged ramrod has been fitted below the barrel. The pistol has a long belt clip on its left-hand side. This type of pistol usually also had a lanyard ring at the bottom of the grip to attach a lanyard.

## Mac Model 1840–1842

**TECHNICAL SPECIFICATIONS**

| | |
|---|---|
| Calibre | : 18 mm (.71") |
| Cartridge capacity | : single-shot, muzzle-loader |
| Operation | : single-action |
| Firing system | : percussion |
| Breach-loading | : N/A |
| Length | : M1840: 148 cm (58.25"); M1842: 140 cm (55.25") |
| Barrel length | : M1840: 108 cm (42.5"); M1842: 103 cm (40.5") |
| Weight | : M1840: 4.3 kg (9.5 lb); M1842: 4.1 kg (9 lb) |
| Sight | : bead |
| Safety | : half-cock hammer |
| Stock | : walnut |

Specific details: It was made at the French national armoury in Chatellerault. The Model 1840, which was the predecessor of the M1842, had a breech chamber that was screwed into the barrel. In the M1842 this was constructed as an integral part of the

barrel. Both models were the first infantry rifles to be introduced by the French Army on a large scale. The M1842 was modified with a barrel with four wide turns of rifling in 1846. The Model 1840 was also made as a carbine: the 'Carbine Tierry' with a barrel length of 82.5 cm (32.5"). The American trading company of Herman Boker imported over 25,000 of these rifles in 1862. This rifle was also much copied by the Belgian firearms industry.

## Moutier dubbelloops kogelgeweer, omstreeks 1850

**TECHNICAL SPECIFICATIONS**

| | |
|---|---|
| Calibre | : 11.4 mm (.450") |
| Cartridge capacity | : double-barrelled, single-shot |
| Operation | : single-action |
| Firing system | : percussion |
| Breach-loading | : N/A |
| Length | : 114 cm (44.9") |
| Barrel length | : 71 cm (28") |
| Weight | : 3.6 kg (7.9 lb) |
| Sight | : fixed sight |
| Safety | : half-cock hammer |
| Stock | : walnut |

Specific details: It was a double-barrelled rifle made by the French gunsmith Moutier of Paris around 1850. This rifle has a straight (English) stock, typical of the time. The lock plates and hammers show beautiful decorations.

Mac Model 1840–1842

Moutier double-barrelled rifle, c. 1850

*Goutelle double-barrelled hunting rifle, c. 1850*

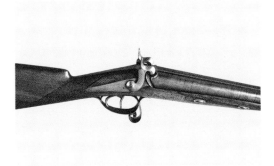

double-barrelled rifles were made in France in those days. Most double-barrelled rifles were shotguns. Except for the curled trigger guard, this rifle shows a very plain design without any further decorations.

## Mas military pistol Model 1850

**TECHNICAL SPECIFICATIONS**

Calibre               : 17.8 mm (.700")
Cartridge capacity : single-shot
Operation            : single-action
Firing system        : percussion
Breach-loading      : N/A
Length                : 350 mm (13.8")
Barrel length        : 200 mm (7.9")
Weight                : 1270 g (45 oz)
Sight                  : fixed notch and bead
Safety                : half-cock hammer
Grip                   : walnut

*Specific details*: This type of military pistol was produced by several French gunmakers.

At the same time a large number of flintlock pistols were also converted into percussion pistols. The back and front of the grip have been reinforced with a steel strip onto which the trigger guard has been mounted as well. Typical of such French weapons are the heavy brass grip caps with brass lanyard rings at the front and the bottom.

## Goutelle double-barrelled hunting rifle, c. 1850

**TECHNICAL SPECIFICATIONS**

Calibre               : 16.5 mm (.65")
Cartridge capacity : double-barrelled, single-shot
Operation            : single-action
Firing system        : percussion
Breach-loading      : N/A
Length                : 120 cm (47.2")
Barrel length        : 76.2 cm (30")
Weight                : 4.1 kg (9 lb)
Sight                  : bead
Safety                : half-cock hammer
Stock                 : walnut

*Specific details*: It was a double-barrelled rifle made by the gunsmith Goutelle of Saint Etienne in France. This was a muzzle-loading weapon which means that its barrel could not be broken to open it. Not many

*Left-hand side of the Goutelle double-barrelled hunting rifle*

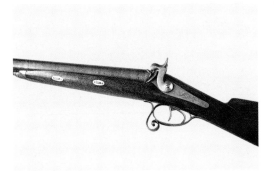

*Mas military pistol, Model 1850*

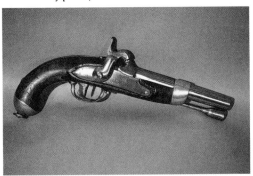

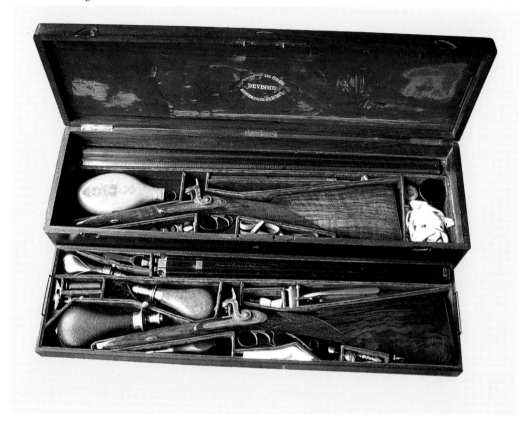

## *Devisme hunting set, 1850*

**TECHNICAL SPECIFICATIONS**

| | |
|---|---|
| Calibre | : shot: 12; bullet: .500 (12.7 mm) |
| Cartridge capacity | : double-barrelled, |
| Operation | : single-action |
| Firing system | : percussion |
| Breach-loading | : barrel lock action |
| Length | : shot: 127 cm (50"); bullet: 107 cm (42") |
| Barrel length | : shot: 81 cm (32"); bullet: 61 cm (24") |
| Weight | : shot: 4.9 kg (11 lb); bullet: 5.4 kg (12 lb) |
| Sight | : bead; bullet: folding sight |
| Safety | : half-cock hammer |
| Stock | : walnut |

*Specific details*: This had a rifle case with detachable tray with a complete rifle set and a complete shotgun set, made by the French gunmaker F.P. Devisme of Paris around 1850. This popular gunsmith made a large variety of firearms, including percussion pistols and double-barrelled rifles and shotguns.

After 1858 Devisme switched to cartridge weapons in various calibres.

*Devisme revolver Model 1855*

119

## Devisme revolver Model 1855

**TECHNICAL SPECIFICATIONS**

| | |
|---|---|
| Calibre | : 11 mm (.43") |
| Cartridge capacity | : 6-shot |
| Operation | : single-action |
| Firing system | : percussion |
| Breach-loading | : N/A |
| Length | : 320 mm (12.6") |
| Barrel length | : 155 mm (6.1") |
| Weight | : 1050 g (37 oz) |
| Sight | : notch and bead |
| Safety | : none |
| Grip | : walnut |

*Specific details*: It was designed by the French gunmaker F.P. Devisme of Paris in 1855. This revolver has a special lever on its left, which allows the gun to be quickly disassembled into three parts: the barrel, the cylinder and the grip. The hammer of the revolver is partially concealed by the grip. Devisme hoped that this weapon would be accepted by the French army as their military revolver, but this never happened. The M1855 was also produced under licence by various gunmakers from Liège in Belgium.

*Le Mat percussion revolver 1856, 1st Model*

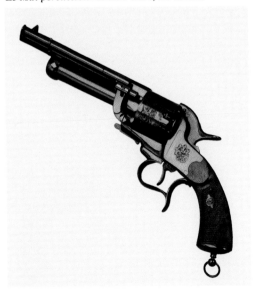

*Le Mat percussion revolver 1856, 2nd Model*

## Le Mat percussion revolver 1856

**TECHNICAL SPECIFICATIONS**

| | |
|---|---|
| Calibre | : see Specific details |
| Cartridge capacity | : 10-shot (9 cylinder chambers; 1 shot barrel) |
| Operation | : double-action |
| Firing system | : percussion |
| Breach-loading | : N/A |
| Length | : 340 mm (13.4") |
| Barrel length | : 165 mm (6.5") bullet barrel; 127 mm (5") shot barrel |
| Weight | : 1450 g (51.1 oz) |
| Sight | : fixed |
| Safety | : half-cock hammer |
| Grip | : nut |

*Specific details*: It was designed by the French military doctor Jean Alexandre Francois Le Mat of Paris in 1856. He later moved to New Orleans in the American state of Louisiana. This revolver was produced by Girard & Fils of Paris and by various manufacturers in Belgium, Great Britain and the United States. The gun has two barrels. The upper barrel is the grooved bullet barrel. The lower barrel, which also acts as the cylinder axis pin, is the shot barrel. The most common calibre combinations are a .36 bullet with .50 shot; a .41 bullet with .66 shot or a .44 bullet with .72 shot. The firing pin point on the barrel must be switched over using the selector on top of the hammer before the shot barrel can be fired. This revolver was converted to .44 pin-fire and .38 centre-fire later. In the first model the bullet guide had been mounted to the right of the barrels and the trigger guard had a knurled hook. The model shown here has the bullet guide on the left and a round trigger guard. Page 120 shows an intermediate type with the bullet guide on the left and a trigger guard as on the first model. The American company Navy Arms has produced a series of excellent replicas of this revolver.

## Manceaux 1862 rifle

**TECHNICAL SPECIFICATIONS**

| | |
|---|---|
| Calibre | : 12 mm (.47") |
| Cartridge capacity | : single-shot |
| Operation | : single-action |
| Firing system | : percussion |
| Breach-loading | : folding bolt lever |
| Length | : 143 cm (56.1") |
| Barrel length | : 92 cm (36.2") |
| Weight | : 4.5 kg (9.88 lb) |
| Sight | : graduated sight |
| Safety | : half-cock hammer, bolt locked when hammer is cocked |
| Stock | : walnut |

*Specific details*: The French company of Manceaux & Vieillard of Paris designed various breech-loading rifles with folding bolt levers from 1860 to 1870. Some of them had a fixed notched sight; while graduated sights were only used on a couple of rifle designs. This rifle is most likely to have been produced by the French MAC: Manufacture d'Armes de Chatellerault. This rifle was tested by the French Army in the period from 1862 to 1864, but the Chassepot rifle was eventually selected. This rifle was also tested by the British Army. A similar rifle, produced by the Belgian Francotte company, was entered in Japanese military testing in 1876. The Manceaux rifle is known to have been made

*Manceaux 1862 rifle*

*Detail of Manceaux 1862 rifle*

in several versions: the Chasseurs carbine with a total length of 132.5 cm (52.2"), the cavalry musket with a total length of 120 cm (47.2"), and the Gardes Mobiles of the French–Prussian War of 1870 and 1871 with a total length of 126.5 cm (49.8").

## Lefaucheux navy revolver Model 1863

**TECHNICAL SPECIFICATIONS**

| | |
|---|---|
| Calibre | : 12 mm |
| Cartridge capacity | : 6-shot |
| Operation | : single-action |
| Firing system | : pin-fire |
| Breach-loading | : N/A |
| Length | : 300 mm (11.8") |
| Barrel length | : 160 mm (6.3") |
| Weight | : 1040 g (36.7 oz) |
| Sight | : notch (in head of hammer) and bead |
| Safety | : half-cock hammer |
| Grip | : walnut |

*Lefaucheux navy revolver Model 1863*

*Specific details*: By E. Lefaucheux of Paris and licensed to Belgian manufacturers in Liège and to Glisenti of Brescia. In 1856 the French Secretary of State of Naval Affairs selected the pin-fire revolver as the first official navy revolver Model 1863. This weapon had been introduced by the French Army five years earlier. This weapon was also used as a military revolver in Spain (1864), Norway (1864) and by the Swedish Artillery (1865). Over 20,000 of these revolvers were supplied to the Northern States during the American Civil War. After 1870 most French revolvers were converted into centre-fire revolvers.

## Mas Chassepot Fusil d'Infanterie Modelle 1866

### TECHNICAL SPECIFICATIONS

| | |
|---|---|
| Calibre | : 11 mm ((.43") |
| Cartridge capacity | : single-shot |
| Operation | : single-action |
| Firing system | : needle-fire |
| Breach-loading | : by bolt lever |
| Length | : 130 cm (51.35") |
| Barrel length | : 81,8 cm (32.3") |
| Weight | : 4.1 kg (9.13 lb) |
| Sight | : graduated sight |
| Safety | : loose locking disc (pièce d'arrêt) between bolt lever and breech |
| Stock | : walnut |

*Specific details*: It was designed by Antoine Alphonse Chassepot in 1857. After several test models the Model 1866 rifle was made. The most peculiar detail of this rifle is the rubber gas sealing ring in the head of the bolt. When the rifle was fired continuously for a long time the steel became too hot and the ring burnt. This rifle was produced by several companies including MAS (Manufacture d'Armes de Saint Etienne), MAC: Manufacture d'Armes de Chatellerault), Tulle, but also in the UK (Birmingham and London), in Venice in Italy and by several factories in Liège, Belgium. The rifles have different manufacturing codes: 'A, B or C' for MAC, 'D or E' for Mutzig, 'F, H, J, N, P or Q' for MAS, 'R, S or T' for Tulle and 'U or V' for the French company Cahen of Lyon. The first series produced was delivered to the French Bataillon de Chasseurs à Pied de la Garde by the end of 1866. Some 1.5 million of these rifles were made from 1865 to 1875. In the French Army it was eventually succeeded by the Gras rifle. The French Navy used the Chassepot until 1879 when it was replaced by the Kropatschek rifle. The remaining rifles produced were sold to China and Japan. Several Chassepot models were produced: Model 1866 Mousqueton d'Artillerie (length 99 cm/39"), Model 1866 Carabine de Cavalerie (length 117.5 cm/46.25"), Model 1866 Carabine de Gendarmerie (length 117.5 cm/46.25"), Model 1866 Cavalerie d'Afrique (length 130 cm/51.35").

*Detail of the Mas Chassepot Rifle M1863*

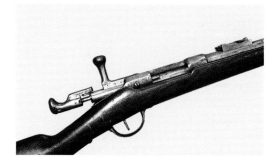

*Lefaucheux double-barrelled shotgun, c. 1870/1840*

*Details of Lefaucheux double-barrelled shotgun*

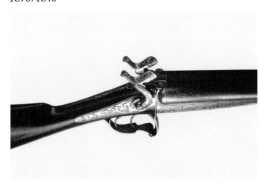

## Lefaucheux double-barrelled shotgun, c. 1870/1840

### TECHNICAL SPECIFICATIONS

Calibre : 20
Cartridge capacity : double-barrelled,
Operation : single-action
Firing system : centre-fire
Breach-loading : barrel catch with lock catch under forward grip
Length : 120 cm (47.2")
Barrel length : 71 cm (28")
Weight : 3.6 kg (6.2 lb)
Sight : bead
Safety : half-cock hammer
Stock : walnut

*Specific details*: Casimir Lefaucheux (1802–1852), a gunsmith from Paris, is considered as the inventor of the pin-fire system. His patent dates from 1832. His son, Eugène Gabriel Lefaucheux (1820–1871), continued his father's craft after his father's death. Together with his father he built various pin-fire revolvers and rifles, including the shotgun shown in the photograph.

This was originally built as a pin-fire shotgun, but was converted to centre-fire by Eugène in 1870. This explains the strangely shaped, mushroom-formed decorations that had to seal the pin-fire holes in the breeches. The firing pins were placed diagonally directly below them.

## Galand double-action revolver 1870

### TECHNICAL SPECIFICATIONS

Calibre : 9 or 11 mm Galand
Cartridge capacity : 6-shot
Operation : double-action
Firing system : centre-fire
Breach-loading : lever
Length : 245 mm (9.6")
Barrel length : 125 mm (4.9")
Weight : 1020 g (36 oz)
Sight : fixed
Safety : half-cock hammer
Grip : ebony or nut

*Galand double-action revolver 1870*

123

*Specific details*: This was produced by the French designer C.F. Galand and license-built by Manufacture Liegeoise a Feu of Liège in Belgium until approximately 1880. The trigger guard folds forward through a lever system, causing the cylinder to slide forward on the cylinder pin for loading or unloading the weapon. This complicated mechanism was the reason that this revolver was not selected as a military weapon. Galand designed another two revolver models that were produced by the Brandlin Armoury Company of Birmingham in Great Britain under the name Galand & Sommerville. With these latter models it is not the trigger guard that folds, but a large lever on the right-hand side of the frame.

## Mas Gras Fusil d'Infanterie Modelle 1874

**TECHNICAL SPECIFICATIONS**

| | |
|---|---|
| Calibre | : 11 x 59R mm |
| Cartridge capacity | : single-shot |
| Operation | : single-action |
| Firing system | : centre-fire |
| Breach-loading | : by bolt lever |
| Length | : 130.5 cm (51.4") |
| Barrel length | : 82 cm (32.3") |
| Weight | : 4.2 kg (9.2 lb) |
| Sight | : graduated sight |
| Safety | : pull the tensioning lever a bit and turn it a quarter turn |
| Stock | : walnut |

*Mas Gras Fusil d'Infanterie Modelle 1874*

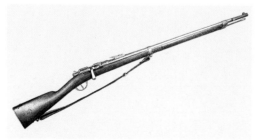

*Detail of Mas Gras Fusil d'Infanterie*

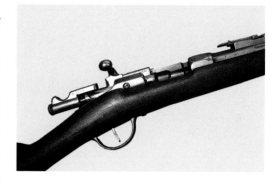

*Mas Gras Fusil d'Infanterie Modelle 1874-82 with straight bolt lever*

*Specific details*: It was designed by the French Army Captain Basile Gras in 1873. The first series had a straight bolt lever. Later models were fitted with curved bolt levers. Gras rifles were produced by the state-owned companies in Chatellerault (MAC), Saint-Etienne (MAS) and Tulle (MAT).

Various types of Gras rifle were made from 1874 to 1887. Initially an unknown number of Chassepot rifles were converted to the Gras system. Other types are: Gras Model 1866 Carabine de Cavalerie (length 117.5 cm/46.25"), Gras Model 1866 Carabine de Gendarmerie à Cheval (mounted police; length 117.5 cm/46.25"), Gras Model 1866 Carabine de Gendarmerie à Pied (regular police; same length), Gras Model 1874 Mousqueton d'Artillerie (length 99 cm/39"), and Gras Fusil Model 1874 M80-M14, and Gras rifles that were converted to 8 mm Lebel (8 x 51R mm) calibre in 1914.

*Lebel Fusil d'Infanterie Modelle 1886*

fitted with a telescopic sight and used for sniping in World War I. In 1935 it was decided to shorten a number of M1886 rifles for use by the cavalry and other motorised military units. This M1886/R35 carbine is shown below. The carbine has a total length of 95.8 cm (37.7"), a barrel length of 45 cm (17.7") and a weight of 3.8 kg (8.3 lb). The capacity of the tubular magazine was reduced to three cartridges. This carbine is shown below.

## Lebel Fusil d'Infanterie Modelle 1886

**TECHNICAL SPECIFICATIONS**

| | |
|---|---|
| Calibre | : 8 x 51R |
| Cartridge capacity | : tubular magazine for 8 cartridges |
| Operation | : single-action |
| Firing system | : centre-fire |
| Breach-loading | : by bolt lever and bolt catch in tailpiece |
| Length | : 130.7 cm (51.45") |
| Barrel length | : 81.5 cm (32.1") |
| Weight | : 4.2 kg (9.2 lb) |
| Sight | : graduated sight |
| Safety | : none |
| Stock | : walnut |

*Specific details*: It was produced by the state-owned companies in Chatellerault, Saint-Etienne and Tulle from 1886 to 1919. Over 4 million of these rifles, and the models derived from it, were produced. The rifle was introduced into the French Army as the Mle 1886 in 1887.

The cartridges in the tubular magazine below the barrel were pushed up by a cartridge lift and fed into the breech by means of the bolt action. Just above the front of the trigger guard there is a button on the action housing. This button could be used to block the supply of cartridges from the tubular magazine, so that a single cartridge could be entered into the breech manually as well. In 1893, the 1886/M93 model was introduced. This rifle had a safety device at the rear end of the bolt that served to block the firing pin. This rifle was

## Mas Ordnance revolver Lebel 1892

**TECHNICAL SPECIFICATIONS**

| | |
|---|---|
| Calibre | : 8 mm Lebel |
| Cartridge capacity | : 6-shot |
| Operation | : double-action |
| Firing system | : centre-fire |
| Breach-loading | : N/A |
| Length | : 240 mm (9.4") |
| Barrel length | : 118 mm (4.6") |
| Weight | : 845 g (29.8 oz) |
| Sight | : fixed |
| Safety | : half-cock hammer, opened loading gate locks hammer |
| Grip | : walnut |

*Specific details*: This was manufactured by Manufacture d'Armes St. Etienne in the period 1886–1938 as the successor to the Chamelot-Delvigne Model 1873 military revolver. This revolver had already been used by French army officers when it was officially issued as a military revolver after some modifications in 1892. The left-hand

*Lebel Modelle 1886-93 carbine*

side of the frame has an inspection plate which can be folded open for maintenance purposes. The 8-mm Lebel cartridge had a lead bullet until 1886, but had a copper-clad bullet after 1892. The weapon and the cartridge were named after the Colonel Lebel, a member of the French arms committee.

## Berthier Model 1892 Artillery carbine

### TECHNICAL SPECIFICATIONS

| | |
|---|---|
| Calibre | : 8 x 51R |
| Cartridge capacity | : internal magazine for 3 cartridges |
| Operation | : single-action |
| Firing system | : centre-fire |
| Breach-loading | : by two bolt lugs and a bolt lever in the tailpiece |
| Length | : carbine: 94.5 cm (37.2"); rifle: 112.5 cm (44.3") |

*Mas Ordnance revolver Lebel 1892*

| | |
|---|---|
| Barrel length | : Barrel length: carbine: 43.3 cm (17.85"); rifle: 63.2 cm (24.9") |
| Weight | : 3 kg (6.7 lb); rifle: 3.6 kg (8 lb) |
| Sight | : graduated sight |
| Safety | : none |
| Grip | : walnut |

*Specfic details*: It was produced in various models by the state armoury in Saint-Etienne from 1890 to 1894. The gun in the photograph is the Model 1892 Artillery carbine. This type has a ring on the left-hand side of the barrel band and a recess in the left-hand side of the stock for the rifle strap.

Other types such as the M1890 cavalry carbine and the M1890 cuirassers carbine or the Gendarmerie carbine have a belt ring at the bottom of the stock. Typical for the Berthiers is the bulging stock section for the internal magazine which could be loaded with a 3-cartridge clip from the top. The clip remained inside the weapon and was held by a catch in the front of the trigger guard. The Berthier M1892 rifle is shown below.

*Berthier Model 1892 rifle*

# 6 British firearms from 1730 to 1900

*Brown Bess 1730*

## Brown Bess 1730

**TECHNICAL SPECIFICATIONS**

| | |
|---|---|
| Calibre | : .75" (19 mm) |
| Cartridge capacity | : single-shot, muzzle-loader |
| Operation | : single-action |
| Firing system | : flintlock |
| Breach-loading | : N/A |
| Length | : 148 cm (58.3") |
| Barrel length | : 116 cm (45.7") |
| Weight | : 4.2 kg (9.26 lb) |
| Sight | : bead |
| Safety | : half-cock |
| Stock | : walnut |

*Specific details*: Brown Bess is the name for a series of flintlock guns that were made

*Details of Brown Bess*

by the Tower of London in the period 1730–1802. 'Bess' is supposed to be a crude form of the German word 'Büchse' whereas 'Brown' refers to the brown colour of the stock.

The name Brown Bess refers to various flintlock rifles and carbines. The first standardisation of military weapons took place in 1763 with the introduction of the Short Land Service Musket. The Brown Bess in the illustration has the letters 'GR' under the crown.

These letters stand for Georgus Rex, the Latin name for King George. The New Land Pattern Musket and its marine version, the Sea Service Musket, were based on the Brown Bess guns.

## Tower cavalry pistol, c. 1760

**TECHNICAL SPECIFICATIONS**

| | |
|---|---|
| Calibre | : .625" (16 mm) |
| Cartridge capacity | : single-shot |
| Operation | : single-action |
| Firing system | : flintlock |
| Breach-loading | : N/A |
| Length | : 552 mm (21.75") |
| Barrel length | : 368 mm (14.5") |
| Weight | : 1420 g (50 oz) |
| Sight | : none |
| Safety | : half-cock |
| Grip: | : walnut with brass grip knob |

*Specific details*: A military pistol from around 1760 with an engraving of a crown and the letters, GR, in the lock plate. These letters stand for Georgus Rex, the King George.

A brass plate on the grip indicates the regiment number..

## Twigg four-barrelled flintlock pistol, c. 1775

**TECHNICAL SPECIFICATIONS**

| | |
|---|---|
| Calibre | : .32" (8,1 mm) |
| Cartridge capacity | : single-shot, four-barrel |
| Operation | : single-action |
| Firing system | : flintlock |
| Breach-loading | : N/A |
| Length | : 254 mm (10") |
| Barrel length | : 89 mm (3.5") |
| Weight | : 850 g (30 oz.) |
| Sight | : none |
| Safety | : half-cock with sliding catch on the neck of the grip; locks both cocks and priming pan lids (steel) |
| Grip | : walnut |

*Specific details*: An English four-barrelled pistol probably made by John Twigg of London. The weapon has four barrels from

*Twigg four-barrelled flintlock pistol, c. 1775*

which a shot can be fired by one of the two cocks. To fire the two lower barrels, a catch on the left-hand side of the box must be turned half a revolution. This releases the two priming pans for the lower barrels. Twigg, who lived from 1732 to 1790, was famous for his multi-barrel guns.

## Twigg double-barrelled flintlock pistol, c. 1780

**TECHNICAL SPECIFICATIONS**

| | |
|---|---|
| Calibre | : .32" (8,1 mm) |
| Cartridge capacity | : single-shot, double-barrelled, |
| Operation | : single-action |
| Firing system | : flintlock |
| Breach-loading | : N/A |
| Length | : 229 mm (9") |
| Barrel length | : 76 mm (3") |
| Weight | : 600 g (21.2 oz) |
| Sight | : none |
| Safety | : sliding sear on the neck of the grip |
| Grip | : walnut |

*Specific details*: A double-barrel pistol with a switching priming pan, made by John Twigg of London in c. 1790. Mr. Twigg had a weapons manufacturing workshop in Angel Court, in the London district of Charing Cross from 1755 to 1759 and on the Strand from 1760 to 1775.

In 1775, he moved to a workshop near Piccadilly Circus. In 1787, Twigg entered into a partnership with John Bass, a weapons smith. Twigg, who died in 1790, is

*Twigg double-barrelled flintlock pistol, c. 1780*

*Right-hand side of the Twigg double-barrelled flintlock pistol*

*London Warranted flintlock pistol 1790*

famous for his duelling pistols and for the weapons he produced for the East India Company.

Around 1785, he made a 7-barrel pepperbox revolver, with barrels that had to be rotated by hand. A famous contemporary and pupil of Twigg was John Manton, who was later to develop a special type of flintlock.

## London Warranted flintlock pistol 1790

### TECHNICAL SPECIFICATIONS
| | |
|---|---|
| Calibre | : .58" (14,7 mm) |
| Cartridge capacity | : single-shot, muzzle-loader |
| Operation | : single-action |
| Firing system | : flintlock |
| Breach-loading | : N/A |
| Length | : 410 mm (16.1") |
| Barrel length | : 203 mm (8") |
| Weight | : 1100 g (38.8 oz) |
| Sight | : fixed |
| Safety | : half-cock |
| Grip | : nut |

*Specific details*: The weapon in the illustration is a travelling pistol with a bronze barrel. The designation 'Warranted' was used by several manufacturers. This type of weapon was also called a Trade Pistol and it was made for sale or barter with Asia, Africa and the Middle East. The flintlocks were mostly made in Belgium and imported by the British.

This type of weapon was produced in unknown quantities between 1790 and 1840.

## London Blunderbuss, c. 1800

### TECHNICAL SPECIFICATIONS
| | |
|---|---|
| Calibre | : .78 – 1.18" (20–30 mm) |
| Cartridge capacity | : single-shot, muzzle-loader |
| Operation | : single-action |
| Firing system | : flintlock |
| Breach-loading | : N/A |
| Length | : 72 cm (28.3") |
| Barrel length | : 38 cm (15") |
| Weight | : 4.5 kg (10 lb) |
| Sight | : fixed |
| Safety | : sliding sear behind tail of cock |
| Stock | : walnut |

*Specific details*: The blunderbuss was developed as a military and civilian short-range self-defence gun. The weapon was

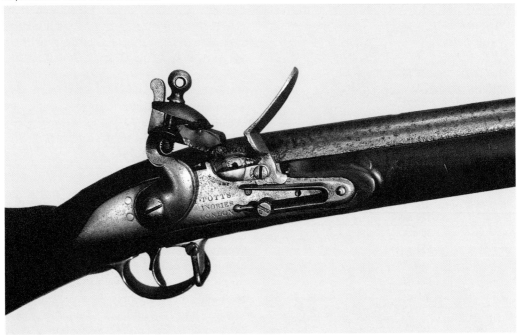

loaded with round lead balls. Some blunderbusses had a spring-loaded folding bayonet. The blunderbuss in the illustration is attributed to Enfield, but they were also produced by English companies such as Bolton, Cornhill of London, Dobson & Baker, Fermoy, Osborne & Jackson, Rea & Sons, Tomlinson, Wogdon & Barton and many others.

The barrel lengths varied from 14 to 16" (36–41 cm). The flaring muzzle was to improve the spread of the coarse shot. The locking lever on the rear of the barrel serves to operate the bayonet that folds forward by spring action.

| Length | : 148.6 cm (58.5") |
| Barrel length | : 106.7 cm (42") |
| Weight | : 4.5 kg (9.9 lb) |
| Sight | : bead |
| Safety | : half-cock |
| Stock | : walnut |

*Specific details*: This was used by the English Army from 1802 to 1838. This rifle was made by several companies.

Since its establishment in 1816, the Royal Armory produced large numbers of this rifle, together with several subcontractors, such as Barnett, Blisset, Bond, Greener,

*Londen Blunderbuss (c. 1800)*

## Enfield New Land Pattern Musket

**TECHNICAL SPECIFICATIONS**

| Calibre | : .75" (19 mm) |
| Cartridge capacity | : single-shot, muzzle-loader |
| Operation | : single-action |
| Firing system | : percussion |
| Breach-loading | : N/A |

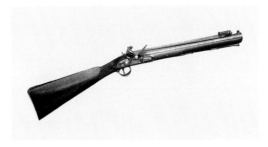

Hollis, Kerr, London Armory, Parker-Field, Potts & Hunt, Pritchett, Wheeler and Wilson.

## *William Bond flintlock travelling pistols, c. 1820*

**TECHNICAL SPECIFICATIONS**

| | |
|---|---|
| Calibre | : .75" (19 mm) |
| Cartridge capacity | : single-shot |
| Operation | : single-action |
| Firing system | : flintlock |
| Breach-loading | : N/A |
| Length | : 210 mm (8.27" |
| Barrel length | : 80 mm (3.15") |
| Weight | : 550 g (19.4 oz) |
| Sight | : bead |
| Safety | : half-cock, to be locked with a sear |
| Grip | : walnut |

*Specific details*: A complete set of travelling pistols made by the London gunsmith, William Bond, around 1820. The Bond family were renowned in those days, especially in their capacity as the supplier to the Tower of London.

This was a national armoury where the weapons components supplied were assembled into army weapons. Together with his cousin Edward Bond, William had a work-

*William Bond flintlock travelling pistols c. 1820*

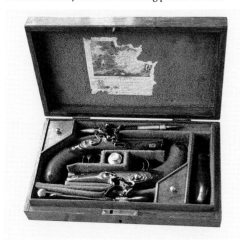

shop on Corn Hill in London where they produced guns. They took over the company from Edward's father Philip Bond in 1815. There is no exact data on how many pistols or sets of this type were made, but we do know that this type of firearm was very popular with travellers who wanted to protect themselves against tramps and wild dogs in the countryside in Great Britain and on the Continent.

## *Day Cane Gun 1825*

**TECHNICAL SPECIFICATIONS**

| | |
|---|---|
| Calibre | : .36" (9,1 mm) |
| Cartridge capacity | : single-shot |
| Operation | : single-action |
| Firing system | : percussion |
| Breach-loading | : N/A |
| Length | : 70 cm (27.6") |
| Barrel length | : 55 cm (21.7") |
| Weight | : 200 g (7.1 oz) |
| Sight | : bead |
| Safety | : none |
| Grip | : walnoten handle |

Specific details: This was designed by John Day from Barnstaple, Devonshire in Great-Britain. In 1823, he patented an under-hammer firing mechanism, of which the cane gun is an example. The weapon had to be loaded through the barrel chamber after which the barrel was screwed onto the handle. To fire the weapon the hammer had

*Day Cane Gun 1825*

to be pulled out so that a percussion cap could be installed. When the hammer was cocked, the trigger folded out as well. In 1858, Remington patented a percussion cane gun in the United States.

## Conway Pepperbox, c. 1830

**TECHNICAL SPECIFICATIONS**

| | |
|---|---|
| Calibre | : .41" (10,4 mm) |
| Cartridge capacity | : 6-shot |
| Operation | : double-action |
| Firing system | : percussion |
| Breach-loading | : N/A |
| Length | : 193 mm (7.6") |
| Barrel length | : 76 mm (3") |
| Weight | : 790 g (28 oz) |
| Sight | : none |
| Safety | : none |
| Grip | : ebony |

*Specific details*: Thomas Conway worked as a gunmaker on Blackfriars Street in Manchester from 1820 to 1850. He mainly made percussion handguns, such as the .44 double-action Tranter revolver, which he produced under a licence, and pepperboxes such as the one shown on this page. The Birmingham proof mark can be clearly seen between the barrels. The percussion caps are carefully enclosed in the protective ring around the barrels. A disadvantage of this weapon was that it was very difficult to load. In those days pepperbox revolvers were popular with travellers who wanted to defend themselves.

*Enfield Victoria M1838 Musket*

## Enfield Victoria M1838 Musket

**TECHNICAL SPECIFICATIONS**

| | |
|---|---|
| Calibre | : .75" (19 mm) |
| Cartridge capacity | : single-shot, muzzle-loader |
| Operation | : single-action |
| Firing system | : percussion |
| Breach-loading | : N/A |
| Length | : 139.7 cm (55") |
| Barrel length | : 99 cm (39") |
| Weight | : 4.35 kg (9.6 lb) |
| Sight | : graduated sight |
| Safety | : half-cock |
| Stock | : walnut |

*Specific details*: Together with the Brunswick M1836 rifle this was one of the first percussion weapons for the English army.

It was designed by George Lovell, the director of the Enfield arms factory and member of the military Small Arms Committee to the Ordnance Board. This is a smooth-barrelled rifle based on the M1802 flintlock

*Conway Pepperbox, c. 1830*

*Detail of the Enfield Victoria M1838 Musket*

rifle. The mark 'VR' on the lock refers to 'Victoria Regina', Queen Victoria who was crowned in 1837. In those days many flintlock muskets were converted into percussion guns to save on costs for arming the military.

Many of these weapons were lost during the great fire of the Tower of London in 1841.

is rather high then. By engaging the trigger accelerator the trigger pressure is at least halved, allowing a much more accurate shot to be fired. Other types of these weapons sometimes had double triggers, with the first trigger serving as an accelerator. The lock has the inscription 'Warranted' which was often used for English-made civilian guns.

## Duelling pistol, c. 1840

**TECHNICAL SPECIFICATIONS**

| | |
|---|---|
| Calibre | : .52" (13,2 mm) |
| Cartridge capacity | : single-shot |
| Operation | : single-action |
| Firing system | : percussion |
| Breach-loading | : N/A |
| Length | : 330 mm (13") |
| Barrel length | : 152 mm (6") |
| Weight | : 1020 g (36 oz) |
| Sight | : bead |
| Safety | : half-cock |
| Grip | : walnut |

*Specific details*: A set of decorated English duelling pistols with a grip that continues up to the muzzle.

The octagonal barrel was made from damask steel. Typical of this weapon is its trigger accelerator: the button before the trigger inside the trigger guard. A trigger accelerator works as follows: after cocking the hammer the weapon can be fired by pushing the trigger, but the trigger pressure

*Duelling pistol c. 1840*

## Baker percussion revolver, c. 1845

**TECHNICAL SPECIFICATIONS**

| | |
|---|---|
| Calibre | : .35–44" (8.9–11.2 mm) |
| Cartridge capacity | : 5-shot |
| Operation | : double-action |
| Firing system | : percussion |
| Breach-loading | : N/A |
| Length | : 290 mm (11.4") |
| Barrel length | : 140 mm (5.5") |
| Weight | : 990 g (35 oz) |
| Sight | : bead |
| Safety | : none |
| Grip | : walnut |

*Specific details*: It was probably made around 1845 by the English gunmaker T.K. Baker of London. The revolver shown has an octagonal barrel, but round or combinations of half-octagonal/half-round barrels also exist.

Other types that are ascribed to Baker are models with a rod-shaped hammer with a spur that was used to cock the hammer before every shot (single-action). This type of revolver was mainly used as a defensive weapon for the private market.

*Baker percussion revolver c. 1845*

*Manton duelling pistol, c. 1850*

## Manton duelling pistol, c. 1850

**TECHNICAL SPECIFICATIONS**

Calibre            : .42" (10.7 mm (.42"))
Cartridge capacity : single-shot
Operation          : single-action
Firing system      : percussion
Breach-loading     : N/A
Length             : 385 mm (15.2")
Barrel length      : 235 mm (9.3")
Weight             : 1050 g (37 oz)
Sight              : keepsight
Safety             : half-cock hammer with safety sear on right-hand lock plate
Grip               : walnut

*Specific details*: A duelling pistol from the Mantons, an English family of gunmakers. John Manton lived in London from 1780 to 1834 and supplied various weapons including hunting guns to the Royal Court. He was succeeded by his younger brother Joseph

*Westley-Richards rifle 1850*

who opened a branch in Calcutta, India, which was an English colony at that time. Joseph developed the disc-priming lock (1816) and the priming tube lock (1818).

## Westley-Richards rifle 1850

**TECHNICAL SPECIFICATIONS**

Calibre            : 8
Cartridge capacity : single-shot
Operation          : single-action
Firing system      : percussion
Breach-loading     : N/A
Length             : 116.8 cm (46")
Barrel length      : 66 cm (26")
Weight             : 4.8 kg (10.6 lb)
Sight              : keepsight
Safety             : half-cock hammer
Stock              : walnut

*Specific details*: A heavy-barrelled rifle, made by the English gunmakers of Westley-Richards, around 1850. The calibre was derived from shot calibre 8. Westley-Richards was founded in Birmingham in 1812. In 1814 the company opened up a branch in Bond Street in the centre of London. The family hired a well-known sportsman, William Bishop, as the branch manager. After he retired the company sold the London branch to Malcolm Lyell, the owner of the Holland & Holland gun factory. John Deeley and William Anson, the inventors of the Anson & Deeley lock, were managers at Westley-Richards at the time when they patented their invention.

*Cogswell pepperbox, c. 1850*

## Cogswell pepperbox, c. 1850

### TECHNICAL SPECIFICATIONS

| | |
|---|---|
| Calibre | : .476" (12,1 mm) |
| Cartridge capacity | : 6 patroonkamers |
| Operation | : double-action |
| Firing system | : percussion |
| Breach-loading | : N/A |
| Length | : 190 mm (7.5") |
| Barrel length | : 76 mm (3") |
| Weight | : 790 g (28 oz) |
| Sight | : none |
| Safety | : none |
| Grip | : walnut |

*Specific details*: This was most likely made by the English gunmaker B. Cogswell of London between 1845 and 1855.

This type of weapon was called a 'revolving pistol'. In the period from 1830 to 1865 many producers manufactured similar pepperbox revolvers, such as Ethan Allen (US), Cooper (GB) and Turner (GB).

## Adams DA-Holster revolver Model 1851

### TECHNICAL SPECIFICATIONS

| | |
|---|---|
| Calibre | : .338, .442 or .500" (8.6, 11.2 or 12.7 mm) |
| Cartridge capacity | : 5-shot |
| Operation | : double-action |
| Firing system | : percussion |
| Breach-loading | : N/A |
| Length | : 340 mm (13.4") |
| Barrel length | : 203 mm (8") |
| Weight | : 1330 g (46.9 oz) |
| Sight | : bead |
| Safety | : none |
| Grip | : walnut |

*Specific details*: This was made by the London-based Deane, Adams & Deane gunmakers from 1851 to circa 1865, and licensed to several gunmaking companies in Birmingham and to Francotte in Liége, Belgium. The weapon was available in three different sizes: the large .500"-calibre

*Adams DA-Holster Revolver Model 1851*

Holster pattern, the intermediate .442"-calibre Belt pattern and the .338"-calibre Pocket size. As all sizes could only be fired in double-action there is no hammer spur. Around 1851, Robert Adams was engaged in fierce competition with Colt. He was highly disappointed when, in 1854, the British Army selected the Colt Navy revolver that was produced in the Colt factory in London. Still many officers in the British Army preferred the man-stopping qualities of the Adams revolver and personally bought such a revolver for their own use.

## Enfield pattern of 1853 rifle

**TECHNICAL SPECIFICATIONS**

| | |
|---|---|
| Calibre | : .577" (14.7 mm) |
| Cartridge capacity | : single-shot, muzzle-loader |
| Operation | : single-action |
| Firing system | : percussion |
| Breach-loading | : N/A |
| Length | : 139,7 cm (55") |
| Barrel length | : 99.1 cm (39") |
| Weight | : 4.3 kg (9.6 lb) |
| Sight | : graduated sight |
| Safety | : half-cock hammer |
| Stock | : walnut |

*Specific details*: This rifle that was produced by various English factories between 1853 and 1864 was also called the Three-Band Musket. There are four different models. The main modifications concern changes to the barrel bands:

*Enfield Pattern of 1853 Rifle*

clamped in the first model; held by a leaf spring in the second model; fixed with screws in the fourth model. The third model had a somewhat shorter stock (1"/2.5 cm).
This rifle was made in very large numbers. During the American Civil War the Southern States imported some 300,000 of these rifles and the Northern army well over 600,000. Most rifles carry the marks 'London Armoury Company' and 'Royal Small Arms Factory'. There are excellent replicas in the .58 Minié calibre. Shown: the Three-Band Musket (above) and the Two-Band Rifle (below).

## Enfield 1853 Volunteer Rifle

**TECHNICAL SPECIFICATIONS**

| | |
|---|---|
| Calibre | : .451" (11.5 mm) |
| Cartridge capacity | : single-shot, muzzle-loader |
| Operation | : single-action |
| Firing system | : percussion |
| Breach-loading | : N/A |
| Length | : 125.7 cm (49.5") |
| Barrel length | : 83.8 cm (33") |
| Weight | : 4.3 kg (9.5 lb) |
| Sight | : graduated sight |
| Safety | : half-cock hammer |
| Stock | : walnut |

*Specific details*: English military rifle with two barrel bands. The bead has a ring around it. Made as a rifle for British volunteer troops that were composed of members of shooting clubs around 1853. The rifle

*Enfield 1853 Volunteer Rifle*

was also manufactured by several small English gunmaking companies and was imported into America by the Confederate Army.

The Gibbs Rifle Company is still making a beautiful replica of an original model with barrels produced by Parker-Hale Ltd of Birmingham (GB).

## Tranter second Model 1855

### TECHNICAL SPECIFICATIONS

| | |
|---|---|
| Calibre | : .497 or .442" (12.6 or 11.2 mm) |
| Cartridge capacity | : 5-shot |
| Operation | : double-action |
| Firing system | : percussion |
| Breach-loading | : N/A |
| Length | : 292 mm (11.5") |
| Barrel length | : 165 mm (6.5") |
| Weight | : 1020 g (36 oz) |
| Sight | : fixed notch |
| Safety | : automatic safety (see Specific details) |
| Grip | : walnut |

Specific details: A revolver based on a patent by Adams with a double-action trigger mechanism by William Tranter, from 1855. Most Tranter revolver types have double triggers.

The upper trigger is located inside the trigger guard, with a second trigger mounted underneath. This second trigger is used to pre-cock and fire the hammer (single-

Tranter Second Model 1855

action) or both triggers are pulled simultaneously (double-action). The typically shaped spring behind the cylinder is a kind of automatic safety. If the hammer is cocked slightly, this spring inserts a pin between the frame and the hammer. As soon as the lower trigger is pulled to cock the hammer, the safety pin is removed. Tranter made three models of these double-trigger revolvers.

The first model is from 1853 and has a removable ramrod. The second model is shown here. It has a fixed ramrod. The ramrod on the third model is locked to the barrel by means of a spring-loaded pawl and the hinge on the lower side has been replaced by a large screw. In 1855, Tranter also designed a small pocket revolver in a .380"/9.7-mm calibre with a 4.5"/114-mm barrel.

## Blissett double-barrel rifle 1856

### TECHNICAL SPECIFICATIONS

| | |
|---|---|
| Calibre | : .450" (11,4 mm) |
| Cartridge capacity | : double-barrelled, single-shot |
| Operation | : single-action |
| Firing system | : percussion |
| Breach-loading | : N/A |
| Length | : 113 cm (44.5") |
| Barrel length | : 71 cm (28") |
| Weight | : 3.9 kg (8.6 lb) |
| Sight | : folding sights for various ranges |
| Safety | : half-cock hammer |
| Stock | : walnut |

Specific details: Blisset was one of a group of gunmakers who supplied parts to the Tower of London Armoury for military guns from 1850 to 1867. He also made a large number of beautiful hunting guns in his own workshop.

As well as his shotguns, the Blisset double-barrelled rifles were very popular. The illustration shows a rifle from 1856 in its original box.

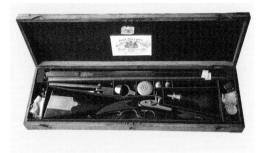

## Tranter Model 1856 army

**TECHNICAL SPECIFICATIONS**

| | |
|---|---|
| Calibre | : .44" (11,1 mm) |
| Cartridge capacity | : 5-shot |
| Operation | : double-action |
| Firing system | : percussion |
| Breach-loading | : N/A |
| Length | : 241 or 298 mm (9.5 or 11.75") |
| Barrel length | : 109 or 152 mm (4.3 or 6") |
| Weight | : 620 or 880 g (22 or 31 oz) |
| Sight | : fixed notch and bead |
| Safety | : half-cock hammer and safety sear on right-hand side of frame |
| Grip | : walnut |

*Specific details*: This was made by William Tranter of Birmingham. He designed this revolver in order to enter a firearms test on the initiative of the British Army who were looking for a new military revolver. There is a ramrod on the left-hand side of the weapon. The model shown is a civilian version of the military revolver. The barrel

*Tranter Model 1856 Army*

may bear the inscriptions of other manufacturers such as Thomas Jackson and Rigby who made this revolver under a licence.

## Enfield pattern of 1858 rifle

**TECHNICAL SPECIFICATIONS**

| | |
|---|---|
| Calibre | : .577" (14,7 mm) |
| Cartridge capacity | : single-shot, muzzle-loader |
| Operation | : single-action |
| Firing system | : percussion |
| Breach-loading | : N/A |
| Length | : 124.5 cm (49") |
| Barrel length | : 83.8 cm (33") |
| Weight | : 3.9 kg (8.5 lb) |
| Sight | : graduated sight |
| Safety | : half-cock hammer |
| Stock | : walnut |

*Specific details*: Other names for this rifle are Two-Band Rifle or Sergeant's Rifle. It was introduced by the British Army in 1856. It was produced from 1856 to 1863 in four different versions, such as the bayonet catch on the barrel, a Navy model in 1858 and a modified graduated rear sight in connection with a new type of gunpowder in 1861.
Before that time the sight had a maximum range of 1100 yards, but thanks to the improved gunpowder this could be increased to 1250 yards. The rifle was imported in large numbers by both sides during the American Civil War, as a result

of which their collector's value is not very high. There are excellent replicas in the .58 Minié calibre.

## Kerr Army Revolver Model 1858

**TECHNICAL SPECIFICATIONS**

| | |
|---|---|
| Calibre | : .380 or .440" (9.7 or 11.2 mm) |
| Cartridge capacity | : 5-shot |
| Operation | : single-action (M1858) or double-action (M1859) |
| Firing system | : percussion |
| Breach-loading | : N/A |
| Length | : 280 mm (11") |
| Barrel length | : 140 mm (5.5") |
| Weight | : 1220 g (43 oz) |
| Sight | : fixed |
| Safety | : half-cock hammer |
| Grip | : nut |

*Specific details*: It was designed by the English gunsmith John Kerr in 1858 and produced by the London Armoury Company. The picture shows the first model.

Later versions had a small sear below the external hammer. After cocking the hammer could be locked with this sear. The pin protruding from behind the hammer is the removable cylinder pin. In 1859, Kerr

*Kerr Army Revolver Model 1858*

built a double-action revolver at the request of the British Army. Although this weapon was not chosen as a military revolver, it was still quite popular, especially in the British colonies.

The .440"-calibre version of this revolver was also used by the Portuguese Army. There are no exact production figures for this revolver, but it is still readily available from antique firearms dealers.

## Enfield-Mortimer Whitworth Rifle Model 1858

**TECHNICAL SPECIFICATIONS**

| | |
|---|---|
| Calibre | : .451" Whitworth (11.5 mm) |
| Cartridge capacity | : single-shot, muzzle-loader |
| Operation | : single-action |
| Firing system | : percussion |
| Breach-loading | : N/A |
| Length | : 133.4 cm (52.5") |
| Barrel length | : 91.4 cm (36") |
| Weight | : 4.4 kg (9.625 lb) |
| Sight | : graduated sight |
| Safety | : half-cock hammer |
| Stock | : walnut |

*Specific details*: An English military rifle with Sir Joseph Whitworth's patent hexagonal rifling. It was imported into America in large numbers. It enabled snipers of the Confederate Army to hit targets at 1000 yards.

The Gibbs Rifle Company makes an excellent replica based on an original model with barrels made by Parker-Hale Ltd from Birmingham (UK).

*Enfield-Mortimer Whitworth Rifle, Model 1858*

## Tower Cavalry Pistol 1859

**TECHNICAL SPECIFICATIONS**

| | |
|---|---|
| Calibre | : .75" |
| Cartridge capacity | : single-shot, muzzle-loader |
| Operation | : single-action |
| Firing system | : percussion |
| Breach-loading | : N/A |
| Length | : 395 mm (15.6") |
| Barrel length | : 230 mm (9.1") |
| Weight | : 1140 g (40.2 oz) |
| Sight | : fixed |
| Safety | : half-cock hammer |
| Grip | : nut with brass grip cap |

*Specific details*: This is a cavalry pistol that was probably designed by Georges Lovell, inspector with the Tower of London, in 1842. The pistol in the picture probably dates from 1859. These pistols originally had a belt guard in the front end of the trigger guard. This was abandoned in later models. A hinged ram has been fitted under the barrel. The grip cap, the trigger guard and the ram guide bushing were made of brass.

*Enfield Pattern of 1861 Cavalry Carbine*

# Enfield Pattern of 1861 Cavalry Carbine

**TECHNICAL SPECIFICATIONS**

| | |
|---|---|
| Calibre | : .58" Minie (14.7 mm) |
| Cartridge capacity | : single-shot, muzzle-loader |
| Operation | : single-action |
| Firing system | : percussion |
| Breach-loading | : N/A |
| Length | : 102.9 cm (40.5") |
| Barrel length | : 61 cm (24") |
| Weight | : 3.2 kg (7 lb) |
| Sight | : graduated sight |
| Safety | : half-cock hammer |
| Stock | : walnut |

*Specific details*: These were largely produced by the London Armoury Company and based on the P1853 carbine. The first version had a folding sight. The barrel had three grooves of progressive depth. Later modifications had a graduated rear sight in combination with a fixed front sight and five grooves of progressive depth in the barrel. During the American Civil War the Southern states imported more than 6000 of these carbines. Perdersoli builds a fine replica which is sold by various dealers in North-America, including Navy Arms.

# Greener double-barrelled rifle, c. 1865

**TECHNICAL SPECIFICATIONS**

| | |
|---|---|
| Calibre | : .500" (12.7 mm) |
| Cartridge capacity | : double-barrelled, single-shot |
| Operation | : single-action |
| Firing system | : percussion |
| Breach-loading | : N/A |
| Length | : 111 cm (43.7") |
| Barrel length | : 71 cm (18") |
| Weight | : 4.6 kg (10.1 lb) |
| Sight | : folding sight for several ranges |
| Safety | : half-cock hammer |
| Stock | : walnut |

*Specific details*: A double-barrelled rifle,

*Detail of the folding sight on a Greener double-barrelled rifle*

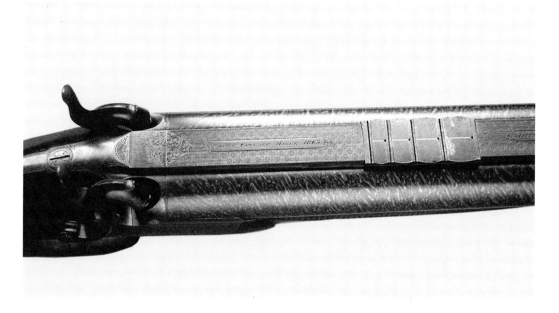

*Greener double-barrelled rifle, c. 1865*

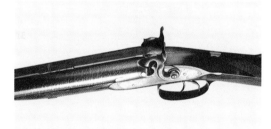

| | |
|---|---|
| Cartridge capacity | : 6-shot |
| Operation | : double-action |
| Firing system | : pin-fire |
| Breach-loading | : N/A |
| Length | : varied |
| Barrel length | : varied |
| Weight | : varied |
| Sight | : none |
| Safety | : none |
| Grip | : nut, rosewood or ebony |

designed and manufactured by the renowned English gunsmith William Wellington (W.W.) Greener of Birmingham. The double-barrelled Greener rifles were frequently used by professional large-game hunters in India and Africa in the 17th century. At the time it was one of the most powerful rifles of its kind. The folding notched sight blades can be used for aiming at distances of 100, 200, 300 and 400 yards.

## Tipping & Lawden Pepperbox 1865

**TECHNICAL SPECIFICATIONS**
Calibre            : .47" (12 mm)

*Tipping & Lawden Pepperbox 1865*

*Specific details*: A pepperbox made by Tipping & Lawden of Birmingham in the period between 1850 and 1877. In addition to building its own firearms, this company also imported and sold firearms made by other European and American gunmakers. The company was taken over by Webley & Son in 1877.

The pepperbox shown is just one of many types of pin-fire guns made by Tipping & Lawden.

## Enfield Snider 1866 trapdoor rifle

**TECHNICAL SPECIFICATIONS**

| | |
|---|---|
| Calibre | : .557" Snider (14.7 MM) |
| Cartridge capacity | : single-shot |
| Operation | : single-action |
| Firing system | : centre-fire |
| Breach-loading | : trapdoor action |
| Length | : 137.8 cm (54.25") |
| Barrel length | : 92.7 cm (36.5") |
| Weight | : 4.1 kg (9.13 lb) |
| Sight | : graduated sight |
| Safety | : half-cock hammer |
| Stock | : walnut |

*Specific details*: In 1864, tests were held in England to select which system was best suited for the conversion of the existing Pattern 1853 percussion rifles. The design by the American engineer Jacob Snider was selected in 1865.

There are a number of versions of this system, identified as Patterns I–IV. In addi-

*Enfield Snider 1866 Trapdoor Rifle*

*Detail of the trapdoor action of the Enfield Snider 1866 Trapdoor Rifle*

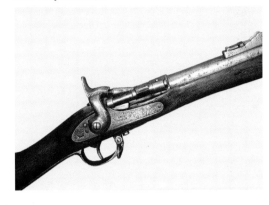

*Open trapdoor action of the Enfield Snider 1866 Trapdoor Rifle*

tion various models were made for specific military units, such as the Converted P/1855 Engineer Carbine: an M1853/1855 percussion rifle, shortened to 47.9" (121.7 cm), the Converted P1856 Cavalry Carbine (length 37.4"/95 cm) and the converted P1860 Sergeant's Rifle (length 48.7"/123.7 cm), next to models such as the Royal Irish Constabulary Pattern, the Yeomanry Carbine and the Civil Guard Carbine. The Snider conversion was built in England up to 1883. Since 1871 they were gradually replaced by the Martini-Henry. The Snider .577 cartridge originally had a cardboard cartridge with a metal base. This was later replaced by a brass case, invented by the English Colonel Boxer.

*Detail of the Enfield Snider 1870 Mark III Pattern*

## Enfield Snider 1870 Mark III pattern

**TECHNICAL SPECIFICATIONS**

| | |
|---|---|
| Calibre | : .577" Snider (14.7 mm) |
| Cartridge capacity | : single-shot |
| Operation | : single-action |
| Firing system | : centre-fire |
| Breach-loading | : trapdoor action with extra lug |
| Length | : 137.2 cm (54") |
| Barrel length | : 99.1 cm (39") |
| Weight | : 3.9 kg (8.6 lb) |
| Sight | : graduated sight |
| Safety | : half-cock hammer |
| Stock | : walnut |

*Specific details*: The Snider trapdoor when worn would sometimes open prematurely all by itself.

The Mark III Snider had an extra lug to lock the breech, developed by the English gunsmith Edward Bond of the London Small Arms Company. The system was approved by the British Army in 1869 and the first Mark III rifles were issued to the military in 1870. As the Martini-Henry rifle was gradually introduced from 1874, the Snider Mark III dropped out of use in the regular army.

However various volunteer and militia units continued to use this weapon until c. 1885.

*Webley British Bulldog 1878*

143

# Webley British Bulldog 1878

## TECHNICAL SPECIFICATIONS

| | |
|---|---|
| Calibre | : .320 CF, .44 RF, .44 CF or .450 CF |
| Cartridge capacity | : 5-shot |
| Operation | : double-action |
| Firing system | : rim-fire or centre-fire |
| Breach-loading | : N/A |
| Length | : 150 or 162 mm (5.9 or 6.4") |
| Barrel length | : 51 or 63.5 cm (2 or 2.5") |
| Weight | : 475 or 505 g (16.8 or 17.8 oz) |
| Sight | : fixed |
| Safety | : half-cock hammer |
| Grip | : walnut |

*Specific details*: This was produced by Webley & Son, later Webley & Scott of Birmingham from 1878 to 1914. Large numbers of this compact revolver were also manufactured by other gunmakers, either under a licence or not, in Belgium, Germany, France and the USA. In this latter country it was so popular that it caused the Peters and Winchester ammunition makers to market special ammunition in the calibre .44 Bulldog. Webley made this revolver with the inscription 'W.R.A. Co.' for the American market where they were sold by the Winchester Repeating Arms Co.

A pivoting ejector rod was attached to the cylinder axis. The revolver in the picture was one of the Bulldogs issued to the London Metropolitan Police. Francotte of Liége in Belgium was also licensed to produce this revolver and made a large number for the Danish Army. The weapon was available in a blued or nickel-plated version.

A third version had a brass hammer. This type was made as a naval revolver. It is very rare.

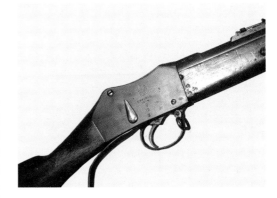

*Details of the Martini-Henry 1881*

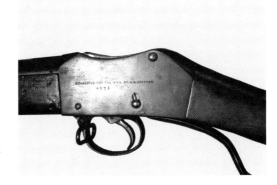

*Details of the Martini-Henry 1881*

*Martini-Henry 1881*

*Barrel inscription on the Martini-Henry 1881*

## Martini-Henry 1881

**TECHNICAL SPECIFICATIONS**

| | |
|---|---|
| Calibre | : .450-577" |
| Cartridge capacity | : single-shot |
| Operation | : single-action |
| Firing system | : centre-fire |
| Breach-loading | : falling-block action |
| Length | : 121.9 cm (48") |
| Barrel length | : 85.1 cm (33.5") |
| Weight | : 3.9 kg (8.6 lb) |
| Sight | : graduated sight |
| Safety | : loading indicator on right hand side of frame |
| Stock | : walnut |

*Specific details*: Development of the Martini-Henry started in 1866 and was completed in 1871. This rifle was a combination of the Martini falling-block action and Henry rifling with seven grooves. Frederich Martini (1832–1897) was a Swiss gunsmith of Hungarian origins, who modified and improved the American Peabody falling-block action.

Alexander Henry (1817–1895) was the owner of gunmaking company in Edinburgh, Scotland. Both arms engineers had submitted their own prototypes for the British Army firearms tests that took place from 1867 to 1869 to find a substitute for the Snider rifle.

The Martin-Henry played a major role in the Second Afghan War and the Zulu War, both in 1878 and in the African Boer War of 1881. It was made in various models, the most important ones being: the Mark I (1871–1876) with a total length of 49" (124.5 cm) and a lanyard eye at the butt of the stock; the Mark I Cavalry Carbine (length 37.7"/95.8 cm); the Mark I Artillery Carbine (length 37.7"/95.8 cm); the Mark II (1877–1881) and the Mark III (1881–1888) with a length of 49.5" (125.7 cm). Several Martini-Henry's were later converted to sporting rifles, such as the rifle in the picture.

## Enfield .476 Army Mark 2 1880

**TECHNICAL SPECIFICATIONS**

| | |
|---|---|
| Calibre | : .476" (12.1 mm) |
| Cartridge capacity | : 6-shot |
| Operation | : single-action |
| Firing system | : centre-fire |
| Breach-loading | : catch on top of barrel |
| Length | : 293 mm (11.5") |
| Barrel length | : 152 mm (6") |
| Weight | : 1130 g (39.9 oz) |
| Sight | : fixed |
| Safety | : half-cock hammer and loading gate lock |
| Grip | : walnut |

*Specific details*: The Enfield Mark 1 .476 revolver was introduced by the British Army in 1880 to replace the Adams .450 service revolver. The model shown in the picture, the Mark 2 was first produced in 1881 to succeed the Enfield Mark 1 revolver. The Mark 2 was manufactured until 1889 when it was succeeded by the Webley Mark 1. The most striking differences with the Mark 1 are: the round bead, the extra screw above the back end of the trigger guard, and the loading plate lock. When the loading gate was opened, the hammer could not be cocked. The Enfield Mark 1 and 2 were used by the British Army and Navy. It also formed part of the armament of the Canadian North-West Mounted Police (marks: 'NWMP' and 'Canada') and the Royal Irish Constabulary (mark: 'RIC').

*Enfield .476 Army Mark 2 1880*

## Moore & Harris double-barrelled rifle, c. 1880

**TECHNICAL SPECIFICATIONS**

| | |
|---|---|
| Calibre | : .500" Nitro Express Blackpowder |
| Cartridge capacity | : double-barrelled, single-shot |
| Operation | : single-action |
| Firing system | : centre-fire |
| Breach-loading | : barrel lugs with catch under top-break pivot |
| Length | : 113 cm (44.5") |
| Barrel length | : 71 cm (28") |
| Weight | : 4.1 kg (9 lb) |
| Sight | : folding sight for various ranges |
| Safety | : half-cock hammer |
| Stock | : walnut |

*Specific details*: Heavy double-barrelled rifle was made by William Moore & William Harris of Birmingham and London around 1880. This type of heavy double-

*Moore & Harris double-barrelled rifle, c. 1880*

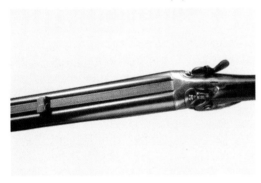

*Detail with cartridge of Moore & Harris double-barrelled rifle*

barrelled rifle was mainly produced for hunting in India, which was a British colony at the time. The ammunition for this rifle was also introduced around 1880. The 380-grain (24.6 g) bullet was propelled by 136 grains (8.8 g) of black powder and had a muzzle velocity of approximately 1800 ft/s (550 m/s). This was a respectable muzzle energy of 3720 joules, which was enough to stop a Bengal tiger, but it was not enough for hunting elephants in Africa. The later version of 1890 with smokeless powder and a heavier bullet head was highly popular in Africa. The 570-grain (37 g) bullet head could reach a muzzle velocity of 2150 feet (655 m) per second, which resulted in a muzzle energy of some 7940 joules: a real 'elephant calibre'. The recoil of this weapon was also phenomenal.

## Lancaster Four-Barrelled pistol 1881

**TECHNICAL SPECIFICATIONS**

| | |
|---|---|
| Calibre | : .380, .476 or .577" (9.7, 12.1 or 14.7 mm) |
| Cartridge capacity | : single-shot (per barrel) |
| Operation | : double-action |
| Firing system | : centre-fire |
| Breach-loading | : grendelhaak |
| Length | : 280 mm (11") |
| Barrel length | : 159 mm (6.25") |
| Weight | : 1150 g (40.6 oz) |
| Sight | : fixed |
| Safety | : none |
| Grip | : nut |

*Specific details*: Charles Lancaster was an English gunsmith from London who specialised in multi-barrel pistols for military purposes and for hunting. After his death in 1878, his business partner Henry Thorn continued the company by the name of Lancaster. Thorn designed the four-barrelled pistol shown in the picture. The .577" calibre version of this pistol is also called 'Howdah' after the saddle on the back of an elephant in which tiger hunters

Lancaster Four-Barrelled pistol, 1881

Webley New Model 1883 R.I.C.

in India travelled. The Lancaster was then used as a back-up weapon. In addition to the four-barrelled model, the company also produced double-barrelled pistols in .380 and .476" calibres. The large calibre models were popular with British Infantry officers who successfully used them in several operations in Sudan from 1882 to 1885.

## Webley New Model 1883 R.I.C.

**TECHNICAL SPECIFICATIONS**

| | |
|---|---|
| Calibre | : .455" (11.6 mm) |
| Cartridge capacity | : 5-shot |
| Operation | : double-action |

| | |
|---|---|
| Firing system | : centre-fire |
| Breach-loading | : N/A |
| Length | : 229 mm (9") |
| Barrel length | : 102 mm (4") |
| Weight | : 825 g (29.1 oz) |
| Sight | : bead |
| Safety | : none |
| Grip | : walnut |

*Specific details*: A revolver for the Royal Irish Constabulary, produced around 1883 by the English gun-making company P. Webley of Birmingham. This revolver was designed as a police and military gun, but

Martini-Metford MkIV 1886

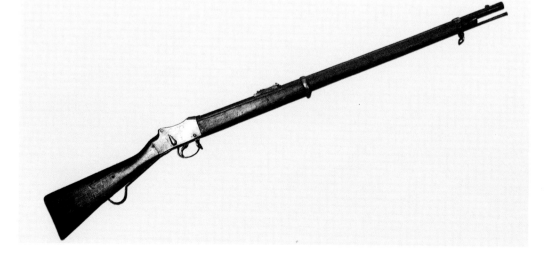

from 1883 to 1898 it was often sold to civilians for defence against thieves and highwaymen. The revolver has a hinged loading gate at the right-hand side, allowing the individual cylinder chambers to be loaded in turns.

## Martini-Metford MkIV 1886

**TECHNICAL SPECIFICATIONS**

| | |
|---|---|
| Calibre | : .402" (10.21 mm) |
| Cartridge capacity | : single-shot |
| Operation | : single-action |
| Firing system | : centre-fire |
| Breach-loading | : falling-block action |
| Length | : 121.9 cm (48") |
| Barrel length | : 85.1 cm (33.5") |
| Weight | : 3.9 kg (8.6 lb) |
| Sight | : graduated sight |
| Safety | : loading indicator on right-hand side frame |
| Stock | : walnut |

*Specific details*: The Martini-Metford rifle consists of the Martini falling-block action and a barrel developed by the British Engineer William Metford. This barrel had five or seven shallow rifling turns. Initially

*Details of the Martini-Metford MkIV 1886*

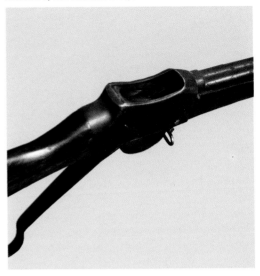

the head of the military did not think that this rifling would be suitable, but the test rifle fired so accurately that it was decided to purchase this rifle in 1886. The Martini-Metford has a straight bolt lever and a straight English stock. This rifle is seen as the intermediate form between the Martini-Henry and the Martini-Enfield of 1889 in the .303 (7.6 mm) calibre.

*Details of the Martini-Metford MkIV 1886*

*Webley New Express No.5 1886*

# Webley New Express No.5 1886

## TECHNICAL SPECIFICATIONS

| | |
|---|---|
| Calibre | : .360" No. 5 Rook (9.1 mm) |
| Cartridge capacity | : 6-shot |
| Operation | : double-action |
| Firing system | : centre-fire |
| Breach-loading | : N/A |
| Length | : 185, 190 or 230 mm (7.3, 7.5 or 9.1") |
| Barrel length | : 71, 76 or 114 mm (2.75, 3 or 4.5") |
| Weight | : 500 to 610 g (17.6 to 21.5 oz) |
| Sight | : fixed |
| Safety | : half-cock hammer |
| Grip | : walnut or ebonite |

*Specific details*: This was produced by

*Webley Army Mark I 1890*

*Webley Army Model Mark IV 1899*

Webley & Scott of Birmingham in the period 1886 to 1913. The uncommon calibre, .360 No. 5 Rook, was quite popular in Great-Britain at that time. It was used for several firearms, including rifles. The first series of revolvers had a typical pointed groove in the cylinder. In later versions this was round, as usual. The weapon could be loaded through a loading gate on the right-hand side of the frame. The swinging ejector rod is stored in the hollow cylinder pin below the barrel. The version with its 152-mm (6") barrel was intended as a match revolver and was provided with an adjustable notched sight.

There is no exact information on how many of these revolvers were produced by Webley, as their serial numbers were similar to the ones used for military revolvers.

## Webley Army Mark I 1886

### TECHNICAL SPECIFICATIONS

| | |
|---|---|
| Calibre | : .476, .455 or .442" (12.1-11.6 or 11.2 mm) |
| Cartridge capacity | : 6-shot |
| Operation | : double-action |
| Firing system | : centre-fire |
| Breach-loading | : bolt rod on upper bridge |

| | |
|---|---|
| Length | : 236 mm (9.3") |
| Barrel length | : 152 mm (6") |
| Weight | : 985 g (34.7 oz) |
| Sight | : fixed |
| Safety | : half-cock hammer |
| Grip | : ebonite |

*Specific details*: An army revolver designed by Henry Webley in 1886. The British Army bought this revolver in 1887 as a replacement for the Enfield Mark 2. The British Navy eventually switched over to this revolver as well. The navy version has an 'N' on the back of the grip, just below the hammer. This revolver was produced between 1887 and 1894. From 1894 to 1897 Webley produced the successor to the Mark I: the Mark II. This revolver had a bigger spur on the hammer and an improved action. The Mark III, introduced in 1897, only had some internal improvements, such as the improved cylinder pin.

## Webley Army Mark IV 1899

**TECHNICAL SPECIFICATIONS**

| | |
|---|---|
| Calibre | : .455" (11.6 mm) |
| Cartridge capacity | : 6-shot |
| Operation | : double-action |
| Firing system | : centre-fire |
| Breach-loading | : bolt on upper bridge |
| Length | : 185, 210, 235 or 260 mm (7.3, 8.3, 9.3 or 10.2") |
| Barrel length | : 76, 102, 127 or 152 mm (3, 4, 5 or 6") |
| Weight | : 1015 g (35.8 oz) with 127-mm/5" barrel |
| Sight | : fixed |
| Safety | : half-cock hammer |
| Grip | : ebonite |

*Specific details*: This was introduced as the successor to the Webley Mark III revolver in 1899. This model has a slightly differently shaped hammer. The Mark IV was mainly used by officers during the South-African Boer War of 1899–1902. This revolver remained a standard item of the British Army arsenal until after World War I.

## Webley-Fosbery Automatic Revolver Model 1900

**TECHNICAL SPECIFICATIONS**

| | |
|---|---|
| Calibre | : .455" or .38" ACP |
| Cartridge capacity | : 6-shot |
| Operation | : single-action |
| Firing system | : centre-fire |
| Breach-loading | : bolt handle on upper bridge |
| Length | : 220, 270 or 307 mm (8.7, 10.6 or 12.1") |
| Barrel length | : 102, 152 or 190 mm (4, 6 or 7.5") |
| Weight | : 33.2 to 37.7 oz (940–1070 g) |
| Sight | : fixed |
| Safety | : rotating safety sear on left-hand side of frame |
| Stock | : walnut |

Specific details: This was produced by Webley & Scott of Birmingham from 1899 to 1939. This weapon was designed by the English officer G. Vincent Fosberry. The revolver's repeating action is based on the recoil energy of the cartridge that has been fired. To fire the first shot the hammer had to be cocked manually into the single-action position. When the shot was fired the barrel and the cylinder were pushed back an inch (20 mm). This cocked the hammer again and rotated the cylinder by 1/12 turn. As soon as the barrel and cylinder had moved back far enough, a catch spring pushed the barrel and the cylinder forwards again, while the cylinder rotated through another 1/12 turn. Now the next cylinder chamber was in front of the barrel. The repeating action to fire the last five shots was carried out automatically thanks to the recoil energy. The cylinder stop that locks the cylinder has been housed in the upper bridge. The stud for the repeating action is located in the frame below the cylinder. This revolver has a rotating sear on the left-hand side of the grip. Due to its complicated construction this revolver was never designated as the official service weapon of the British army, but many officers paid for their own Webley-Fosberry's, which were used until after World War I.

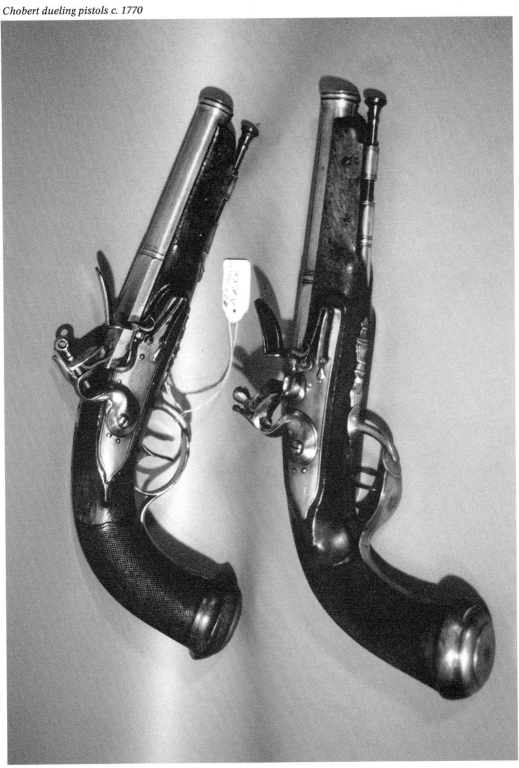

# 7 Italian firearms from 1865 to 1891

*Guerriero pin-fire revolver 1865*

*Detail of Guerriero pin-fire revolver*

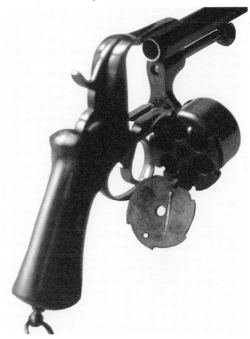

## Guerriero pin-fire revolver 1865

### TECHNICAL SPECIFICATIONS

| | |
|---|---|
| Calibre | : 9 mm pin-fire (.35") |
| Cartridge capacity | : 6-shot |
| Operation | : double-action |
| Firing system | : pin-fire |
| Breach-loading | : spring-loaded pin below barrel |
| Length | : 255 mm (10") |
| Barrel length | : 150 mm (5.9") |
| Weight | : 880 g (31 oz) |
| Sight | : fixed sight |
| Safety | : half-cock hammer |
| Grip | : walnut |

*Specific details*: A pin-fire revolver with closed frame by the Italian designer Alessandro Guerriero of Genoa. He was granted an American patent on this revolver in 1865.

When the cylinder was swivelled away a rear plate could be opened to load the cylinder chambers. The rim of the this plate also houses the cylinder transport lugs. This system is quite rare.

## Vetterli Infantry rifle Model 1870

### TECHNICAL SPECIFICATIONS

| | |
|---|---|
| Calibre | : 10.35 x 47R |
| Cartridge capacity | : single-shot |
| Operation | : single-action |
| Firing system | : centre-fire |
| Breach-loading | : two lugs forward on the bolt |
| Length | : 134.5 cm (52.95") |
| Barrel length | : 86 cm (33.85") |
| Weight | : 4.1 kg (9 lb) |
| Sight | : graduated sight |
| Safety | : sear on left-hand side, behind the bolt lever |
| Stock | : walnut |

*Specific details*: It was produced by the arms factories of Beretta in Turin and Torre

Annunziata and Officina Construzione d'Artiglieria in Rome. This weapon resembles the Swiss Vetterli rifle, but then without a magazine. The Vetterli initially had a graduated sight with a 1000-m range. In 1881, it was replaced by the Vecchi sight with a range of 1200 m. The weapon in the photograph has the old sight.

## Bodeo Model 1889, officers model

**TECHNICAL SPECIFICATIONS**

| | |
|---|---|
| Calibre | : 10.4 mm (.41") |
| Cartridge capacity | : 6-shot |
| Operation | : single-action |
| Firing system | : centre-fire |
| Breach-loading | : N/A |
| Length | : 267 mm (10.5") |
| Barrel length | : 114 mm (4.5") |
| Weight | : 910 g (32 oz.) |
| Sight | : fixed |
| Safety | : half-cock hammer and sear on left-hand side of frame |
| Stock | : walnut or ebonite |

*Specific details*: This was made from 1888 to 1910 in two versions: a standard model with an octagonal barrel and a folding trigger, and the officers model (shown) with a round barrel and a trigger guard. The 10.4-mm cartridge is often referred to as the 10.35 Glisenti and is almost identical to the .44 S&W Russian cartridge. The loading gate is mounted on the right-hand side of the frame. When this was opened the

hammer was blocked immediately. By pulling the trigger the chambers could be rotated in front of the barrel. The sear disconnected the hammer from the trigger. The revolver was officially introduced into the Italian Army in 1889. It was replaced by the Glisenti pistol in 1910.

## Mannlicher Carcano M1891 rifle

**TECHNICAL SPECIFICATIONS**

| | |
|---|---|
| Calibre | : 6.5 x 52 mm Mannlicher-Carcano |
| Cartridge capacity | : 6 cartridges (internal magazine) |
| Operation | : bolt action |
| Firing system | : centre-fire |
| Breach-loading | : 2-lug action (Mauser-type) |
| Length | : 129 cm (50.8") |
| Barrel length | : 78 cm (30.7") |
| Weight | : 3.9 kg (8.6 lb) |
| Sight | : graduated sight (500–2000 m) |
| Safety | : wing catch at rear end of bolt |
| Stock | : wood |

*Specific details*: This was produced in large numbers (over 4 million) by the Regia Fabbrica d'Armi in Brescia and Turin from 1892 to 1937. The bolt-action rifle Model 1891 was developed by Salvatore Carcano, an artillery lieutenant-colonel and weapons engineer in the Italian state armoury in Turin. He developed this rifle on the basis of a modified form of the Mauser 1888 bolt action, combined with the Mannlicher cartridge magazine, which could be loaded with a six-cartridge clip. In spite of the designation '1891', the weapon was officially selected as a new army rifle in March 1892 after which it was not introduced until 1894. In 1905, the weapon was modified with the introduction of another hand guard, followed by a new type of cartridge ejector in 1907.

## Mannlicher Carcano M1891 carbine

**TECHNICAL SPECIFICATIONS**

| | |
|---|---|
| Calibre | : 6.5 x 52 mm Mannlicher-Carcano |
| Cartridge capacity | : 6 patronen (internal magazine) |
| Operation | : bolt action |
| Firing system | : centre-fire |
| Breach-loading | : 2-lug action (Mauser-type) |
| Length | : 92 cm (36.2") |
| Barrel length | : 45 cm (17.7") |
| Weight | : 3.0 kg (6.6 lb) |
| Sight | : graduated sight (500–1500 m) |
| Safety | : wing catch at rear end of bolt |
| Stock | : wood |

*Specific details*: This was introduced for certain military units such as the cavalry,

Carabineri (mounted police) and bicycle battalions in 1893. Some 750,000–1,000,000 of these carbines were produced by the Fabbrica Naizonale d'Armi Brescia and the Regia Fabbrica d'Armi of Terni (inscription 'R.E. TERNI' with crown) between 1891 and 1940.

The carbine has a long, folding spike bayonet. The pitch of the rifling is shortened towards the muzzle of the barrel. The magazine of the carbine could be loaded with a six-cartridge clip.

*Mannlicher Carcano M1891 carbine*

*Mannlicher Carcano M1891 rifle*

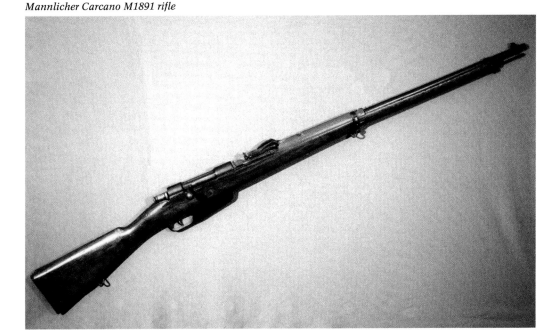

*Hellmann double-barrelled rifle, c. 1770*

# 8 Dutch Firearms from 1822 to 1895

*Dutch Artillery Carbine flintlock system 1822*

*Details of Dutch Artillery Carbine*

## Dutch artillery carbine flintlock system 1822

**TECHNICAL SPECIFICATIONS**

| | |
|---|---|
| Calibre | : 17.5 mm (.69") |
| Cartridge capacity | : single-shot, muzzle-loader |
| Operation | : single-action |
| Firing system | : flintlock |
| Breach-loading | : N/A |
| Length | : 110 cm (43.3") |
| Barrel length | : 76 cm (29.9") |
| Weight | : 3.2 kg (7.1 lb) |
| Sight | : none |
| Safety | : half-cock |
| Stock | : walnut |

*Specific details*: This artillery carbine was derived from the French M1777 flintlock rifle. There was a similar gun for the cavalry, but then with a carrying rod and a saddle ring on the left-hand side of the rifle. The protruding part below the barrel, close to the muzzle is a lug for a so-called spike bayonet. This type of weapon was made in The Netherlands and also in Belgium, which was part of The Netherlands from the time of Napoleon until 1830. Both carbines were converted to the percussion system after 1841.

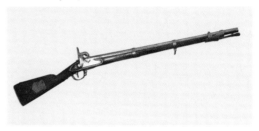

*Dutch Army Rifle 1816/1841*

## Dutch army rifle 1816/1841

**TECHNICAL SPECIFICATIONS**

| | |
|---|---|
| Calibre | : 17.5 cm (.69") |
| Cartridge capacity | : single-shot, muzzle-loader |
| Operation | : single-action |
| Firing system | : flintlock, converted to percussion later |
| Breach-loading | : N/A |
| Length | : 142 cm (56") |
| Barrel length | : 102,9 cm (40.5") |
| Weight | : 4.2 kg (9.26 lb) |
| Sight | : notch and bead |
| Safety | : half-cock hammer |
| Stock | : nut |

*Specific details*: This was originally a flintlock rifle that was converted into a percussion rifle around 1841. An interesting feature is the copper plate on the side of

*Detail of Dutch Army Rifle 1816/1841*

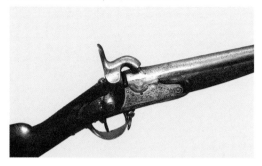

*Dutch Lancers carbine 1822/1841*

*Detail of Dutch Army Rifle 1816/1841*

Netherlands and Belgium from 1870 to 1871.

## Dutch Lancers carbine 1822/1841

**TECHNICAL SPECIFICATIONS**

| | |
|---|---|
| Calibre | : .69" (17.5 mm) |
| Cartridge capacity | : single-shot, muzzle-loader |
| Operation | : single-action |
| Firing system | : initially flintlock, later percussion |
| Breach-loading | : N/A |
| Length | : 147 cm (58") |
| Barrel length | : 108 cm (42.5") |
| Weight | : 3.9 kg (8.6 lb) |
| Sight | : notch and bead |
| Safety | : half-cock |
| Stock | : walnut |

*Specific details*: A flintlock carbine that was converted to the percussion system in or after 1841. A brass inset was placed in

*Dutch Lancers carbine 1822/1841 with extended bayonet*

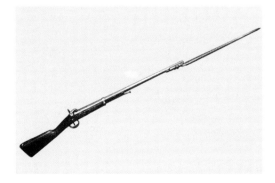

the stock. When Belgium separated itself from The Netherlands and declared its independence, William I, the Dutch King, sent an army to the province which fought a number of battles, one of which was the Ten-Day Battle of August 1831. In those days the rifle, in the photograph, still had a flintlock. In 1841 it was converted to the percussion system and, as engraved in the plaque, it served on the border between The

front of the priming pan and the touchhole to seal the barrel. An extra part with a nipple was placed on the breech for the percussion system. The lock plate and the cock were modified as well, but the rest of the carbine remained unchanged. The detail shows the brass inset.

An interesting and rare feature is the long folding bayonet, with its spring pressure mechanism close to the muzzle. This weapon is also shown with the bayonet extended.

## *Dutch artillery carbine 1825/1841*

**TECHNICAL SPECIFICATIONS**

| | |
|---|---|
| Calibre | : .69" (17.5 mm) |
| Cartridge capacity | : single-shot, muzzle-loader |
| Operation | : single-action |
| Firing system | : percussion |
| Breach-loading | : N/A |
| Length | : 95.6 cm (37.25") |
| Barrel length | : 60 cm (23.6") |
| Weight | : 2.9 kg (6.4 lb) |
| Sight | : notch and bead |
| Safety | : half-cock hammer |
| Stock | : walnut |

*Specific details*: A flintlock carbine that was converted to the percussion system in or after 1841. A brass inset was placed in front of the priming pan and the touchhole to seal the barrel.

An extra part with a nipple was placed on the breech for the percussion system. The lock plate and the cock were modified as

*Dutch Artillery Carbine 1825/1841*

*Detail, of the Dutch Artillery Carbine 1825/1841*

well, but the rest of the carbine remained unchanged. The detail shows the brass inset.

## *Dutch Cavalry carbine Model 1841*

**TECHNICAL SPECIFICATIONS**

| | |
|---|---|
| Calibre | : .66" (16.7 mm) |
| Cartridge capacity | : single-shot, muzzle-loader |
| Operation | : single-action |
| Firing system | : percussion |
| Breach-loading | : N/A |
| Length | : 84 cm (33.1") |
| Barrel length | : 45 cm (17.7") |
| Weight | : 2.75 kg (6.1 lb) |
| Sight | : notch and bead |
| Safety | : half-cock hammer |
| Stock | : walnut |

*Specific details*: The existing flintlock carbines were converted to the percussion system in 1841. The original cock was

*Dutch Cavalry carbine Model 1841*

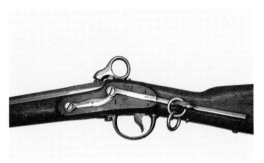

replaced by a distinct, ring-shaped cock. This weapon was used by the Dutch and Belgian armies and by the Gendarmery (police forces). An iron carrying rod with a saddle ring is mounted on the left-hand side of the stock, at the lock plate level. Such weapons were made by the P. Stevens arms company of Maastricht, The Netherlands and by Francotte of Liège, Belgium.

## Dutch 'Boom' rifle 1864

### TECHNICAL SPECIFICATIONS

| | |
|---|---|
| Calibre | : .496" (12.6 mm) |
| Cartridge capacity | : single-shot, muzzle-loader |
| Operation | : single-action |
| Firing system | : percussion |
| Breach-loading | : N/A |
| Length | : 146 cm (57.5") |
| Barrel length | : 105 cm (41.3") |
| Weight | : 4.6 kg (10.1 lb) |
| Sight | : arc-shaped folding sight |

*Dutch 'Boom' rifle 1864*

| | |
|---|---|
| Safety | : half-cock hammer |
| Stock | : walnut |

*Specific details*: This is a military rifle from 1864. The name 'boom' refers to the long forward grip of the rifle. A typical element is the curved end at the bottom of the trigger guard. The weapon in the photograph was made by the P. Stevens gun factory of Maastricht. Although this weapon was initially intended as a military rifle, it was hardly used as such as some 70,000 muzzle-loading rifles were converted to breech loaders, using the Snider action, in 1867.

## Dutch Tirailleur (Sniper) rifle, Snider system, 1867

### TECHNICAL SPECIFICATIONS

| | |
|---|---|
| Calibre | : .67" (17 mm) |
| Cartridge capacity | : single-shot, muzzle-loading |
| Operation | : single-action |
| Firing system | : centre-fire |
| Breach-loading | : hinged bolt |
| Length | : 146 cm (57.5") |
| Barrel length | : 105 cm (41.3") |
| Weight | : 4.6 kg (10.1 lb) |
| Sight | : arc-shaped folding sight |
| Safety | : half-cock hammer |
| Stock | : nut |

*Specific details*: An army rifle that was converted in 1867 using the Snider system. The rear end of the barrel was replaced by

*Dutch Tirailleur (Sniper) rifle, Snider system, 1867*

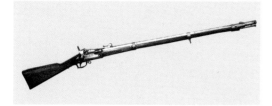

*Details of Dutch Tirailleur (Sniper) rifle, Snider system, 1867*

*Dutch Tirailleur (Sniper) rifle, Snider system, 1867 with open bolt*

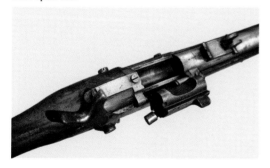

*Details of Dutch Tirailleur (Sniper) rifle, Snider system, 1867*

a hinged bolt that housed the firing pin. The rifle still had a ramrod, but this was only used for cleaning the barrel. These rifles are often still indicated by their original model designations, with the year when the original weapon was built. From 1867 to 1870 some 70,000 rifles were fitted with the Snider system. The Snider rifle was only used for a couple of years; as from 1870, it was gradually replaced by the Beaumont bolt action rifle.

## Beaumont Model 1871 army rifle

**TECHNICAL SPECIFICATIONS**

| | |
|---|---|
| Calibre | : 11.3 x 50R |
| Cartridge capacity | : single-shot |
| Operation | : single-action |
| Firing system | : centre-fire |
| Breach-loading | : bolt lever |
| Length | : 132 cm (51.95") |
| Barrel length | : 83 cm (32.7") |
| Weight | : 4.38 kg (9.66 lb) |
| Sight | : graduated sight |
| Safety | : sear, on the right-hand side of the tailpiece |
| Stock | : nut |

*Specific details*: This was issued to the Dutch Army from 1870. This rifle is virtually identical to the Chassepot, but with another graduated sight and with a curved rear trigger guard bridge. This rifle was produced by the gun factories of Beaumont and Stevens in Maastricht and J.J. Bär of Delft. The sear was abandoned in 1876 and

*Beaumont Model 1871 Army Rifle*

another type of sight was introduced in 1879. This allowed a range of 1300 m. A new cartridge was also introduced that year, the 1878 Harsveldt cartridge. This was called for modifications to the breech. This type of rifle is usually referred to as the Beaumont M1871/79 rifle. The M1871 was used as a practice rifle in a special version, using a barrel insert and a folding connector that could be used as a kind of cartridge ejector.

This rifle was called the Beaumont M1871-KSO. KSO stands for *Kamer Schiet Oefening* which is Dutch for Breech Shooting Practice. The 6-mm Flobert rimfire ammunition was used for this purpose. A detail of such a KSO rifle is shown above.

*Specific details*: This rifle was introduced to the Dutch Navy in 1871. The bayonet lug on the front end of the barrel is different from the Army model, since the Navy used different bayonets. In addition this rifle has a simple graduated sight.

## Beaumont Model 1871 carbine

**TECHNICAL SPECIFICATIONS**

| | |
|---|---|
| Calibre | : 11.3 x 50R |
| Cartridge capacity | : single-shot |
| Operation | : single-action |
| Firing system | : centre-fire |
| Breach-loading | : bolt action |
| Length | : 94.5 cm (37.2") |
| Barrel length | : 45.5 cm (17.9") |
| Weight | : 3.2 kg (7.1 lb) |
| Sight | : graduated sight |
| Safety | : sear on the right-hand side of the tailpiece |
| Stock | : nut |

*Specific details*: A carbine version of the

## Beaumont Model 1871 navy rifle

**TECHNICAL SPECIFICATIONS**

| | |
|---|---|
| Calibre | : 11.3 x 50R |
| Cartridge capacity | : single-shot |
| Operation | : single-action |
| Firing system | : centre-fire |
| Breach-loading | : bolt lever |
| Length | : 132 cm (51.95") |
| Barrel length | : 83 cm (32.7") |
| Weight | : 4.38 kg (9.66 lb) |
| Sight | : graduated sight |
| Safety | : sear on the right-hand side of the tailpiece |
| Stock | : nut |

*Beaumont Model 1871 Carbine*

Beaumont M1871 rifle. This carbine was made as a cadet and a pupil type for training purposes. Both types were mainly produced by the de Beaumont gun factory of Maastricht.

## Dutch Marechaussee (Military Police) Carbine Model 1872 - Remington system

**TECHNICAL SPECIFICATIONS**

| | |
|---|---|
| Calibre | : 11 mm (.433") |
| Cartridge capacity | : single-shot, breech-loading |
| Operation | : single-action |
| Firing system | : centre-fire |
| Breach-loading | : rolling bolt |
| Length | : 90 cm (35.4") |
| Barrel length | : 54 cm (21.3") |
| Weight | : 3.3 kg (7.3 lb) |
| Sight | : arc-shaped folding sight |
| Safety | : half-cock hammer |
| Stock | : nut |

*Specific details*: A military police carbine from 1872 with a folding bayonet. The MP version fired the same calibre projectile as the Beaumont rifle, but then in a cylindrical case.
Similar weapons were used by the Dutch Cavalry and the Engineers, but then without the folding bayonet and prepared for the Beaumont cartridge with a bottle-neck case. The carbine in the photograph was built under licence by the Nagant arms company of Liège.

*Dutch Marechaussee (Military Police) Carbine Model 1872 - Remington system*

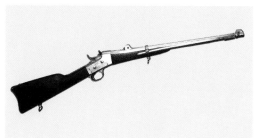

*Detail of Dutch Marechaussee (Military Police) Carbine Model 1872 - Remington system*

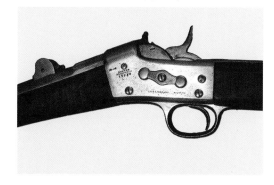

*Dutch Military revolver Model 1873 OM (Old Model)*

## Dutch Military revolver Model 1873 OM (old model)

**TECHNICAL SPECIFICATIONS**

| | |
|---|---|
| Calibre | : .37" (9.4 mm) centre-fire |
| Cartridge capacity | : 6 cartridges |
| Operation | : single-action |
| Firing system | : centre-fire |
| Breach-loading | : cylinder stops |
| Length | : 280 mm (11") |
| Barrel length | : 160 mm (6.3") |
| Weight | : 1300 g (45.9 oz) |
| Sight | : fixed notch and bead |
| Safety | : hammer blocking rod |
| Stock | : nut grip plates |

*Specific details*: A Dutch military revolver from 1873. The revolver in the photograph was made in 1878 by the P. Stevens arms company of Maastricht. In total Stevens

*Left-hand side of the Dutch Military revolver Model 1873 OM (Old Model)*

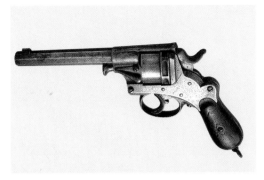

*Details of the Dutch Military revolver Model 1873 OM (Old Model)*

*Loading gate of the Dutch Military revolver Model 1873 OM (Old Model)*

made 3750 of these revolvers before the production was taken over by other factories such as Eduard de Beaumont (Maastricht), Leonard Soleil and J.F.J. Bär of Delft. The total production was well over 13,000 of these revolvers. From 1880

onwards the revolver was fitted with a lighter, round barrel. This was the Revolver M73 new model. Both models were used by the Dutch military forces and the Royal Dutch–Indonesian Army (KNIL) until 1940. There is a very extensive description of these revolvers in the books by the Dutch authors Martens and de Vries (*Nederlandse Vuurwapens Marine 1896– 1942*: ISBN 90-6706-448-9 and *Nederlandse Vuurwapens KNIL 1897–1942*: ISBN 90-6707-401-2).

## Dutch Military revolver Model 1873 NM (new model)

**TECHNICAL SPECIFICATIONS**

| | |
|---|---|
| Calibre | : .37" (9.4 mm) |
| Cartridge capacity | : 6 cartridges |
| Operation | : single-action |
| Firing system | : centre-fire |
| Breach-loading | : cylinder stops |
| Length | : 272 mm (10.7") |
| Barrel length | : 156 mm (6.1") |
| Weight | : 1200 g (42.3 oz) |
| Sight | : fixed notch and bead |
| Safety | : hammer blocking rod |
| Stock | : nut grip plates |

*Specific details*: A Dutch military revolver from 1873. This is the successor of the M1873 OM (old model) with an octagonal barrel. The new model has a round barrel, but for the rest it is almost identical to the old model. The revolver in the photograph was made by the Dutch arms company Bär of Delft.

*Dutch Military revolver Model 1873 NM (New Model)*

## Dutch Rijksveldwacht (Constabulary) revolver Model 1875

*Dutch Rijksveldwacht revolver Model 1875*

### TECHNICAL SPECIFICATIONS

| | |
|---|---|
| Calibre | : .37" (9.4 mm) centre-fire |
| Cartridge capacity | : 6 cartridges |
| Operation | : single-action |
| Firing system | : centre-fire |
| Breach-loading | : cylinder stops |
| Length | : 180 mm (7.1") |
| Barrel length | : 77 mm (3") |
| Weight | : 560 g (19.8 oz) |
| Sight | : fixed notch and bead |
| Safety | : lever on left-hand side of frame to block the cylinder |
| Stock | : nut grip plates |

*Specific details*: A Dutch revolver from 1875 made by Leopold Ancion-Marx (logo: LAM in a triangle) of Liège. The calibre is identical to that of the Dutch 1873 military revolver. This revolver was the service weapon of the state police. It was made under contract from a Dutch gun-trading company: the Nederlands Wapenmagazijn, with branches in Haarlem, The Hague, Amsterdam and Arnhem. The typical safety lever was not uncommon in those days and is a typical feature of the state police revolver. Other gunmakers of Liège such as Henrion, Dassy & Heuschen (HDH) applied this simple system as well. This revolver was also referred to as the Constabulary Model.

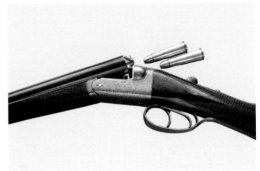

Barrel inscription on Rijksveldwacht (Constabulary)
revolver Model 1875

## Nowotny double-barrelled rifle, King William III, c. 1880

**TECHNICAL SPECIFICATIONS**

| | |
|---|---|
| Calibre | : 11.3 x 50R Beaumont M71 |
| Cartridge capacity | : double-barrelled, single-shot |
| Operation | : single-action |
| Firing system | : centre-fire |
| Breach-loading | : barrel latch and 'dolls head' |
| Length | : 115 cm (45.3") |
| Barrel length | : 71 cm (28") |
| Weight | : 3.2 kg (7.1 lb) |
| Sight | : folding sight |
| Safety | : sliding sear on neck of stock |
| Stock | : walnut |

*Specific details*: One of a series of double-barrelled rifles made by the Czech rifle maker Nowotny of Prague. This series was made for King William III (1817–1890) for hunting in the grounds of Loo Palace in Apeldoorn, The Netherlands. The rifle had the same calibre as its contemporary, the Dutch Beaumont M71 military rifle. The barrels are locked to the frame by latches at the bottom of the barrel block and a so-called 'doll's head': a lug that seals the top. King William III was a fervent hunter, a tradition that has been continued by the Dutch royals to this very day.

The rear side of the back of the stock carries a Dutch military escutcheon with the engraving 'JE MAINTAINDRAI': 'I will uphold'.

*Detail of the escutcheon on the stock of the Nowotny rifle*

*Donaghy revolver, c. 1880*

## Donaghy revolver, c. 1880

**TECHNICAL SPECIFICATIONS**

| | |
|---|---|
| Calibre | : 9.4 mm |
| Cartridge capacity | : 5-shot |
| Operation | : single-action |
| Firing system | : centre-fire |
| Breach-loading | : N/A |
| Length | : 210 mm (8.3") |
| Barrel length | : 90 mm (3.5") |

*Donaghy target pistol, c. 1880*

| | |
|---|---|
| Weight | : 800 g (28.2 oz.) |
| Sight | : fixed notch, bead |
| Safety | : rotating sear on left-hand side of frame |
| Stock | : walnut |

*Specific details*: This was produced in Amsterdam by the Irish gunsmith Donaghy. This revolver was intended for private use, presumably in the former Dutch Indies. Donaghy was renowned for his beautiful hunting rifles and target pistols, but he also made simple revolvers.

*Dutch police revolver, c. 1885*

## Donaghy target pistol, c. 1880

**TECHNICAL SPECIFICATIONS**

| | |
|---|---|
| Calibre | : 6 mm Flobert |
| Cartridge capacity | : single-shot |
| Operation | : single-action |
| Firing system | : rim-fire |
| Breach-loading | : simple falling block |
| Length | : 290 mm (11.4") |
| Barrel length | : 152 mm (6") |
| Weight | : 1080 g (38 oz) |
| Sight | : fixed notch, bead |
| Safety | : none |
| Stock | : walnut |

*Specific details*: A beautiful target-shooting pistol, made by the Irish gunsmith Donaghy who lived in Amsterdam. The barrel is beautifully engraved and inlaid with gold thread. Such pistols were mostly used by wealthy gentlemen for indoor target shooting.

## Dutch police revolver, c. 1885

**TECHNICAL SPECIFICATIONS**

| | |
|---|---|
| Calibre | : .380 |
| Cartridge capacity | : 5-shot |
| Operation | : single-action |
| Firing system | : centre-fire |
| Breach-loading | : N/A |
| Length | : 210 mm (8.3") |
| Barrel length | : 90 mm (3.5") |
| Weight | : 790 g (28 oz.) |
| Sight | : fixed notch, bead |
| Safety | : rotating sear on left-hand side of frame |
| Stock | : walnut |

*Specific details*: A Dutch police revolver from c. 1890 to 1895. This revolver was made by Leopold Ancion-Marx of Liège. This revolver was probably used as a service weapon by a local police department of that time.

A similar type, but then with a milled cylinder and an extra finger hook on the trigger guard is shown in the top left corner.

## Beaumont–Vitali M1871/88 carbine

**TECHNICAL SPECIFICATIONS**

| | |
|---|---|
| Calibre | : 11.3 x 50R |
| Cartridge capacity | : 4 patronen |
| Operation | : single-action |
| Firing system | : centre-fire |
| Breach-loading | : bolt action with breech-sealing lugs |
| Length | : 94.5 cm (37.2") |
| Barrel length | : 45.5 cm (17.9") |
| Weight | : 3.2 kg (7.1 lb) |
| Sight | : graduated sight |
| Safety | : safety catch on the right-hand side of the tailpiece |
| Stock | : walnut |

*Specific details*: The single-shot Beaumont M1871 carbine was converted into a multi-

*Beaumont-Vitali M1871/88 carbine*

168

## Beaumont–Vitali M1871/88 rifle

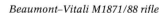

**TECHNICAL SPECIFICATIONS**

| | |
|---|---|
| Calibre | : 11.3 x 50R |
| Cartridge capacity | : cartridge magazine for 4 cartridges |
| Operation | : single-action |
| Firing system | : centre-fire |
| Breach-loading | : bolt lever |
| Length | : 132 cm (51.95") |
| Barrel length | : 83 cm (32.7") |
| Weight | : 4.38 kg (9.66 lb) |
| Sight | : graduated sight |
| Safety | : safety catch on the right-hand side of the tailpiece |
| Stock | : nut |

shot bolt action gun in 1888 by preparing it for the integration of a Vitali cartridge magazine.

This magazine had a cartridge lift which was pushed up by a coiled spring, around a spring guide rod. This explains the typical bulge in the centre of the magazine. The picture shows a Beaumont–Vitali M1871/88 carbine.

*Specific details*: The Beaumont M1871's were prepared for the integration of a Vitali cartridge magazine from 1888. This magazine had a cartridge lift which was pushed up by a coiled spring, around a spring guide rod. The spring was housed in the side of the magazine. The tailpiece of the gun was fitted with a sear that locked the cartridge lift to allow the weapon to be loaded manually, shot-by-shot. A loading clip is shown below the rifle. This is a simple device consisting of two tin plate U-sections,

*Beaumont–Vitali M1871/88 rifle*

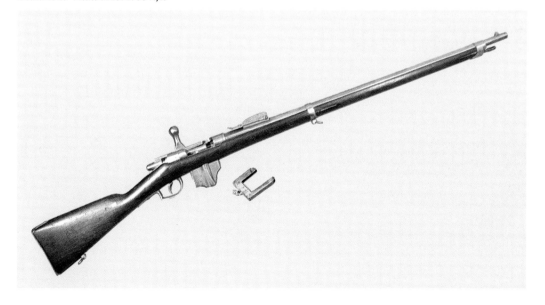

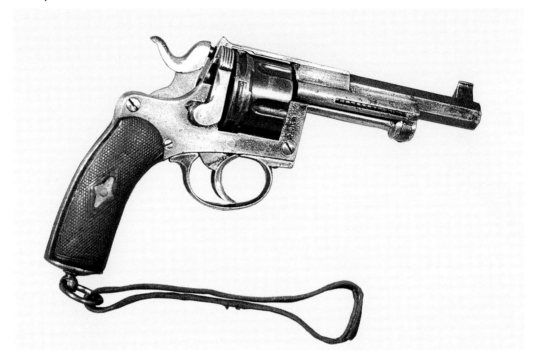

riveted to a coarsely finished fir block. This made it easier to load the four cartridges into the magazine.

## *Dutch police revolver Model 1891*

**TECHNICAL SPECIFICATIONS**

| | |
|---|---|
| Calibre | : 10 mm (10 x 27 Rand) |
| Cartridge capacity | : 6 cartridges |
| Operation | : single-action |
| Firing system | : centre-fire |
| Breach-loading | : N/A |
| Length | : 222 mm |
| Barrel length | : 113 mm |
| Weight | : 820 g |
| Sight | : fixed notch and bead |
| Safety | : none |
| Stock | : walnut |

*Specific details*: A police revolver made by the Dutch arms company J.F.J. Bär of Delft. This revolver is virtually identical to the so-called M91 KNIL revolver that was used by the Royal Dutch–Indonesian Army (KNIL) and the Indonesian police forces. The M91 KNIL revolver was also produced by Vickers Ltd from the UK.

The police revolver was also made in the older 9.4-mm calibre used for the M1873 revolvers.

## *Dutch police revolver, c. 1891*

**TECHNICAL SPECIFICATIONS**

| | |
|---|---|
| Calibre | : 9.4 mm |
| Cartridge capacity | : 5-shot |
| Operation | : single-action |
| Firing system | : centre-fire |
| Breach-loading | : N/A |
| Length | : 203 mm (8") |
| Barrel length | : 85 mm (3.3") |
| Weight | : 790 g (28 oz.) |
| Sight | : fixed notch, bead |
| Safety | : rotating sear on left-hand side of frame |
| Stock | : walnut |

*Dutch police revolver, c. 1891*

*Specific details*: A Dutch police revolver from c. 1890 to 1895. This revolver was made by the Dutch arms company J.F.J. Bär of Delft and has the same calibre as the military revolvers of the time.

This revolver was probably used as a service weapon by a local police department of that time.

## Steyr/Hembrug Model M1895 rifle

**TECHNICAL SPECIFICATIONS**
Calibre    : 6.5 x 53R

*Steyr/Hembrug Model M1895 rifle*

| | |
|---|---|
| Cartridge capacity | : 5 cartridges (internal magazine) |
| Operation | : bolt-action |
| Firing system | : centre-fire |
| Breach-loading | : bolt action with breech-sealing lugs |
| Length | : 129.5 cm (51") |
| Barrel length | : 79 cm (31.1") |
| Weight | : 4.4 kg (9.7 lb) |
| Sight | : graduated sight |
| Safety | : winged catch on rear end of bolt |
| Stock | : wood |

*Specific details*: A military rifle that was introduced by the Dutch Army in 1895. It was made by the Austrian Steyr company from 1895 to 1902 and by the Artillerie-Inrichtingen Hembrug from 1901 to 1920. The internal magazine could be loaded using clips for five cartridges.

Some of these rifles were converted to the 7.92 Mauser calibre (8 x 57 mm) in 1917. Several types of carbine were derived from the M1895.

One of them is the Model 1895 Carbine No. 5 for the Dutch Air Force and Artillery. This carbine was a shortened M1895 rifle. It was introduced in 1938.

# 9 American Firearms from 1836 to 1896

*Colt 1836 Paterson (Model No. 5)*

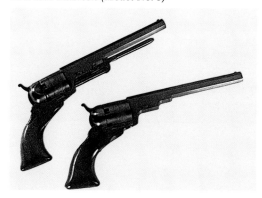

## Colt 1836 Paterson (Model No. 5)

### TECHNICAL SPECIFICATIONS

| | |
|---|---|
| Calibre | : .36" (9.1 mm) |
| Cartridge capacity | : 5-shot |
| Operation | : single-action |
| Firing system | : percussion |
| Breach-loading | : N/A |
| Length | : 292 mm (11.5") (with 191 mm/7.5" barrel) |
| Barrel length | : 102–305 mm (4–12") |
| Weight | : 1157 g (40.8 oz) with 191 mm/7.5" barrel) |
| Sight | : fixed |
| Safety | : half-cock hammer |
| Grip | : walnut grip plates |

*Specific details*: This is the first cylinder revolver designed and built by Colt in the Patent Arms Manufacturing Company in Paterson, New Jersey from 1836 to 1842. The Colt Paterson was built both with and without a loading cylinder and the guardless trigger is rotated out of the frame when the hammer is cocked. Some 2500 of these revolvers were built before the company went bankrupt in 1843. Related models are the Pocket Model or the Baby Paterson in .28, .31 and .34 calibres and the Holster Model in a .36 calibre, made from 1836 to 1841. The company Hege-Uberti builds high-quality replicas in a .36 calibre.

## Allen & Wheelock large frame pocket revolver Model 1845

### TECHNICAL SPECIFICATIONS

| | |
|---|---|
| Calibre | : .34" (8.6 mm) |
| Cartridge capacity | : 5-shot |
| Operation | : double-action |
| Firing system | : percussion |
| Breach-loading | : N/A |
| Length | : 176–227 mm (6.9–8.9") |
| Barrel length | : 76–127 mm (3–5") |
| Weight | : 900 g (31.8 oz) |
| Sight | : none |
| Safety | : none |
| Grip | : walnut |

*Specific details*: This was made by the American company Allen & Wheelock from 1857 to 1860. The total output was approximately 1500 pieces. The inscription

*Allen & Wheelock Large Frame Pocket revolver Model 1845*

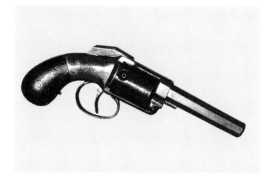

on the barrel reads: 'Patented April 16, 1845' followed by the company name. The design was based on the well-known Ethan Allen pepperbox revolvers. This revolver was mainly intended for the civilian market.

## Colt 1846 Walker

**TECHNICAL SPECIFICATIONS**

| | |
|---|---|
| Calibre | : .44" (11.2 mm) |
| Cartridge capacity | : 6-shot |
| Operation | : single-action |
| Firing system | : percussion |
| Breach-loading | : N/A |
| Length | : 400 mm (15.75") |
| Barrel length | : 229 mm (9") |
| Weight | : 1995 g (70.4 oz) |
| Sight | : fixed |
| Safety | : half-cock hammer |
| Grip | : walnut grip plates |

*Specific details*: A design from 1846 by the cavalry officer and Texas Ranger Capt. Samuel Walker. Roughly 1000 of these revolvers were made by Colt in 1847. Walker himself was killed in the Battle of Juamantha in Mexico in 1847. Today this is a much sought after collector's item with a high price (US$ 50,000 to US$ 300,000). One of these revolvers, which was in a reasonable state was sold for US$ 143,000 at an auction in 1995. The Italian company

Uberti builds a very good replica in the same calibre. As the Paterson branch had gone bankrupt, Colt did not build this model itself but had them produced by E. Whitney of Whitneyville, Connecticut, with the cylinders and barrels being made by Slate & Brown of Hartford. Therefore this revolver is sometimes also referred to as the Whitneyville-Walker. The company Hege-Uberti also builds high-quality replicas of this revolver.

## Colt 1848 Dragoon

**TECHNICAL SPECIFICATIONS**

| | |
|---|---|
| Calibre | : .44" (11.2 mm) |
| Cartridge capacity | : 6-shot |
| Operation | : single-action |
| Firing system | : percussion |
| Breach-loading | : N/A |
| Length | : 343 mm (13.5") |
| Barrel length | : 191 mm (7.5") |
| Weight | : 1770 g (62.4 oz) |
| Sight | : fixed |
| Safety | : half-cock hammer |
| Grip | : walnut grip plates |

*Specific details*: Produced from 1848 to 1863 and derived from the Colt Walker. There are three Dragoon models. The first

*Colt 1848 Dragoon*

*Colt 1846 Walker*

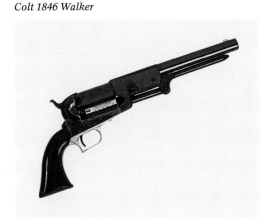

model, of which some 5000 pieces were made, comes in a military version with a brass trigger guard, which is nickel plated in the civilian version. The second version, of which some 2700 pieces were made in 1850 and 1851, has rectangular cylinder lock holes (in the first model they are oval). The third model was built from 1852 to 1861 and has a round trigger guard. It was made in approximately10,500 pieces, a small number of which have a slot in the frame to fit an extra stock. Hege-Uberti builds excellent replicas of the three models: 1st, 2nd and 3rd Model Dragoon. The first and the second model are shown in the photographs.

## Colt 1848 Baby Dragoon

**TECHNICAL SPECIFICATIONS**

| | |
|---|---|
| Calibre | : .31" (7.9 mm) |
| Cartridge capacity | : 5- or 6-shot |
| Operation | : single-action |
| Firing system | : percussion |
| Breach-loading | : N/A |
| Length | : 216, 241, 267 or 292 mm (8.5, 9.5, 10.5 or 11.5") |
| Barrel length | : 76, 102, 127 or 152 mm (3, 4, 5 or 6") |
| Weight | : 650 g (22.9 oz) with a 102-mm (4") barrel |

*Colt 1848 Baby Dragoon*

| | |
|---|---|
| Sight | : fixed |
| Safety | : half-cock hammer |
| Grip | : walnut grip built in one piece |

*Specific details*: Some 15,500 of these revolvers were made between 1847 and 1850. The first 10,000 had a rectangular trigger guard and a scene of a battle between Indians and Texas Rangers engraved on the cylinder. Later models have an etching of a raid on a stage-coach and a round trigger guard. It was a highly valued gun for the pioneers who followed the Oregon Trail. A small number of these revolvers have a loading ramrod. This model was made by many companies, including Belgiun gunsmiths in the Liège area. Hege-Uberti builds excellent replicas of this revolver. Shown from left to right are: Colt 1848 Dragoon, the 1849 Wells Fargo and the 1849 Pocket Model.

## Colt 1848 Pocket (Dragoon)

**TECHNICAL SPECIFICATIONS**

| | |
|---|---|
| Calibre | : .31" (7.9 mm) |
| Cartridge capacity | : 5 or 6-shot |
| Operation | : single-action |
| Firing system | : percussion |
| Breach-loading | : N/A |
| Length | : 216, 241, 267 or 292 mm (8.5, 9.5, 10.5 or 11.5") |
| Barrel length | : 76, 102, 127 or 152 mm (3, 4, 5 or 6") |
| Weight | : 650g (22.9 oz) with a 102-mm (4") barrel |
| Sight | : fixed |
| Safety | : half-cock hammer |
| Grip | : walnut grip built in one piece |

*Specific details*: This was a highly successful Colt model. Some 325,000 of these revolvers were made from 1850 to 1875 in about 150 variations, such as with square or round trigger guards. The model with the 3" (76 mm) barrel usually has no loading ramrod. The cylinder has an engraving of a raid on a stage-coach. One of the many variations is the so-called Wells Fargo

*Colt 1848 Pocket (Dragoon)*

*Warner-Springfield Model Navy 1851*

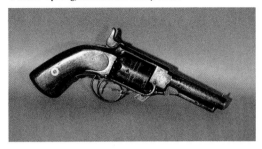

| | |
|---|---|
| Safety | : half-cock hammer |
| Grip | : walnut |

*Specific details*: This was designed by James Warner who produced over 9500 of these revolvers in the period 1852 to 1856. Most Warner revolvers have a so-called open frame, which was also customary for Colt revolvers. The revolver in the photograph has a closed frame which makes it a rare piece. The name 'Navy' is somewhat misleading as it was never officially used as a navy revolver. Warner allegedly infringed on several patent rights owned by other manufacturers, as a result of which he had to cease production of these revolvers. This is thought to be the reason why the successors of this model were made by the Springfield Arms Company.

version with a 3" or 4" barrel (76 or 102 mm). Henry Wells and William G. Fargo of San Francisco started a major stage-coach company in 1851. To allow the coachmen to defend themselves they were armed with light revolvers. However, prominent American historians claim that Colt never made a special model for Wells Fargo. Hege-Uberti builds excellent replicas of these revolvers.

### Colt 1851 Navy Model

**TECHNICAL SPECIFICATIONS**

| | |
|---|---|
| Calibre | : .36" (9.1 mm) |
| Cartridge capacity | : 6-shot |
| Operation | : single-action |
| Firing system | : percussion |
| Breach-loading | : N/A |
| Length | : 330 mm (13") |
| Barrel length | : 191 mm (7.5") |
| Weight | : 1200 g (42.3 oz) |
| Sight | : fixed |
| Safety | : half-cock |
| Grip | : walnut grip plates |

*Specific details*: Some 215,000 of these

### Warner-Springfield Model Navy 1851

**TECHNICAL SPECIFICATIONS**

| | |
|---|---|
| Calibre | : .28, .31, .34 or .44" (7.1, 7.9, 8.6 or 11.2 mm) |
| Cartridge capacity | : 6-shot |
| Operation | : single-action |
| Firing system | : percussion |
| Breach-loading | : N/A |
| Length | : 213, 231, or 253 mm (8.4, 9.1 or 10") |
| Barrel length | : 58, 76 or 95 mm (2-2/3, 3 or 3-3/4") |
| Weight | : 950 g (33.5 oz) |
| Sight | : fixed |

*Colt 1851 Navy Model*

*Colt 1851 Navy Model*

highly popular revolvers were built between 1850 and 1873. The cylinder is engraved with a picture of the naval battle between Mexico and Texas in 1843. The revolver has an octagonal barrel and a brass grip end. This revolver was made in a blued and a blank version. During the American Civil War this model was copied by various manufacturers from the Southern States: Dance Brothers, Griswold & Grier, Rigdon & Ansley and Spiller & Burr. It was also extensively copied by Belgian gunsmiths from Liège. These revolvers have a Liège proof mark and the inscription 'Colt Breveté'. Some models bear the inscription 'Col. Colt London'. They are worth considerably less than other 1851 Navy Models. Hege-Uberti builds an excellent replica.

## Colt Navy London Model 1853

**TECHNICAL SPECIFICATIONS**

| | |
|---|---|
| Calibre | : .36" (9.1 mm) |
| Cartridge capacity | : 6-shot |

*Colt Navy London Model 1853*

| | |
|---|---|
| Operation | : single-action |
| Firing system | : percussion |
| Breach-loading | : N/A |
| Length | : 330 mm (13") |
| Barrel length | : 191 mm (7.5") |
| Weight | : 1190 g (42 oz) |
| Sight | : bead |
| Safety | : half-cock hammer |
| Grip | : nut |

*Specific details*: When Colonel Colt entered his robust percussion revolvers in the international arms exhibition at Hyde Park, London in 1851, they were a great success. The demand from European countries was so high, that he decided to set up a manufacturing base for this market in Pimlico, Great Britain, under American management in 1852. There he produced the Navy revolver 1853 and the Pocket model with barrel lengths of 102, 127 or 152 mm (4, 5 and 6"). The military officials were especially impressed by the fact that the components could be exchanged quite easily, which was not yet common practice in these early days of mass production. After testing by the Board of Ordnance, the British government decided to order 4000 Navy revolvers for the Royal Navy. Shortly after this they ordered another 5500 for the fleets in the Baltic Sea and the Black Sea, and over 14,000 for the military forces in the Crimean. The British switched to the Beaumont-Adams revolver in 1855 after which they placed no further orders for the 1853 Navy. The production of both models started in 1852. When the weapon was found to be outdated in 1856, Colt wound down his production facilities in Great Britain that same year.

## Sharps Model 1853 single shot pistol

**TECHNICAL SPECIFICATIONS**

| | |
|---|---|
| Calibre | : .31, .34 or .36" (7.9, 8.6 or 9.1 mm) |
| Cartridge capacity | : single-shot |
| Operation | : single-action |
| Firing system | : percussion |
| Breach-loading | : falling block action |
| Length | : 297 or 307 mm (10.6 or 12.1") |
| Barrel length | : 127 or 165 mm (5 or 6.5") |
| Weight | : 960 g (34 oz) with a 5"/127-mm barrel |
| Sight | : bead |
| Safety | : half-cock hammer |
| Grip | : walnut |

*Specific details*: An unknown number of these pistols were built by C. Sharps & Co. between 1854 and 1857. The trigger guard of this pistol also acts as the lever-action lever which lowers the falling block to provide access to the breech. Christian Sharps is mainly known for his Sharps rifles.

*Sharps Model 1853 Single Shot Pistol*

*Volcanic Navy Pistol 1854*

## Volcanic Navy Pistol 1854

**TECHNICAL SPECIFICATIONS**

| | |
|---|---|
| Calibre | : .41" Volcanic (10.4 mm) |
| Cartridge capacity | : tubular magazine for 8 cartridges |
| Operation | : single-action |
| Firing system | : centre-fire with priming pellet |
| Breach-loading | : lever action |
| Length | : 325 or 376 mm (12.8 or 14.8") |
| Barrel length | : 152 or 203 mm (6 or 8") |
| Weight | : 1220 or 1360 g (43 or 48 oz) |
| Sight | : fixed notch |
| Safety | : half-cock hammer |
| Grip | : walnut |

*Specific details*: It was designed by Horace Smith and Daniel Baird Wesson and produced by their company Volcanic Repeating Arms Company of New Haven, Connecticut. It was made by this company from 1854 to 1857. Some 1200 of these pistols were produced with a 6"(152-mm) barrel and in addition there was the 8" (203-mm) Navy Model, of which some 1500 pieces were made. Finally there was another Navy model with a 16" barrel and a detachable stock, of which only 300 pieces were made. In 1857 the company was reorganised by its major shareholder, Oliver F. Winchester and the name of the company was changed to the New Haven Arms Company. Smith and Wesson retired from the company and started the Smith & Wesson Company in 1858. From 1857 to 1860 the Volcanic pistol was made by the

*The .41 Valconic cartridge*

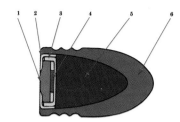

new company in several versions. The most striking difference with the older model was the narrower butt. The various models of this new type were as follows:

Volcanic Lever-Action No. 1 Pocket Pistol in a .31 calibre with a 3.5" (89-mm) barrel (approx. 850 pcs) and a target version with a 6" (152-mm) barrel (approx. 225 pcs).

Volcanic Lever-Action Navy Pistol in a .41 calibre with a 6" (152-mm) barrel (approx. 300 pcs) or an 8" (203-mm) barrel (approx. 1000 pcs) or a 16" (406-mm) barrel and a detachable stock (approx. 200 pcs).

The .41 Volcanic cartridge consisted of a hollow bullet point, without a case. Inside the hollow bullet there was a black powder charge and a kind of percussion cap in the form of a priming pellet. A drawing of this caseless cartridge is shown above:
1. cork seal, 2. brass cup, 3. seat for the priming pellet, 4. priming pellet, 5. black powder charge, bullet point.

*Pettengill Navy Revolver 1856*

## Pettengill Navy Revolver 1856

### TECHNICAL SPECIFICATIONS

| | |
|---|---|
| Calibre | : .34" (8.6 mm) |
| Cartridge capacity | : 6-shot |
| Operation | : double-action |
| Firing system | : percussion |
| Breach-loading | : N/A |
| Length | : 265 mm (10.4") |
| Barrel length | : 114 mm (4.5") |
| Weight | : 685 g (24.2 oz) |
| Sight | : fixed notch and bead |
| Safety | : none |
| Grip | : walnut |

*Specific details*: It was designed by the arms engineer C.S. Pettengill of New Haven, Connecticut. The revolver was produced by Rogers & Spencer of Willowvale, New York. It has a hammer integrated into the neck of the grip, hence its nickname, 'Hidden Hammer Revolver'. It is also referred to as the 'Belt Revolver'. Historically this is more exact, as the Navy revolver was never used as a navy weapon. Some 900 of these revolvers were made from 1856 to 1860. Pettengill also designed the Army revolver in 1856. This is a similar model in a .44 calibre and with a 7.5" barrel.

During the American Civil War the Northern Army ordered 5000 Army Model Revolvers, but this order was revoked after Rogers & Spencer had delivered 2000 of them in 1862 and 1863. The remaining 1400 revolvers that had already been produced were sold to civilians.

## Savage & North (Figure 8) Navy First Model 1856

### TECHNICAL SPECIFICATIONS

| | |
|---|---|
| Calibre | : .36" (9.1 mm) |
| Cartridge capacity | : 6-shot |
| Operation | : double-action |
| Firing system | : percussion |
| Breach-loading | : N/A |

| | |
|---|---|
| Length | : 355 mm (14") |
| Barrel length | : 181 mm (7-1/8") |
| Weight | : 1560 g (55 oz) |
| Sight | : fixed notch |
| Safety | : none |
| Grip | : walnut |

*Specific details*: Designed by Henry S. North in 1856 and produced by the North & Savage Company in Middletown, Connecticut from 1856 to 1859, the first series of this revolver had a bronze frame. In the later series the mouth of the cylinder chambers had been drilled out diagonally to ensure a better gas seal. In 1857, the American Navy bought some 360 of these revolvers.

The total production is estimated at some 500. A third variety of the First Model had an iron frame and the hinge mechanism of the ramrod was enclosed by a fixed housing below the barrel. In addition the grip was placed on the frame at a straighter angle. Some 100 of these revolvers were made. The fourth version had a bronze frame again, but with flattened sides. The total production of this modified version was some 400.

The fifth and last version is almost identical to the fourth, but reverting to an iron frame again. Only 50 of these revolvers were made. This revolver works as follows: the middle finger is placed in the lower ring and the 8-shaped trigger is pulled back. This cocks the hammer and releases the

*Savage & North (Figure 8) Navy First Model 1856*

cylinder. When the trigger is released it assumes its forward position again due to spring pressure.

The cylinder is now rotated one revolution to bring the new chamber in front of the barrel. The cylinder then slides forward slightly, until it is tight against the barrel. To fire the shot, the small trigger in the upper ring must be pushed. In 1859 the name of the company was changed to the Savage Revolving Firearms Company. Around 1861 the new company introduced the Navy Second Model, an improved version of the First Model.

The most striking difference is the trigger system. Savage maintained the figure 8, but built a large, wide trigger guard around it. Some 20,000 of these revolvers were made, largely intended for the American Army and Navy.

## Smith 1857 Carbine

**TECHNICAL SPECIFICATIONS**

| | |
|---|---|
| Calibre | : .50" (12.7 mm) |
| Cartridge capacity | : single-shot |
| Operation | : single-action |
| Firing system | : percussion |
| Breach-loading | : top-breaking barrel with bolt lug in trigger guard |
| Length | : 99.1 cm (39") |
| Barrel length | : 54.6 cm (21.5") |
| Weight | : 3.5 kg (7.75 lb) |
| Sight | : graduated sight |
| Safety | : none |
| Stock | : walnut |

*Smith 1857 Carbine*

*Specific details*: This was made during the American Civil War and used by the Northern troops. The American government bought some 30,000 of these carbines at $ 24, each from the Poultney & Trimble trading company of Baltimore, Maryland, which is why their name is inscribed on the barrel of the carbine. It fires a bullet encased in rubber and a black powder charge. There are two versions: a Cavalry model with a saddle rod and ring on the left-hand side of the weapon, and an Artillery model with rifle belt rings. Authentic replicas are marketed in North America by Navy Arms. This replica is sold in Europe by Hege-Uberti, Frankonia and Kettner.

## Remington Model 1858 new army

**TECHNICAL SPECIFICATIONS**

| | |
|---|---|
| Calibre | : .44" (11.2 mm) |
| Cartridge capacity | : 6-shot |
| Operation | : single-action |
| Firing system | : percussion |
| Breach-loading | : N/A |
| Length | : 337 mm (13.25") |
| Barrel length | : 203 mm (8") |
| Weight | : 1202 g (42.4 oz) |
| Sight | : fixed |
| Safety | : half-cock hammer |
| Grip | : walnut grip plates |

*Remington Model 1858 New Army*

*Specific details*: Some 132,000 of these revolvers were built by Remington between 1863 and 1873. The revolver has an octagonal barrel. The .36 calibre version is known as the Model 1858 Navy. It was highly valued by the soldiers during the American Civil War due to its strong closed frame.

A high-quality replica in a .44 calibre is made by Uberti, Italy. The barrel of the original revolver bears the inscription: 'Patented Sept. 14, 1858 E. Remington & Sons, Ilion, New York, U.S.A. New Model'.

## Allen & Wheelock Army Revolver Model 1858

**TECHNICAL SPECIFICATIONS**

| | |
|---|---|
| Calibre | : .36 or .44" (9.1 or 11.2 mm) |
| Cartridge capacity | : 5-shot |
| Operation | : single-action |
| Firing system | : percussion |
| Breach-loading | : N/A |
| Length | : 258, 335 or 385 mm (11.2, 13.2 or 15.2") |
| Barrel length | : 102, 152 or 190.5 mm (4, 6 or 7.5") |
| Weight | : 1020 to 1300 g (36 to 45.9 oz) |
| Sight | : fixed |
| Safety | : half-cock hammer |
| Grip | : walnut |

*Specific details*: It was made by Allen & Wheelock of Worcester, Mass. from 1858

*Allen & Wheelock Army revolver Model 1858*

to 1861. The first models had a hammer mounted to the left of the frame. Afterwards Allen made a revolver with a centrally mounted hammer. The construction of the ramrod of this revolver is quite peculiar: the front of the trigger guard can be disconnected and rotated down in a forward movement.

A rod with the bullet guide is connected to this trigger guard section. It slides towards the cylinder opening. By pulling the lug below the cylinder axis pin down, the pin is released and can be pulled out of the revolver.

Now the entire cylinder can be taken out of the weapon. The last version of this model was made in various Lip-Fire cartridge calibers in 1861. However Smith & Wesson objected, as this model violated their Rollin-White patent. As a result Allen & Wheelock ceased production of this revolver in 1863.

## Whitney Model 1858 Navy

### TECHNICAL SPECIFICATIONS

| | |
|---|---|
| Calibre | : .36" (9.1 mm) |
| Cartridge capacity | : 6-shot |
| Operation | : single-action |
| Firing system | : percussion |
| Breach-loading | : N/A |
| Length | : 330 mm (13") |
| Barrel length | : 190 mm (7.5") |
| Weight | : 1270 g (45 oz) |
| Sight | : fixed notch and bead |
| Safety | : half-cock hammer |
| Grip | : walnut |

*Specific details*: This was made between 1858 and 1862 in two models with a total volume of 33,000 revolvers. The first model had 4 modified versions and the second model was made in six. The revolver has an iron grip section. The revolver in the photograph is a second model, first variation. Some 1200 revolvers of this specific version were made.

*Whitney Model 1858 Navy*

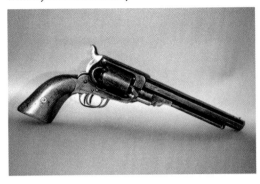

## Sharps 1859 Infantry Carbine

### TECHNICAL SPECIFICATIONS

| | |
|---|---|
| Calibre | : .54" (13,7 mm) |
| Cartridge capacity | : single-shot |
| Operation | : single-action |
| Firing system | : percussion |
| Breach-loading | : falling block action |
| Length | : 118.8 cm (46.75") |
| Barrel length | : 76.2 cm (30") |
| Weight | : 3.9 kg (8.5 lb) |
| Sight | : fixed |
| Safety | : half-cock hammer |
| Stock | : nut |

*Specific details*: A successful military rifle used by the Union Army during the American Civil War. This rifle has three barrel bands. Sharps produced this model from 1859 to 1862. American Navy Arms has an excellent replica for sale. The pictures show: Model Sharps 1859 Infantry Carbine (below) and the 1863 Cavalry Carbine.

*Sharps 1859 Infantry Carbine*

*Sharps Pepper box Pistol 1859*

sponding inscriptions on the side of the frame;

–2nd model: calibre .30 rim-fire with a 2.5"/64-mm barrel. Made from 1861 to 1862 by C. Sharps & Co and from 1862 to 1865 by Sharps & Hankins with the corresponding inscriptions on the side of the frame;

–3rd model: calibre .32 Short rim-fire with a 3.5"/90-mm barrel. Made by Sharps & Hankins from 1863 to 1866;

–4th model: calibre .32 Long rim-fire with a 2.5"/64-mm, 3"/76-mm or 3.5"/90-mm barrel and a round grip section. Produced by Sharps & Hankins from 1863 to 1866 and by C. Sharps & Co from 1866 to 1874.

## Sharps Pepperbox Pistol 1859

**TECHNICAL SPECIFICATIONS**

| | |
|---|---|
| Calibre | : .22 Short, .30, .32 Short or .32" Long |
| Cartridge capacity | : single-shot (per barrel) |
| Operation | : single-action |
| Firing system | : rim-fire |
| Breach-loading | : bolt pin below grip section |
| Length | : 95, 108 or 120 mm (3.7, 4.3 or 4.7") |
| Barrel length | : 64, 76 or 90 mm (2.5, 3 or 3.5") |
| Weight | : 295 to 325 g (10.4 to 11.5 oz) |
| Sight | : bead |
| Safety | : half-cock hammer |
| Grip | : walnut |

*Specific details*: A 4-barrel pepperbox, made in the period between 1859 and 1874. Produced by C. Sharps & Co. from 1859 to 1862. In 1862 this company merged with Hankins of Philadelphia and the name was changed to Sharps & Hankins Company. The two companies split up again in 1866 and Sharps continued the company in his own name, until he died in 1874. This pistol is known to exist in four models:

–1st model: calibre .22 Short with a 2.5"/64-mm barrel. Made from 1859 to 1862 by C. Sharps & Co and from 1862 to 1865 by Sharps & Hankins with the corre-

## Starr Model 1859 Navy

**TECHNICAL SPECIFICATIONS**

| | |
|---|---|
| Calibre | : .36" (9.1 mm) |
| Cartridge capacity | : 6-shot |
| Operation | : double-action |
| Firing system | : percussion |
| Breach-loading | : N/A |
| Length | : 305 mm (12") |
| Barrel length | : 152 mm (6") |
| Weight | : 1450 g (51.1 oz) |
| Sight | : bead |
| Safety | : half-cock hammer |
| Grip | : walnut |

*Specific details*: The Starr Arms Company of New York made this revolver based on a patent of 1856. A similar revolver, the Starr Model 1859 Army had a .44 calibre and was

*Starr Model 1859 Navy*

made in some 50,000 pieces, whereas only 3000 Navy models were made. When the trigger is pulled, the hammer is first cocked. The little lug on the rear side of the trigger is provided for firing the weapon. Next to Starr, the Savage Revolving Fire Arms Company of Middletown, Connecticut also made this weapon.

## Colt 1860 Army Model

**TECHNICAL SPECIFICATIONS**

| | |
|---|---|
| Calibre | : .44" (11.2 mm) |
| Cartridge capacity | : 6-shot |
| Operation | : single-action |
| Firing system | : percussion |
| Breach-loading | : N/A |
| Length | : 337 or 350 mm (13.25 or 13.75") |
| Barrel length | : 191 or 203 mm (7.5 or 8") |
| Weight | : 1202 g (42.4 oz) with a 203 mm (8") barrel |
| Sight | : fixed |
| Safety | : half-cock hammer |
| Grip | : walnut grip in one piece |

*Specific details*: The most used revolver by the Union Army during the American Civil War. Colt delivered some 127,000 of these revolvers in this period. A total number of

*Colt 1860 Army Model*

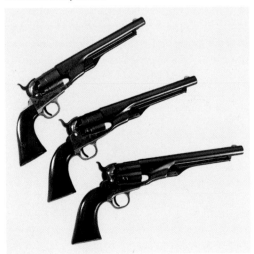

*Civilian version of the Colt 1860 Army Model*

200,500 of these revolvers were manufactured from 1860 to 1873. This model has an iron grip frame and a brass trigger guard. The Army version came in two types: one with an opening in the grip frame to fit an extra stock (lower model in the photograph) and one without this facility (centre revolver). The upper revolver in the photograph is the Civilian Model with a brass grip frame. The Civilian Model with an opening for an extra stock is very rare. The cylinder has been engraved with a picture of a naval battle. In addition the lower revolver features a milled cylinder. This version is quite rare as well. Hege-Uberti builds some excellent replicas of this revolver. The picture shows, from top to bottom: Civilian Model, Army Model and Army Model with a provision for an extra stock and a milled cylinder. The photograph at the top of this page is a civilian version of the Colt 1860 Army Revolver.

*Spencer 1860 Carbine*

## Spencer 1860 Carbine

**TECHNICAL SPECIFICATIONS**

| | |
|---|---|
| Calibre | : .44, .50 or .52" rim-fire (11.2, 12.7 or 13.2 mm) |
| Cartridge capacity | : 7 cartridges |
| Operation | : single-action |
| Firing system | : rim-fire |
| Breach-loading | : falling block action |
| Length | : 99.1 cm (39") |
| Barrel length | : 55.9 cm (22") |
| Weight | : 3.7 kg (8.23 lb) |
| Sight | : graduated sight |
| Safety | : half-cock hammer |
| Stock | : nut |

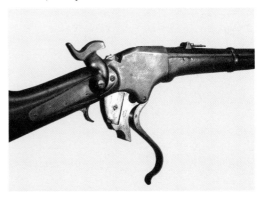

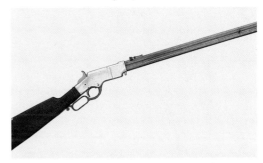

*Winchester 1860 Henry Rifle*

*Specific details*: Designed by Christopher M. Spencer, this carbine has a detachable tubular magazine in its stock. It was initially made in the .52 rim-fire calibre, but the cartridge is commonly designated as the .56–56 Spencer or 56 for short. The .44 and .50 (.56–50 and .56–52) calibres were added later.

This type of weapon exists in several versions, such as the 1860 Navy Model with a 76-cm (30") barrel and the 1865 carbine with a magazine lock, a patent by Edward Stabler. This allowed the falling block to move only partially, so that no new cartridge could be supplied from the tubular magazine.

The weapon then had to be loaded by hand, shot-by-shot. This system was intended to save on ammunition. All models were produced by the Spencer Repeating Arms Company of Boston Massachusetts. In addition to military weapons, Spencer also made sporting guns, including a .56–46 rim-fire calibre with a bottle-neck case.

At least 100,000 M1860 carbines were made. At the end of the American Civil War, Christopher M. Spencer encountered serious financial difficulties and his company's inventory was then bought by Oliver Winchester.

## Winchester 1860 Henry Rifle

**TECHNICAL SPECIFICATIONS**

| | |
|---|---|
| Calibre | : .44" Henry rim-fire |
| Cartridge capacity | : 15 cartridges |
| Operation | : single-action |
| Firing system | : rim-fire |
| Breach-loading | : lever action |
| Length | : 110 cm (43.3") |
| Barrel length | : 61 cm (24") |
| Weight | : 4.0 kg (8.8 lb) |
| Sight | : graduated sight |
| Safety | : half-cock hammer |
| Stock | : walnut |

*Specific details*: Derived from the Volcanic rifle in combination with the new rim-fire cartridge developed by B. Tyler Henry, the first series had a round stock plate and were produced by the New Haven Arms Company from 1860 to 1862, followed by the sharp-plated version from 1863 to 1866.

*The 7th Illinois Infantry, armed with Winchester 1860 Henry rifles (photograph courtesy of Cimarron Firearms)*

In 1860 and 1861 the frames were made of iron (some 300 of them were made) and then of brass until 1866. The total number of Winchester 1860 Henry Rifles produced numbers about 14,000. The military version has lanyard rings. Beautiful replicas of these weapons are produced by Cimarron Arms and Hege-Uberti in a .44-40 WCF calibre.

## Colt 1861 Navy Model

### TECHNICAL SPECIFICATIONS

| | |
|---|---|
| Calibre | : .36" (9.1 mm) |
| Cartridge capacity | : 6-shot |
| Operation | : single-action |
| Firing system | : percussion |
| Breach-loading | : N/A |
| Length | : 330 mm (13") |
| Barrel length | : 191 mm (7.5") |
| Weight | : 1200 g (42.3 oz) |
| Sight | : fixed |
| Safety | : half-cock hammer |
| Grip | : walnut grip in one piece |

*Specific details*: This revolver manufactured between 1861 and 1873, has a round barrel. The cylinder has been engraved with

a picture of a naval battle. The total number produced was approximately 38,500. About 100 of them have a facility to fit an extra stock, which makes them very rare and valuable. This model never rivalled its predecessor's popularity, mainly because the percussion era was nearing its end and due to a fire which destroyed the major part of the Colt factory in Hartford in 1864. Hege-Uberti builds an excellent replica of this revolver. The picture shows the Colt 1851 (top) and the 1861 Navy (bottom).

*Colt 1861 Navy Model*

## Springfield 1861 Rifle

**TECHNICAL SPECIFICATIONS**

| | |
|---|---|
| Calibre | : .58" Minie (14.7 mm) |
| Cartridge capacity | : single-shot, muzzle-loader |
| Operation | : single-action |
| Firing system | : percussion |
| Breach-loading | : N/A |
| Length | : 142.2 cm (56") |
| Barrel length | : 101.6 cm (40") |
| Weight | : 4.6 kg (10.25 lb) |
| Sight | : graduated sight |
| Safety | : half-cock hammer |
| Stock | : walnut |

*Specific details*: This was produced between 1861 and 1863. The Springfield Armory produced some 256,000 of these rifles. Other manufacturers made 750,000 of these rifles under licence. All metal parts are blank, but some 2,000 rifles have a blued sight and a blued lock plate. A typical feature is the rear belt ring, which is attached to the trigger guard. American Navy Arms produces a beautiful replica. The picture shows: the Springfield M1861 (bottom) and the M1863 (top).

*Smith & Wesson Model No. 2 Old Army*

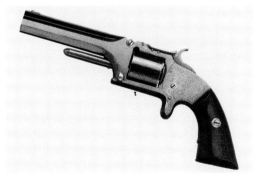

# Smith & Wesson Model No. 2 Old Army

**TECHNICAL SPECIFICATIONS**

| | |
|---|---|
| Calibre | : .32" rim-fire |
| Cartridge capacity | : 6-shot |
| Operation | : single-action |
| Firing system | : rim-fire |
| Breach-loading | : bolt lug below frame, in front of cylinder |
| Length | : 217–318 mm (8.5–12.5") |
| Barrel length | : 102, 127, 152 or 203 mm (4, 5, 6 or 8") |
| Weight | : 710 to 850 g (25 to 30 oz) |
| Sight | : fixed |
| Safety | : half-cock hammer |
| Grip | : walnut, mahogany, mother of pearl or ivory |

*Specific details*: This revolver was a major success for Smith & Wesson who produced over 88,700 of them from 1861 to 1874. The most common barrel lengths were 5 or 6", whereas the 4" and 8" models are quite rare. The weapon can be blued or nickel plated and some – albeit very few – revolvers are even silver or gold plated. Up to about serial number 3000 of this revolver the upper bridge over the cylinder is fitted with two pins. Later series have three pins that support the cylinder lock. In spite of its Army designation, this revolver was never officially purchased by the American Army. However, the revolver did play a role in the American Civil War because many soldiers bought it themselves. In those days the rim-fire cartridge provided a major head-start

*Right-hand side of the Smith & Wesson Model No. 2 Old Army*

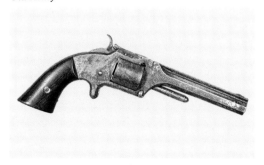

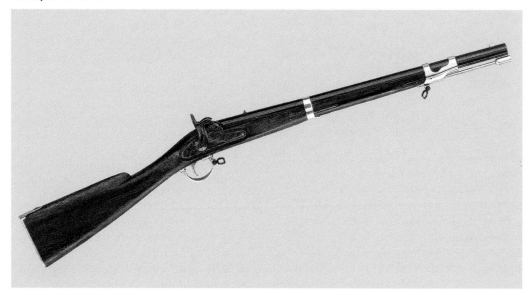

over ordinary muzzle loaders. This weapon was extensively copied by many factories including some in the Liège area in Belgium.

## *Murray 1862 Carbine*

**TECHNICAL SPECIFICATIONS**

Calibre : .58" Minie (14.7 mm)
Cartridge capacity : single-shot, muzzle-loader
Operation : single-action
Firing system : percussion
Breach-loading : N/A
Length : 99.7 or 101 cm (39.25 or 39.75")
Barrel length : 59.7 or 61 cm (23.5 or 24")
Weight : 3.4 kg (7.5 lb)
Sight : fixed
Safety : half-cock hammer
Stock : walnut

*Specific details*: This was made by J.P. Murray of Columbus, Georgia from 1862 to 1864. Murray made a cavalry carbine with a saddle rod and a ring, an infantry model with a 24" (61-cm) barrel and a rifle version with a 32.75" (83.2-cm) barrel. The stock plate, trigger guard and both barrel rings are made of brass. American Navy

Arms has a beautiful replica of the carbine version.

## *Colt 1862 Pocket Navy Model*

**TECHNICAL SPECIFICATIONS**

Calibre : .36' (9.1 mm)
Cartridge capacity : 5-shot
Operation : single-action
Firing system : percussion
Breach-loading : N/A
Length : 241, 267 or 292 mm (9.5, 10.5 or 11.5")
Barrel length : 114, 140, or 165 mm (4.5, 5.5 or 6.5")
Weight : 765 g (27 oz)
Sight : fixed
Safety : half-cock Hammer
Grip : walnut grip in one piece

*Specific details*: The 1862 Pocket Navy Model strongly resembles the 1851 Navy and the 1849 Pocket revolver. The cylinder is engraved with a raid on a stage-coach. The grip frame and the trigger guard are silver-plated brass. Some 19,000 of these revolvers were produced between 1861 and 1873. A large number of them were later converted into cartridge revolvers, so that

*Colt 1862 Pocket Navy Model*

*Springfield 1863 Rifle*

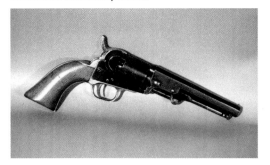

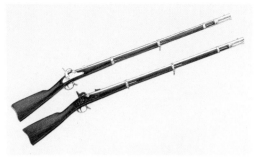

original percussion models have become very scarce. Excellent replicas with 5.5 or 6.5" barrels are available from Hege-Uberti.

## Colt 1862 Police Model

**TECHNICAL SPECIFICATIONS**

| | |
|---|---|
| Calibre | : .36" (9.1 mm) |
| Cartridge capacity | : 5-shot |
| Operation | : single-action |
| Firing system | : percussion |
| Breach-loading | : N/A |
| Length | : 216, 241, 267 or 292 mm (8.5, 9.5, 10.5 or 11.5") |
| Barrel length | : 89, 114, 140, or 165 mm (3.5, 4.5, 5.5 or 6.5") |
| Weight | : 725 g (25.6 oz) with a 3.5" barrel |
| Sight | : fixed |
| Safety | : half-cock hammer |
| Grip | : walnut grip in one piece |

*Colt 1862 Police Model*

*Specific details*: The 1862 Police Model has a nicely styled frame with a milled cylinder.

This revolver was also referred to as the Colt New Model Police Pistol or the Colt 1862 Belt Model. Some 28,000 of them were made between 1861 and 1873, of which a large number were later converted into cartridge revolvers. The model with a 3.5"/89-mm barrel does not have a ramrod. A small number were sold in a red leather book-shaped case with the titles "Colt's Pocket Companion" and "Colt on the Constitution of higher Law and irrepress-ible Conflict".

Hege-Uberti makes excellent replicas of this exquisite Colt with 5.5 or 6.5" (140- or 165-mm) barrels. The picture shows: Model 1861 Pocket Navy (top) and the Model 1862 Police.

## Springfield 1863 rifle

**TECHNICAL SPECIFICATIONS**

| | |
|---|---|
| Calibre | : .58" Minie (14.7 mm) |
| Cartridge capacity | : single-shot, muzzle-loader |
| Operation | : single-action |
| Firing system | : percussion |
| Breach-loading | : N/A |
| Length | : 142.2 cm (56") |
| Barrel length | : 101.6 cm (40") |
| Weight | : 4.3 kg (9.5 lb) |
| Sight | : graduated sight |
| Safety | : half-cock hammer |
| Grip | : walnut |

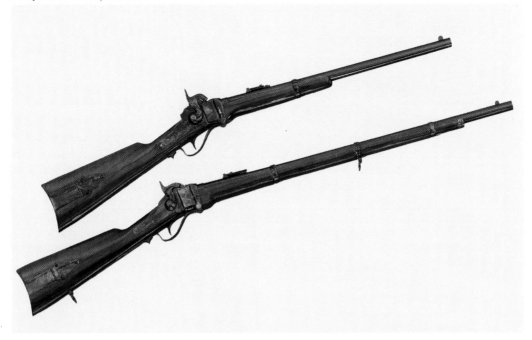

*Specific details*: It was produced between 1863 and 1865 in two types: type I with the year '1863' stamped in and type II with the year stamp '1864' or '1865'. Some 275,000 type I rifles were made and some 225,000 type II's. Type II has a single notched leaf and was the last American Army rifle to be built as a muzzle-loader.

The metal parts are blank, except for the blued sight. American Navy Arms produces a beautiful replica. The picture shows the Springfield M1861 (bottom) and the M1863 (top).

*Richmond 1863 Rifle*

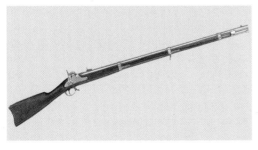

# Sharps 1863 cavalry carbine

**TECHNICAL SPECIFICATIONS**

| | |
|---|---|
| Calibre | : .54" (13.7 mm) |
| Cartridge capacity | : single-shot |
| Operation | : single-action |
| Firing system | : percussion |
| Breach-loading | : falling block action |
| Length | : 99.1 cm (39") |
| Barrel length | : 56 cm (22") |
| Weight | : 3.5 kg (7.75 lb) |
| Sight | : fixed |
| Safety | : half-cock hammer |
| Stock | : nut |

*Specific details*: A military cavalry carbine that was used by both sides during the American Civil War. The rifle has been fitted with a saddle rod and a ring on the left. American Navy Arms makes an excellent replica of this rifle.

The picture shows: Model Sharps 1859 Infantry Rifle (bottom) and the 1863 Cavalry Carbine (top).

## Richmond 1863 Rifle

**TECHNICAL SPECIFICATIONS**

Calibre : .58" (14.7 mm)
Cartridge capacity : single-shot, muzzle-loader
Operation : single-action
Firing system : percussion
Breach-loading : N/A
Length : 142.2 cm (56")
Barrel length : 101.6 cm (40")
Weight : 4.6 kg (10.25 lb)
Sight : folding sight
Safety : half-cock hammer
Stock : walnut

*Specific details*: It was produced from 1861 to 1865 using machines that were seized from Harpers Ferry Armory of Harpers Ferry in Virginia. In 1861, the machines were brought to Richmond, Virginia by the Virginia militia. The first production series of the Richmond 1863 was composed of confiscated parts of the Harpers Ferry M1855 rifle. Navy Arms make a beautiful replica of this rifle, complete with a lock plate for the 1855 rifle marked with the year '1863'.

## Remington 1863 New Model Army

**TECHNICAL SPECIFICATIONS**

Calibre : .44" (11.2 mm)
Cartridge capacity : 6-shot
Operation : single-action
Firing system : percussion

*Remington 1863 New Model Army*

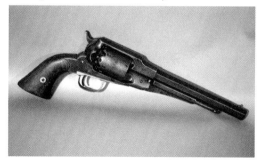

Breach-loading : N/A
Length : 324 mm (12.8")
Barrel length : 203 mm (8")
Weight : 1305 g (46 oz)
Sight : fixed notch and bead
Safety : half-cock hammer
Grip : walnut

*Specific details*: A total number of 132,000 of these revolvers were produced by Remington between 1863 and 1873. The rear end of the cylinder has been milled at the nipples as a kind of safety feature. As a result this modification was given the designation 'New Model'. The numbers engraved in these revolvers are sometimes higher than their actual production number. The reason for this is that Remington did not start with a new series of numbers, but continued from the Remington-Beal Revolver of 1860.

## Merwin & Bray Model 1863 cup-primer revolver

**TECHNICAL SPECIFICATIONS**

Calibre : .28, .30 or .42" (7.1, 7.6 or 10.7 mm)
Cartridge capacity : 6-shot
Operation : single-action
Firing system : cup-primer (see below)
Breach-loading : N/A
Length : 230 or 245 mm (9 or 9.6")
Barrel length : 121 or 133 mm (4.75 or 5.25")
Weight : 710 or 740 g (25 or 26.1 oz)
Sight : fixed notch and bead
Safety : half-cock hammer
Grip : walnut

*Specific details*: This was produced by the Plant Manufacturing Company of New Haven (Connecticut) for the New York Trading Company Merwin & Bray. This revolver was made in a blued version, but several other versions exist as well. The weapon in the photograph has been gold plated. The revolver cylinder was loaded from the front, using cup-primer cartridges.

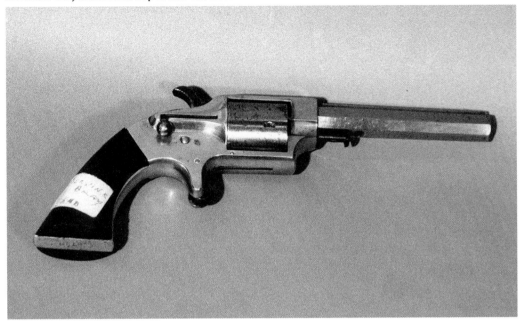

This system was intended to evade the patent rights that Smith & Wesson had on a drilled-through cylinder. The latch on the right-hand side of the frame is the case ejector. The drawing below shows the cup-primer cartridge: A. the case, B. the bullet point, C. the black powder charge and D. the primer. This is a rim-fire cartridge.

*Drawing of the cup-priming cartridge: A. case, B. bullet point, C. black powder charge, D. primer*

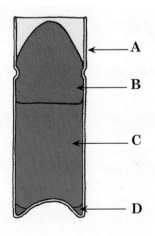

## Plant Cup-Primer Revolver 1863

### TECHNICAL SPECIFICATIONS

| | |
|---|---|
| Calibre | : .28, .38, .40 or .42" cup-primer (7.1, 9.7, 10.2 or 10.7 mm) |
| Cartridge capacity | : 6-shot |
| Operation | : single-action |
| Firing system | : rim-fire cup-primer |
| Breach-loading | : N/A |
| Length | : 275 mm (10.8") |
| Barrel length | : 152 mm (6") |
| Weight | : 900 g (31.7 oz) |
| Sight | : fixed |
| Safety | : half-cock hammer |
| Grip | : walnut |

*Specific details*: It was produced by Plant's Manufacturing Company of New Haven, Connecticut. Strangely this revolver is often referred to as the Plant Army Revolver although it was never used as a service weapon.

The Plant revolver is often inscribed with the name of the New York Trading Company Merwin & Bray. They financed its manufacture from 1864. The ammuni-

*Plant Cup-Primer Revolver 1863*

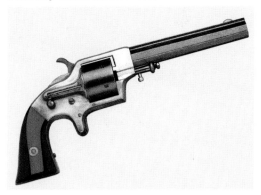

## Pond Muzzle-Loading Revolver 1863

**TECHNICAL SPECIFICATIONS**

| | |
|---|---|
| Calibre | : .22 of .32" rim-fire |
| Cartridge capacity | : .22: 7-shot; .32: 6-shot |
| Operation | : single-action |
| Firing system | : rim-fire |
| Breach-loading | : N/A |
| Length | : 204, 217, 242 or 267 mm (8, 8.5, 9.5 or 10.5") |
| Barrel length | : 89, 102, 127 or 152 mm (3.5, 4, 5 or 6") |
| Weight | : 720 to 860 g (25.4 to 30 oz) |
| Sight | : fixed |
| Safety | : half-cock hammer |
| Grip | : walnut |

tion for this weapon is rather special. It resembles a rim-fire cartridge, but then with a hollow bottom. The bullet point is fully contained inside the case. This cartridge was invented by Plant and his business partners. The revolver design was a successful attempt to evade the Rollin-White patent right due to which the Plant revolver could not have drilled-through cylinder chambers.

The cup-primer cartridge was loaded from the front. Small slots for the firing pin point had been milled into the rear end of the cylinder chambers. The typical latch on the right-hand side of the frame is used to eject the cases from the cylinder chambers. After the Plant factory was destroyed by fire, the Marlin Firearms Company continued the production of this revolver and marketed it as the Eagle Arms Pocket Revolver.

*Specific details*: It was designed and produced by Lucius William Pond of Worcester, Massachusetts from 1863 to 1870. He made some 2000 of these revolvers in a .22 calibre and over 5000 in .32. The revolver was an attempt to evade the patent right of Rollin White, who was granted the patent to drilled-through cylinder chambers in 1855.

In 1856 White made this patent available to Smith & Wesson against a payment of 50 cents per weapon that was produced. This allowed Smith & Wesson to dominate the revolver market until 1872, when the patent right expired. This is why the cylinder chambers of the Pond revolver are not drilled through.

The rear ends of the chambers have a small opening for the firing pin point. The cartridges have to be inserted into the cylinder chambers from the front. The cylinder has loose chamber cases and is loaded as follows: a loose, steel chamber case is placed on the rod below the barrel for every cylinder chamber. The cartridge can then be slid into the chamber case bottom down. The chamber case is then pushed back into the cylinder chamber. This procedure is repeated until all chambers have been loaded.

*Pond Muzzle-Loading Revolver 1863*

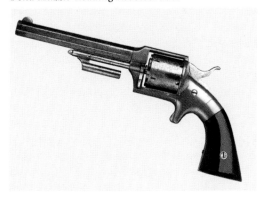

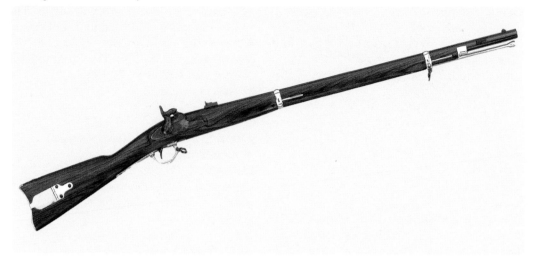

## Remington 1863 Zouave Rifle

**TECHNICAL SPECIFICATIONS**

| | |
|---|---|
| Calibre | : .58" (14.7 mm) |
| Cartridge capacity | : single-shot, muzzle-loader |
| Operation | : single-action |
| Firing system | : percussion |
| Breach-loading | : N/A |
| Length | : 124.5 cm (49") |
| Barrel length | : 83.8 cm (33") |
| Weight | : 4.1 kg (9 lb) |
| Sight | : folding sight |
| Safety | : half-cock hammer |
| Stock | : walnut |

*Specific details*: It was produced from 1862 to 1865 by Springfield in a total number of 12,500. Both barrel bands, the stock plate and the patchbox are made of brass. Perdersoli makes an authentic replica that is marketed by a number of companies including Navy Arms.

*Teat-fire cartridge: 1. case, 2. bullet point, 3. black powder charge, 4. primer*

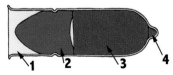

## Moore Teat Revolver 186

**TECHNICAL SPECIFICATIONS**

| | |
|---|---|
| Calibre | : .30 Teat, .32 Teat of .42" Teat |
| Cartridge capacity | : 6-shot |
| Operation | : single-action |
| Firing system | : Teat ignition |
| Breach-loading | : N/A |
| Length | : 178 mm (7") |
| Barrel length | : 82.5 mm (3.25") |
| Weight | : 400 g (14.1 oz) |
| Sight | : fixed |
| Safety | : half-cock hammer |
| Grip | : walnut |

*Specific details*: It was produced by Moore's Patent Firearms Company from 1864 to 1867 and by the National Arms Company of Brooklyn, New York from 1867 to 1871. This revolver fired the Teat cartridge.

Its case has a fully countersunk bullet point. The rear end of the case ends in a tip in which the primer is contained. The cylinder of the revolver had to be loaded from the front. The cylinder was not fully drilled through.

A small opening for the firing pin point was made at the rear end of the cylinder chamber. This complicated construction had been devised to evade the existing Rollin-White patent owned by Smith & Wesson. The original name of this cartridge is the 'Central Fire Waterproof Copper Shell Cartridge'.

When Moore's factory went bankrupt in 1867 its production was continued by the National Arms Company.

## Manhattan Model 1864 Navy

**TECHNICAL SPECIFICATIONS**

| | |
|---|---|
| Calibre | : .36" (9.1 mm) |
| Cartridge capacity | : 5 of 6-shot |
| Operation | : single-action |
| Firing system | : percussion |
| Breach-loading | : N/A |
| Length | : 232, 257 or 295 mm (9.1, 10.1 or 11.6") |
| Barrel length | : 102, 127 or 165 mm (4, 5 or 6.5") |
| Weight | : 905 g (32 oz) with a 6.5"/165-mm barrel |
| Sight | : fixed notch and bead |
| Safety | : half-cock hammer |
| Grip | : walnut |

*Specific details*: It was produced between 1859 and 1868 by the Manhattan Fire Arms Company of Newark, New Jersey. Some 78,000 of these revolvers were made in total, divided over five different versions

with minor modifications. The serial numbers of Model 1 end with 4200. The numbers for the second model continue to 14,500; the third model to 45,200, the fourth model to 69,200. The fifth model is only made with a six-shot cylinder and its serial numbers run from 1 to 9000.

## Cooper Double-Action Pocket Revolver 1864

**TECHNICAL SPECIFICATIONS**

| | |
|---|---|
| Calibre | : .31" (7.9 mm) |
| Cartridge capacity | : 6-shot |
| Operation | : double-action |
| Firing system | : percussion |
| Breach-loading | : N/A |
| Length | : 180, 205 or 230 mm (7.1, 8.1 or 9.1") |
| Barrel length | : 102, 127 or 152 mm (4, 5 or 6") |
| Weight | : 980—1100 g (34.6—38.8 oz) |
| Sight | : bead |
| Safety | : half-cock hammer |
| Grip | : walnut |

*Specific details*: It was made by J.M. Cooper & Co in the period 1864 to 1869. The company name with the extension 'Pittsburgh Pennsylvania' was engraved in this gun in the period 1864–1866, after which the company moved to Philadelphia. The total number produced is approxi-

*Manhattan Model 1864 Navy*

*Cooper Duoble-Action Pocket Revolver 1864*

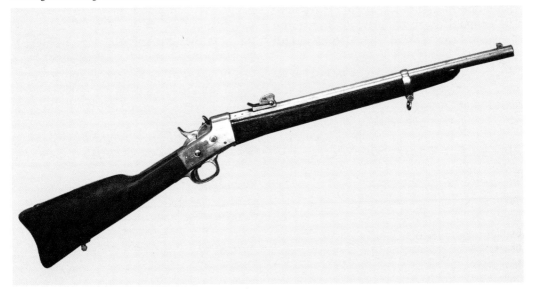

mately 15,000. This revolver resembles the various Colt models, which were all single action however. The collector's value of the Cooper Pocket Revolver is considerably lower than that of the Colt revolvers.

## Remington Rolling Block 1864 Carbine

### TECHNICAL SPECIFICATIONS

| | |
|---|---|
| Calibre | : .46" Rim-fire or .56-50" Spencer Rim-fire |
| Cartridge capacity | : single-shot |
| Operation | : single-action |
| Firing system | : rim-fire |
| Breach-loading | : rolling block action |
| Length | : 87 cm (34.25") |
| Barrel length | : 50.4 cm (19.85") |
| Weight | : 3.2 kg (7 lb) |
| Sight | : arc-shaped folding sight |
| Safety | : half-cock hammer |
| Stock | : nut |

*Specific details*: This was based on the design by Leonard Geiger and the patents owned by Joseph Rider. Remington made many weapons with this action type, including various sporting rifles. The

*Detail of the Remington Rolling Block 1864 Carbine*

*Breech opening of the Remington Rolling Block 1864 Carbine*

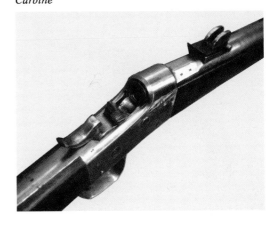

picture shows the carbine model of 1864. Other important models are the Navy Rifle 1870 (total length 48.65"/123.6 cm) and the army rifle Model 1871 (total length 51.75"/131.5 cm).

The weapon was produced by several arms manufacturers in many companies, sometimes under licence.

## Rogers & Spencer Army Model 1865

**TECHNICAL SPECIFICATIONS**

| | |
|---|---|
| Calibre | : .44" (11.2 mm) |
| Cartridge capacity | : 6-shot |
| Operation | : single-action |
| Firing system | : percussion |
| Breach-loading | : N/A |
| Length | : 340 mm (13.4") |
| Barrel length | : 191 mm (7.5") |
| Weight | : 1420 g (50 oz) |
| Sight | : fixed notch and bead |
| Safety | : half-cock hammer |
| Grip | : walnut |

*Specific details*: This was made by Rogers & Spencer from Utica, New York from 1863 to 1865. The name of this weapon comes from an order from the army for 5000 revolvers that was placed in 1865. A total of 5800 of these revolvers were produced.

A typical feature is the bullet guide, that is attached to the drum pin.

*Rogers & Spencer Army Model 1865*

## Smith & Wesson Model 1-⅕ 1865

**TECHNICAL SPECIFICATIONS**

| | |
|---|---|
| Calibre | : .32" RF-Short |
| Cartridge capacity | : 5-shot |
| Operation | : single-action |
| Firing system | : rim-fire |
| Breach-loading | : tip-up revolver with latch at the bottom of the barrel frame |
| Length | : 207 mm (8.15") |
| Barrel length | : 89 or 102 mm (3.5 of 4") |
| Weight | : 425 g (14.9 oz) |
| Sight | : bead |
| Safety | : half-cock hammer |
| Grip | : rosewood, walnut, mother of pearl or ivory |

Specific details: This was assembled by Smith & Wesson from parts produced by the King & Smith arms company of Middletown in Connecticut between 1865 and 1868. Initially the revolver was only sold with an octagonal 3.5"/89-mm barrel. A version with a 4"/102-mm barrel was produced for a while in 1866. The serial numbers run from 1 to 26,300. This revolver greatly resembles the No. 2 Army or old model. With the Model 1-1/5 the cylinder stop is located at the bottom of the revolver frame, where the No. 2 has a cylinder stop in the upper bridge. Over 26,000 revolvers of this model were built, including some 200 with a 4"/102-cm barrel.

## Remington 1866 Deringer

**TECHNICAL SPECIFICATIONS**

| | |
|---|---|
| Calibre | : .41" rim-fire |
| Cartridge capacity | : double-barrelled, |
| Operation | : single-action |
| Firing system | : rim-fire |
| Breach-loading | : sear on right-hand side of grip section |
| Length | : 121 mm (4.75") |
| Barrel length | : 76 mm (3") |
| Weight | : 340 g (12 oz.) |
| Sight | : fixed |
| Safety | : none |
| Grip | : ebonite, walnut or mahogany |

*Specific details*: This was designed by H. Elliot of Remington Arms Co. Some 150,000 of these revolvers were produced by Remington from 1866 to 1935 in .41 rim-fire. Various modifications were implemented during the production period: Type 1- first series without ejector; Type 1- central series with ejector (c. 1865–1870); Type 1-late production with automatic ejector.

Types 2 and 3 only differ with regard to the inscriptions: Type 2: 'Remington Arms Co., Ilion, N.Y.', Type 3: 'Remington Arms-U.M.C. Co., Ilion, N.Y.'. The sear on the right-hand side of the grip section was used to release the barrel section. The sliding sear on the left-hand side is the ejector. The .41 Short rim-fire, made from 1863 to 1942, was a popular cartridge for such weapons at the time. The cartridge has a muzzle velocity (V0) of 129.5 m/s (425 fps) and a muzzle energy (E0) of 70.4 J.

## Winchester 1866 Sporting Rifle

**TECHNICAL SPECIFICATIONS**

| | |
|---|---|
| Calibre | : .44" (11,2 mm) Henry rim-fire |
| Cartridge capacity | : 17 cartridges |
| Operation | : single-action |
| Firing system | : rim-fire |
| Breach-loading | : lever action |
| Length | : 110 cm (43.3") |
| Barrel length | : 61 cm (24") |
| Weight | : 4.0 kg (8.8 lb) |
| Sight | : graduated sight |
| Safety | : half-cock hammer |
| Stock | : walnut |

*Specific details*: In 1866 the name New Haven Arms Company was changed to Winchester Repeating Arms Company. The Model 1866 was the first rifle to be produced by this new company. New

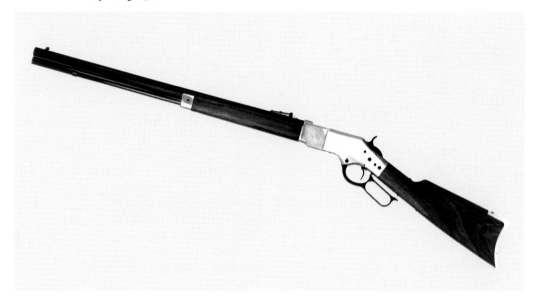

features were the improved tubular magazine and the improved loading system, patented by the plant manager Nelson King. In the period 1866 to 1898, three versions were made of the model 1866: approximately 28,000 Sporting Rifles with octagonal barrels, some 127,000 number of 1866 Carbines with round barrels and some 14,000 rifles of the military version with round barrels. Beautiful replicas are built by Cimarron Arms and Hege-Uberti in the .44-40 WCF calibre.

*Specific details*: In 1866 the name New Haven Arms Company was changed to Winchester Repeating Arms Company. The carbine version has a barrel band and a saddle ring on the left. Just like the Sporting Rifle, the carbine features the improved tubular magazine and the improved loading system.

The 1866 Carbine has a round barrel. About 127,000 of these carbines were made in the period 1866 to 1898. Cimarron Arms and Hege-Uberti make a beautiful replica in the .44-40 WCF calibre.

## Winchester 1866 Yellowboy Carbine

*Luxury version of the Winchester 1866 Yellowboy Carbine*

**TECHNICAL SPECIFICATIONS**

| | |
|---|---|
| Calibre | : .44" (11.2 mm) Henry rim-fire |
| Cartridge capacity | : 13 cartridges |
| Operation | : single-action |
| Firing system | : rim-fire |
| Breach-loading | : lever action |
| Length | : 99.8 cm (39.3") |
| Barrel length | : 50 cm (20") |
| Weight | : 3.5 kg (7.75 lb) |
| Sight | : folding sight |
| Safety | : half-cock hammer |
| Stock | : walnut |

## Wesson Derringer 1868

**TECHNICAL SPECIFICATIONS**

Calibre : .22 RF, .32 RF or .41" RF
Cartridge capacity : double-barrelled, single-shot
Operation : single-action
Firing system : rim-fire
Breach-loading : sear in frame below barrel section
Length : 100 or 113 mm (3.9 or 4.4")
Barrel length : 51 or 64 mm (2 or 2.5")
Weight : 85–180 g (3–6.3 oz)
Sight : bead
Safety : half-cock hammer
Grip : walnut, mother of pearl or ivory

*Specific details*: Designed by Frank Wesson of Springfield, Mass. and produced by Wesson in the period 1868 to circa 1880, the Derringer was made in three model sizes. To load the gun the barrel section had to be pivoted around its longitudinal axis over 90 degrees to provide access to both breeches. The Wesson Derringers often had a small dagger or blade in the hollow barrel shaft as an extra weapon for self-defence. These extra weapons had to be removed by hand. The specific details of the various models are:

Small Frame: calibre .22 Short RF; 2 or 2.5" (51- or 64-mm) barrel; some 3500 pieces were made from 1868 to 1880.
Medium Frame: calibre .32 RF; 2.5 or 3.5" (64- or 89- mm) barrel; some 3800 pieces were made between 1869 and 1880.
Large Frame: calibre .41 RF with only a 3" (76-mm) barrel; some 2000 of these Derringers were made from 1870 to 1880.

## Colt Cloverleaf or House Pistol 1871

**TECHNICAL SPECIFICATIONS**

Calibre : .41" (10.4 mm)
Cartridge capacity : 4 cartridges
Operation : single-action
Firing system : rim-fire
Breach-loading : N/A
Length : 133 or 171.5 mm (5.25 or 6.75")
Barrel length : 38 or 76 mm (1.5 of 3")
Weight : 397 of 454 g (14 or 16 oz)
Sight : bead
Safety : half-cock hammer
Grip : walnut or rosewood

*Specific details*: About 7500 of these pistols were produced by Colt from 181 to

*Wesson Derringer 1868*

1876. The 1.5"/38-mm barrel is quite rare. It was either octagonal or round. The 3"/76-mm version was only produced with a round barrel. Both types were available in various finishes: with a bronze frame and a blued barrel and cylinder, fully blued or fully nickel-plated. The revolver shown in the picture is an early type as indicated by its raised hammer spur.

This was modified afterwards, so that it points back more. From 1875 the House Pistol was also produced in a five-shot version with a round cylinder. Some 2500 revolvers of this version were made with serial numbers reaching over 6100. This weapon was only provided with a 2-7/8" (73-mm) barrel.

*Smith & Wesson Schofield 2nd Model Revolver 1871*

## Smith & Wesson Schofield 2nd Model Revolver 1871

**TECHNICAL SPECIFICATIONS**

| | |
|---|---|
| Calibre | : .45" S&W |
| Cartridge capacity | : 6-shot |
| Operation | : single-action |
| Firing system | : centre-fire |
| Breach-loading | : latch on frame |
| Length | : 321 mm (12 5/8") |
| Barrel length | : 178 mm (7") |
| Weight | : 1161 g (40.9 oz) |
| Sight | : fixed |
| Safety | : half-cock hammer |
| Grip | : walnut grip plates |

*Specific details*: This is derived from the S&W Model 3 top-break revolver and modified by the American Army Major George W. Schofield with a latch on the frame. There are two models: first model with a square lever on the latch, second model with a round lever.

It was manufactured between 1871 and 1877 and 3000 first model versions were made for the military and only 35 for the civilian market. In the second version: 4000 army revolvers and approx. 645 civilian ones were made. A high-quality replica is produced by Uberti-Italy in the .44-40 Win and .45 LC calibres.

## Wesson & Harrington Model 1871

### TECHNICAL SPECIFICATIONS

| | |
|---|---|
| Calibre | : .22 of .32" RF |
| Cartridge capacity | : 5-shot |
| Operation | : single-action |
| Firing system | : rim-fire |
| Breach-loading | : N/A |
| Length | : 192 mm (7.5") |
| Barrel length | : 76 mm (3") |
| Weight | : 550 g (19.4 oz) |
| Sight | : fixed |
| Safety | : half-cock hammer |
| Stock | : nut of hardgummi |

*Special details:* this revolver is the result

*Wesson & Harrington Model 1871*

of cooperation between Wesson and Harrington of Worcester, Massachusetts in 1871. The revolver has an unusual form of ejector which runs over an extension of the cylinder. The ejector can be operated with the thumb and forefinger to empty the chambers.

The empty shell or the cartridge is forced out of the chamber and slides along a recess on the right of the frame. This revolver was available in various models: No. 1 was only available in .22 Rimfire and 2,500 were made from 1871–1873. Model No. 2 was also available in .22 Rimfire and 15,000 were made in 1874–1879.

Model No. 3 Wesson & Harrington was also made in 1874–1879 in .32 Rimfire-Short when more than 15,000 were produced. Model 3 is illustrated.

## Marlin Model 1872 XXX Standard Pocket Revolver

### TECHNICAL SPECIFICATIONS

| | |
|---|---|
| Calibre | : .30" RF |
| Cartridge capacity | : 5-shot |
| Operation | : single-action |
| Firing system | : rim-fire |
| Breach-loading | : tip-up revolver |
| Length | : 200 mm (7.9") |
| Barrel length | : 83 mm (3.25") |
| Weight | : 354 g (12.5 oz) |
| Sight | : fixed notch and bead |
| Safety | : half-cock hammer |
| Grip | : rosewood or ebonite |

*Specific details*: This was made by the Marlin Fire Arms Company between 1872 and 1877. The total production was some 5000 of these revolvers in various modified models. The revolver is also called the 'Triple-X'.

The first model had an octagonal barrel and a smooth cylinder. The second model had a round barrel and a smooth cylinder. The third model had a round barrel and a semi-grooved cylinder and the fourth model

*Marlin Model 1872 XXX Standard Pocket Revolver*

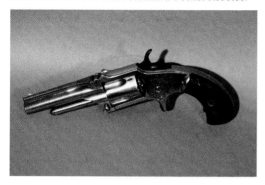

*Marlin Model 1872 XXX Standard Pocket Revolver tipped open*

*Several versions of the Colt M1873: from top to bottom: the M1873 with a 7.5" barrel, the 5.5" version, the 4.75" and the M1873 Storekeeper with a 3" barrel*

reverted to a round barrel and a cylinder but with long grooves. The weapon in the photographs is clearly a fourth model. In 1875, Marlin also introduced the same model in a .32 RF (rim-fire) calibre. This Marlin revolver has been inspired by the Smith & Wesson tip-up revolvers of the time.

A version of this revolver is the Marlin Model 1873 XX Standard Pocket revolver in a .22 LR calibre. In 1878 Marlin launched a similar revolver into the market in the .38 S&W centre-fire calibre.

## Colt Model 1873 Single-Action Army ('Peacemaker')

**TECHNICAL SPECIFICATIONS**

| | |
|---|---|
| Calibre | : originally .45 LC and .44-40 Win. |
| Cartridge capacity | : 6-shot |
| Operation | : single-action |
| Firing system | : originally centre-fire |
| Breach-loading | : N/A |
| Length | : 330 mm (13"): see Specific details |
| Barrel length | : 191 mm (7.5"): see Specific details |
| Weight | : 1050 g (37 oz) |
| Sight | : fixed |
| Safety | : half-cock hammer |
| Grip | : walnut grip in one piece |

*Specific details*: This was produced from 1873 to 1941 (some 360,000 pcs) and from 1955 until today in a wide range of calibres including: .22 Long, .22 LR, .32WRF, .32 Colt, .32 S&W, .32-20 WCF, .38 S&W, .38 Special, .357 Magnum, .41 S&W, .44 S&W special, .44 Magnum, .44–40 WCF, .45 ACP, .455 Eley etc.

The Colt 1873 SAA has been made in many versions, which sometimes have very special names. The barrel lengths vary from 3"(76 mm) to 18" (457 mm). The most well-known versions are the Storekeeper (without an ejector rod), Sherif's Model, Frontier (in .44-40 Win. calibre), Bisley Model and Buntline (from 12"/305-mm barrel length), and a couple are shown below.

### NEW FRONTIER
### SINGLE ACTION ARMY
.45 Colt, .357 Mag.
BARRELS: 5½", 7½"

A proud descendant of the famous "Frontier" of 1873.

### BUNTLINE SCOUT '62
.22 Short, Long, Long Rifle or New .22 Mag. Rimfire
BARREL: 9½"
A new version of the dependable Buntline Scout.

(Midnight Blue)

with extra .22 L. R. Cylinder    (Nickel)

### SINGLE ACTION ARMY
.45 Colt, .357 Mag.
BARRELS: 4¾", 5½", 7½" in .45 Colt and .357 Mag. 5½".

The gun that won the West here again from Colt's.

### FRONTIER SCOUT (Blue)
.22 Short, Long, Long Rifle or New .22 Mag. Rimfire
BARREL: 4¾"
The classic lines and dependable action of the single action army. Now available in .22 Mag. with extra fitted .22 long rifle cylinder.

with extra .22 L. R. Cylinder

### BUNTLINE SPECIAL
.45 Long Colt
BARREL: 12"

This fine reproduction of a famous early Western .45 makes an excellent collector's item.

### FRONTIER SCOUT
### (All Nickel)
.22 Short, Long, Long Rifle or New .22 Mag. Rimfire
BARREL: 4¾"
A nickel plated version of the single action army. Also available in .22 Mag. with extra fitted .22 long rifle cylinder.

with extra .22 L. R. Cylinder

### BUNTLINE SCOUT (Blue)
.22 Short, Long, Long Rifle or New .22 Mag. Rimfire
BARREL: 9½"

This long barrel Buntline allows near rifle accuracy.

### FRONTIER SCOUT '62
.22 Short, Long, Long Rifle or New .22 Mag. Rimfire
BARREL: 4¾"
This finely balanced single action revolver is an ideal handgun for hunting and plinking. Also available in .22 Mag. with extra fitted .22 long rifle cylinder.

*Special anniversary version of the Colt M1873*

Hege-Uberti builds some excellent replicas. This revolver is the most well-known and most famous Colt Model and has been produced in large numbers by several manufacturers, not always under licence from Colt.

*Colt Model 1873 Custer 7th U.S. Cavalry Single Action Army*

Colt discontinued the production of the Model 1873 on several occasions. It was produced from 1899 to 1940, from 1956 to 1975 and from 1977 to now.

## Colt Model 1873 Custer 7th U.S. Cavalry Single-Action Army

### TECHNICAL SPECIFICATIONS

| | |
|---|---|
| Calibre | : .45 Colt |
| Cartridge capacity | : 6-shot |
| Operation | : single-action |
| Firing system | : centre-fire |
| Breach-loading | : N/A |
| Length | : 330 mm (13"): see Specific details |
| Barrel length | : 191 mm (7.5"): see Specific details |
| Weight | : 1050 g (37 oz) |
| Sight | : fixed |
| Safety | : half-cock hammer |
| Grip | : walnut grip in one piece |

*Specific details*: This was the first series of 1873 Army Models manufactured by Colt. A number of these revolvers were bought by Gen. George Armstrong Custer's 7th Cavalry Regiment. They bear the proof mark of the Ordnance Inspector Orville W. Ainsworth. The frame is marked 'U.S.' and the name of the 7th Cavalry regiment has been engraved into the back of the grip. The serial numbers run up to approximately 25,000.

One such revolver in a good state sold for a price of US\$ 20,700 at an auction held by the Rock Island Auction Company in 1996. The American Cimarron Firearms Company produces an authentic replica, including the proof and regiment marks.

*Springfield 1873 Tapdoor Carbine*

## Springfield 1873 Trapdoor Carbine

**TECHNICAL SPECIFICATIONS**

| | |
|---|---|
| Calibre | : .45-70 Government |
| Cartridge capacity | : single-shot |
| Operation | : single-action |
| Firing system | : centre-fire |
| Breach-loading | : folding lever |
| Length | : 102.9 cm (40.5") |
| Barrel length | : 55.9 cm (22") |
| Weight | : 3.2 kg (7 lb) |
| Sight | : graduated sight |
| Safety | : half-cock hammer |
| Stock | : nut |

Specific details: This was made by Springfield Armory in the period 1873–1877. The total output was 73,000 including some 20,000 carbines and 3000 cadet rifles.

The military rifle and the cadet rifle both had two barrel bands. The carbine only had one. This carbine was issued to the legendary 7th Cavalry in 1863. It had a saddle rod and a ring. Pedersoli makes a

*Detail of the bolt of a Springfield 1873 Trapdoor Carbine*

beautiful replica of the carbine model, that is marketed in North America by Navy Arms.

*Replica of the Springfield 1873 Trapdoor Carbine*

## Winchester 1873 Carbine

**TECHNICAL SPECIFICATIONS**

| | |
|---|---|
| Calibre | : .44-40 WCF; see Specific details |
| Cartridge capacity | : 12 cartridges |
| Operation | : single-action |
| Firing system | : centre-fire |
| Breach-loading | : lever action |
| Length | : 99.8 cm (39.3") |
| Barrel length | : 50.8 cm (20") |
| Weight | : 3.3 kg (7.25 lb) |
| Sight | : graduated sight |
| Safety | : half-cock hammer |
| Stock | : walnut |

*Winchester 1873 Carbine*

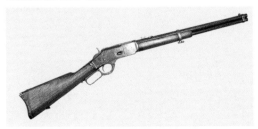

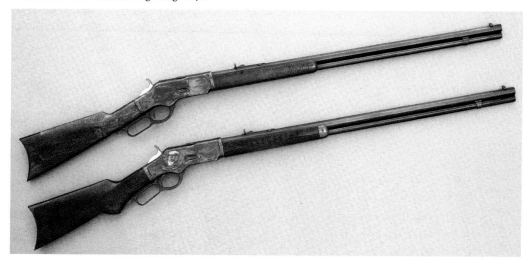

*Specific details*: Over 720,000 of these weapons were produced from 1873 to 1919. Other calibres include: .38-40 (1879), .32-20 (1882), .22 LR (1884). The model 1873 was made in three different versions: the Sporting Rifle with a 24" (61-cm) octagonal, round or partially octagonal barrel and a straight English stock; the carbine with a 20" (51-cm) round barrel and the musket with a 30" (76.2-cm) round barrel that was attached to the stock by three barrel bands. In addition there are three different model varieties with only minor modifications. Cimarron Arms and Hege-Uberti produce beautiful replicas in the calibres .357 Magnum, .44-40 WCF and .45 LC.

*Winchester 1873 Sporting Rifle in the 'One of One Thousand' version*

# Winchester 1873 Musket long range rifle

### TECHNICAL SPECIFICATIONS

| | |
|---|---|
| Calibre | : .44-40 WCF; see Specific details |
| Cartridge capacity | : 15 cartridges |
| Operation | : single-action |
| Firing system | : centre-fire |
| Breach-loading | : lever action |
| Length | : 125.2 cm (49.3") |
| Barrel length | : 76.2 cm (30") |
| Weight | : 4.3 kg (9.5 lb) |
| Sight | : graduated sight |
| Safety | : half-cock hammer |
| Stock | : walnut |

Specific details: Over 720,000 of these weapons were produced from 1873 to 1919. Other calibres include: .38-40 (1879), .32-20 (1882), .22 LR (1884).

The model 1873 was made in three different versions: the Sporting Rifle with a 24" (61-cm) octagonal, round or partially octagonal barrel and a straight English stock; the carbine with a 20" (51-cm) round barrel and the musket with a 30" (76.2-cm) round barrel that was attached to the stock by three barrel bands.

In addition there are three different model versions with only minor modifications.

Cimarron Arms and Hege-Uberti produce beautiful replicas in the calibres .44-40 WCF and .45 LC.

## Winchester 1873 Sporting Rifle

**TECHNICAL SPECIFICATIONS**

| | |
|---|---|
| Calibre | : .44-40 WCF; see Specific details |
| Cartridge capacity | : 15 cartridges |
| Operation | : single-action |
| Firing system | : centre-fire |
| Breach-loading | : lever action |
| Length | : 110 cm (43.3") |
| Barrel length | : 61 cm (24") |
| Weight | : 3.9 kg (8.5 lb) |
| Sight | : graduated sight |
| Safety | : half-cock hammer |
| Stock | : walnut |

*Specific details*: Over 720,000 of these weapons were produced from 1873 to 1919. Other calibres include: .38-40 (1879), .32-20 (1882), .22 LR (1884).

The model 1873 was made in three different versions: the Sporting Rifle with a 24" (61-cm) octagonal, round or partially octagonal barrel and a straight English stock; the carbine with a 20" (51-cm) round barrel and the musket with a 30" (76.2-cm) round barrel that was attached to the stock by three barrel bands.

In addition there are three different model versions with only minor modifications. The third model was also built as a luxury Sporting Rifle with a stock including a pistol grip. In 1878 Winchester issued a special version, the 'One of One Thousand',

only 136 of which were made. Such a Sporting Rifle sold for US$ 75,000 at an auction in 1991. Cimarron Arms and Hege-Uberti produce beautiful replicas in the calibres .357 Magnum, .44-40 WCF and .45 LC.

## Sharps 1874 buffalo rifle

**TECHNICAL SPECIFICATIONS**

| | |
|---|---|
| Calibre | : .45-70 Government, .44-90 Sharps |
| Cartridge capacity | : single-shot |
| Operation | : single-action |
| Firing system | : centre-fire |
| Breach-loading | : falling block action |
| Length | : 116.8 cm (46") |
| Barrel length | : 71.1 cm (28") |
| Weight | : 4.8 kg (10.1 lb) |
| Sight | : fixed or with graduated eye cap sight |
| Safety | : half-cock hammer |
| Stock | : nut |

*Sharps 1874 Buffalo Rifle*

*Winchester 1873 Sporting Rifle*

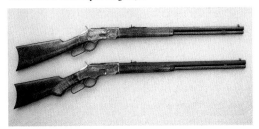

*Specific details*: This was a popular hunting rifle among buffalo hunters. It had a heavy octagonal barrel, sometimes with an adjustable, graduated eye cap sight. The trigger section is fitted with an accelerator (double triggers). This weapon was derived from the Sharps 1874 Business Rifle. Pedersoli makes an excellent replica that is marketed by Navy Arms in North America. The photograph shows the Sharps 1874 Plains Rifle (left) and the 1874 Buffalo Rifle (right).

## Sharps 1874 Cavalry Carbine

**TECHNICAL SPECIFICATIONS**

| | |
|---|---|
| Calibre | : .45-70 Government |
| Cartridge capacity | : single-shot |
| Operation | : single-action |
| Firing system | : centre-fire |
| Breach-loading | : falling block action |
| Length | : 99 cm (39") |
| Barrel length | : 55.9 cm (22") |
| Weight | : 3.5 kg (7.75 lb) |
| Sight | : fixed |
| Safety | : half-cock |
| Stock | : nut |

*Specific details*: The Sharps 1874 Cavalry Carbine was the standard weapon of the Frontier Cavalry during the Indian Wars of 1870-1880. The carbine played a major role at Little Big Horn, where it was used by Gen. Custer's 7th Cavalry. Sharps made thousands of these carbines in the period 1874 to 1877. The Italian arms company

*Sharps 1874 Infantry Rifle*

Pedersoli makes an excellent replica that is marketed by Navy Arms in North America. The photograph shows from the left to the right: Sharps 1874 Infantry Rifle, Sharps 1874 Cavalry Carbine and the Springfield 1873 Cavalry Carbine.

## Sharps 1874 Infantry Rifle

**TECHNICAL SPECIFICATIONS**

| | |
|---|---|
| Calibre | : .45-70 Government |
| Cartridge capacity | : single-shot |
| Operation | : single-action |
| Firing system | : centre-fire |
| Breach-loading | : falling block action |
| Length | : 118.8 cm (46.75") |
| Barrel length | : 76.2 cm (30") |
| Weight | : 3.9 kg (8.5 lb) |
| Sight | : fixed |
| Safety | : half-cock hammer |
| Stock | : nut |

*Specific details*: The Sharps Model 1874 was made in many different versions and calibres. The military cartridge versions usually have the .45-70 Government calibre. The Sharps 1874 Infantry Rifle has three barrel bands. Some 1800 of these rifles were made from 1871 to 1877 and it was the standard weapon of the New York State Militia. In addition there are four different versions of the Model 1874 Creedmoor, intended for military shooting competitions. The Italian arms company Pedersoli makes an excellent replica that is marketed by Navy Arms in North America. The photograph shows from the left to the right: Sharps 1874 Infantry Rifle, Sharps 1874 Cavalry Carbine and the Springfield 1873 Cavalry Carbine.

## Sharps 1874 Plains Rifle

**TECHNICAL SPECIFICATIONS**

| | |
|---|---|
| Calibre | : .45-70 Government, .45-75 Sharps |
| Cartridge capacity | : single-shot |

*Sharps 1874 Plains Rifle*

| Operation | : single-action |
|---|---|
| Firing system | : centre-fire |
| Breach-loading | : falling block action |
| Length | : 124.5 cm (49") |
| Barrel length | : 81.3 cm (32") |
| Weight | : 4.3 kg (9.5 lb) |
| Sight | : fixed |
| Safety | : half-cock hammer |
| Stock | : nut |

*Specific details*: One of the most popular hunting rifles of the Wild West period. The weapon was used by Frontier Scouts, pioneers and Indians alike. Belly Dixon, a famed soldier of that time, shot an enemy at a distance of 1538 yards using this rifle during the fighting at Adobe Walls. Pedersoli makes an excellent replica that is marketed by Navy Arms in North America. The photograph shows the Sharps 1874 Plains Rifle (left) and the 1874 Buffalo Rifle (right).

*Remington Model 1875 Single-Action Army*

## Remington Model 1875 Single-Action Army

**TECHNICAL SPECIFICATIONS**

| | |
|---|---|
| Calibre | : .44 Colt, .44 Remington-CF, .44-40 Win. or .45 LC |
| Cartridge capacity | : 6-shot |
| Operation | : single-action |
| Firing system | : centre-fire |
| Breach-loading | : N/A |
| Length | : 324 or 330 cm (12.8 or 13") |
| Barrel length | : 140 or 191 mm (5.5 or 7.5") |
| Weight | : 1130 or 1250 g (40 or 44 oz) |
| Sight | : fixed |
| Safety | : half-cock hammer |
| Grip | : hard-wood grip plates |

*Specific details*: Some 25,000 of these revolvers were made by Remington in the period 1875–1889 in a blued and a nickel-plated version. Due to its use – mostly in a 5.5" (14-cm) barrelled version – along the American-Mexican border it was nick-named 'Outlaw'. High-quality replicas are still made by Uberti-Italy in the calibres .357 Magnum, .44-40 Win., .45 ACP and .45 LC.

## Merwin & Hulbert Pocket Model 1875

**TECHNICAL SPECIFICATIONS**

| | |
|---|---|
| Calibre | : .32MH, .38MH, .44-40 WCF, .44 Henry RF |
| Cartridge capacity | : 5, 6 of 7-shot |
| Operation | : single-action |
| Firing system | : centraal- of rim-fire |
| Breach-loading | : quarter turn bolt |
| Length | : 186.5 of 250 mm (7.3 or 9.8") |
| Barrel length | : 76 or 140 mm (3 or 5.5") |
| Weight | : 850 or 1040 g (30 or 36.7 oz) |
| Sight | : fixed |
| Safety | : half-cock hammer |
| Grip | : ebonite, ivory or mother of pearl |

*Specific details*: This was made from 1875 to about 1886, with the folding hammer spur being introduced in 1885. This model

*Merwin & Hulbert Pocket Model 1875*

was made both with or without a trigger guard. The .32 and .38 Merwin-Hulbert cartridges are identical to the Smith & Wesson calibres.

This designation was used to avoid conflicts with Smith & Wesson who held the patent rights. The Merwin-Hulbert cartridges were made by American Metallic Cartridge Co., Union Cartridge Co. and Winchester Repeating Arms Co. until World War I. Most of them are nickel-plated.

## Smith & Wesson Pocket Model 1876 Baby Russian

**TECHNICAL SPECIFICATIONS**

| | |
|---|---|
| Calibre | : .38 Smith & Wesson |
| Cartridge capacity | : 5-shot |
| Operation | : single-action |
| Firing system | : centre-fire |
| Breach-loading | : bolt latch on upper bridge |
| Length | : 210 or 225 mm (8.3 or 8.9") |
| Barrel length | : 82,5 or 102 mm (3.25 or 4") |
| Weight | : 640 g (22.6 oz) |
| Sight | : fixed |
| Safety | : half-cock hammer |
| Grip | : walnut, ebonite, mother of pearl or ivory |

*Specific details*: The Pocket Model 1876 is also called the Baby Russian or Smith &

*Smith & Wessen Pocket Model 1876 Baby Russian*

*Colt 1876 APC U.S. Cavalry Model*

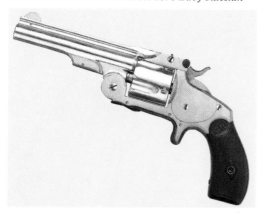

Wesson Model Number 2. The weapon was derived from the Smith & Wesson army revolver in a .44 Russian calibre. This model was introduced for the civilian market in 1876.

In total Smith & Wesson produced 25,548 Baby Russians until the end of 1877, when it was modified and produced as the Second Model-2nd Issue until 1891 and renumbered from 1 to 108255. The second model has a shorter ejector rod housing below the barrel and a modified trigger system.

A third version, the Third Model of 1891, was made from 1891 to 1911 with the serial numbers 1 to 28107. This type does have a trigger guard.

## Colt 1876 APC U.S. Cavalry Model

**TECHNICAL SPECIFICATIONS**

| | |
|---|---|
| Calibre | : .45 Colt |
| Cartridge capacity | : 6-shot |
| Operation | : single-action |
| Firing system | : centre-fire |
| Breach-loading | : N/A |
| Length | : 330 mm (13") |
| Barrel length | : 191 mm (7.5") |
| Weight | : 1050 g (37 oz) |
| Sight | : fixed |
| Safety | : half-cock hammer |
| Grip | : walnut grip in one piece |

Specific details: A.P. Casey was an army officer who was posted to Colt as an arms inspector for the military.

This revolver model was used by the American cavalry from 1876 until the end of the Indian wars. Most military weapons of that time were branded with the APC inspection mark.

## Colt Model 1877 Thunderer and Lightning

**TECHNICAL SPECIFICATIONS**

| | |
|---|---|
| Calibre | : .38 CF (Lightning) or .41 CF (Thunderer) |
| Cartridge capacity | : 6-shot |
| Operation | : double-action |
| Firing system | : centre-fire |
| Breach-loading | : N/A |
| Length | : 167–306 mm (6.6–12") |
| Barrel length | : 51, 64, 89, 114, 127, 152, 178 or 191 mm (2, 2.5, 3.5, 4.5, 5, 6, 7 or 7.5") |
| Weight | : 1050 g (37 oz) with a 3.5"/89-mm barrel |
| Sight | : fixed |
| Safety | : half-cock |
| Stock | : mahogany (early models) or ebonite grip plates |

*Colt Model 1877 Thunderer & Lighting*

(51–89 mm) have no ejector rod. Hege-Uberti builds some excellent replicas in single-action in the calibres: .44-40 Win., .44 S&W, .45 ACP and .45 LC.

## Colt Model 1878 Frontier Six-Shooter Single Action Army

**TECHNICAL SPECIFICATIONS**

| | |
|---|---|
| Calibre | : .44-40 Win |
| Cartridge capacity | : 6-shot |
| Operation | : single-action |
| Firing system | : centre-fire |
| Breach-loading | : N/A |
| Length | : 260.4 mm (10.25") |
| Barrel length | : 120.7 mm (4.75") |
| Weight | : 960 g (33.9 oz) |
| Sight | : fixed |
| Safety | : half-cock hammer |
| Grip | : walnut grip in one piece |

*Specific details*: The first double-action revolver by Colt. Some 166,000 pieces were made between 1877 and 1909. The 1877 Thunderer was made in a .41 Colt calibre and the 1877 Lightning in the .38 Colt calibre. Models with barrel lengths of 2–3.5"

*Specific details*: The Colt Frontier was intended for the frontier troops. The

*Colt Model 1878 Frontier Six-Shooter Single Action Army*

*Colt Model 1878 Frontier with a 7.5"/190.5-mm barrel*

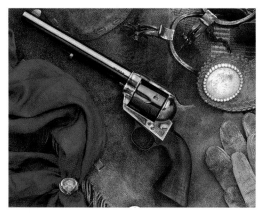

| Operation | : single-action |
|---|---|
| Firing system | : centre-fire |
| Breach-loading | : N/A |
| Length | : 279.4 mm (11") |
| Barrel length | : 139.7 mm (5.5") |
| Weight | : 1020 g (36 oz) |
| Sight | : fixed |
| Safety | : half-cock hammer |
| Grip | : walnut grip in one piece |

*Specific details*: This was made in various barrel lengths over the period 1878–1882. The serial numbers of the Colt 1873 are continued in this series, from approx. 45,000 to 65,000. After World War II the Frontier Six-Shooter has repeatedly been included in Colt's production range, in many calibres from .22 LR to .44 Magnum. The American Cimarron Firearms Company makes an authentic replica.

revolver was built in the calibre .44-40 or .44 WCF (Winchester Center Fire). A major logistic advantage of this ammunition was that it could be used both for the Colt revolver and the Winchester M1873 lever-action repeating carbine. The American Cimarron Firearms Company makes an authentic replica. The Colt 1878 Frontier in the picture below has a 190.5-mm/7.5" barrel.

# Colt Model 1878 Frontier Six-Shooter

## TECHNICAL SPECIFICATIONS

| Calibre | : .44-40 Win |
|---|---|
| Cartridge capacity | : 6-shot |

*Colt Model 1878 Frontier Six-Shooter with a 5.5"/140-mm barrel*

# Merwin-Hulbert Army Revolver Model 1878

## TECHNICAL SPECIFICATIONS

| Calibre | : .44-40 Win. |
|---|---|
| Cartridge capacity | : 6 cartridges |
| Operation | : single-action |
| Firing system | : centre-fire |
| Breach-loading | : lug on top of cylinder bridge with latch in front of cylinder |
| Length | : 315 mm (12.4") |

*Merin-Hulbert Army Revolver Model 1878*

*From the top to the bottom: Colt Kodiak Double Rifle, Sharps Plains Rifle and the Sharps Buffalo Rifle*

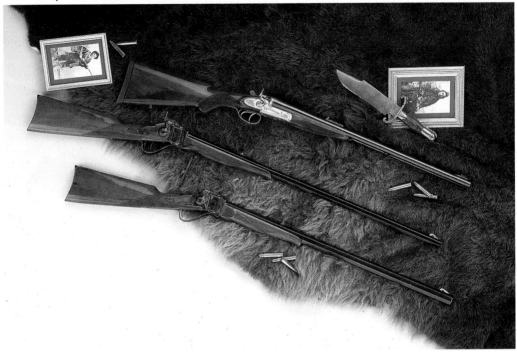

| | |
|---|---|
| Barrel length | : 178 mm (7") |
| Weight | : 1200 g (42.3 oz) |
| Sight | : fixed |
| Safety | : half-cock hammer |
| Grip | : ebonite or walnut |

*Specific details*: This was produced in the period 1878 to about 1884 by Hopkins & Allen of Norwich, Conn. for the trading company Merwin-Hulbert of New York. This trading company was the sales office for the weapons made by Hopkins & Allen and the Evans Rifle Company. In spite of the designation 'Army Revolver' this revolver was never selected as an official military weapon.

Various Pocket models of this revolver were built as well. To load or unload the revolver, the latch in front of the cylinder had to be pushed first. The barrel/cylinder section could then be rotated around the cylinder axis through 90 degrees and slid forward to provide access to the cylinder chambers.

## Colt 1879 Kodiak Double Rifle

**TECHNICAL SPECIFICATIONS**

| | |
|---|---|
| Calibre | : .45-70 Government |
| Cartridge capacity | : double-barrelled, |
| Operation | : single-action |
| Firing system | : centre-fire |
| Breach-loading | : double barrel hooks |
| Length | : 101 cm (39.75") |
| Barrel length | : 61 cm (24") |
| Weight | : 4.6 kg (10.2 lb) |
| Sight | : fixed |
| Safety | : half-cock hammer |
| Stock | : nut stock with pistol grip |

*Specific details*: This was designed by Caldwell Hart Colt, Samuel Colt's son. Some 35 of these weapons were made in the period 1879–1885. Most pieces form part of major arms collections and are extremely valuable. These weapons are sometimes offered for sale, but they are mostly converted versions of the Colt Model 1878 shotgun. From the top to the

216

bottom the photograph shows: Colt Kodiak Double Rifle, Sharps Plains Rifle and the Sharps Buffalo Rifle. The Italian arms company Pedersoli makes an excellent replica that is marketed by Navy Arms in North America.

## Colt 1882 Sheriff's or Storekeeper's

**TECHNICAL SPECIFICATIONS**

| | |
|---|---|
| Calibre | : .44-40 Win |
| Cartridge capacity | : 6-shot |
| Operation | : single-action |
| Firing system | : centre-fire |
| Breach-loading | : N/A |
| Length | : 216 mm (8.5") |
| Barrel length | : 76.2 mm (3") |
| Weight | : 950 g (33.5 oz) |
| Sight | : fixed |
| Safety | : half-cock hammer |
| Grip | : walnut grip in one piece |

*Specific details*: This was derived from the 1873 SAA model, with serial numbers over 73,000. Produced by Colt in many versions and calibres in the period 1882–1898. This revolver has no ejector rod. The American Cimarron Firearms Company makes an authentic replica.

*Colt 1882 Sheriff's or Storekeeper's*

*Winchester Hotchkiss Model 1883*

## Winchester Hotchkiss Model 1883

**TECHNICAL SPECIFICATIONS**

| | |
|---|---|
| Calibre | : .45-70 Government |
| Cartridge capacity | : 5-shot |
| Operation | : single-action |
| Firing system | : centre-fire |
| Breach-loading | : bolt action with breech-sealing lugs |
| Length | : 112 cm (44.1") |
| Barrel length | : 61 cm (24") |
| Weight | : 3.6 kg (7.9 lb) |
| Sight | : graduated sight |
| Safety | : rotating sear on right-hand side, over trigger guard |
| Stock | : nut |

Specific details: This was developed by Benjamin B. Hotchkiss in 1876 and produced by Winchester from 1878. In 1881 the Chinese government ordered 16,000 Hotchkiss carbines. This weapon was originally intended as a military carbine for the American army, but it was never used as such. After several modifications the name of the weapon was shortened to Winchester Model 1883. The safety sear on the right of the stock, over the trigger guard, also serves to lock the magazine so that the bolt carbine can be loaded manually for every single shot. The photograph shows the first model whose serial numbers run from 1 to 6419. For the second model the safety sear and the magazine lock were moved to both sides of the tailpiece. Its serial numbers run from 6420 to 22521. The third model has a metal action frame separating the stock and the forward grip. The serial numbers for this

model run from 22552 to 84555. Winchester also made long-barrelled sporting rifles of these three models, with the barrel lengths varying from 26 to 32" (66 to 81.3 cm). These weapons were produced until about 1899.

## Stevens Single-Shot Diamond No. 43 1886

**TECHNICAL SPECIFICATIONS**

| | |
|---|---|
| Calibre | : .22 LR or .25 Stevens RF |
| Cartridge capacity | : single-shot |
| Operation | : single-action |
| Firing system | : rim-fire |
| Breach-loading | : lug on grip section, just below the hammer |
| Length | : 235 or 337 mm (9.25 or 13.25") |
| Barrel length | : 152 or 254 mm (6 or 10") |
| Weight | : 500 to 680 g (17.6 to 24 oz) |
| Sight | : simple adjustable sight |
| Safety | : half-cock hammer |
| Grip | : walnut |

*Specific details*: J. Stevens & Co started to produce simple single-shot pocket pistols in 1864. In 1888 the company was renamed to J. Stevens Arms & Tools Company. It was located in Chicopee Falls, Massachusetts. Until 1920 this company also made a series of target-shooting pistols with 6–12" barrels. The pistol in the photograph is the Diamond 1st Issue with a brass frame. The second model had a steel frame. Both versions have no trigger guard. A total of 95,000 Diamonds were produced

*Stevens Single-Shot Diamond No. 43 1886*

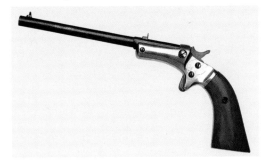

*Springfield 1873/1884 Trapdoor Rifle*

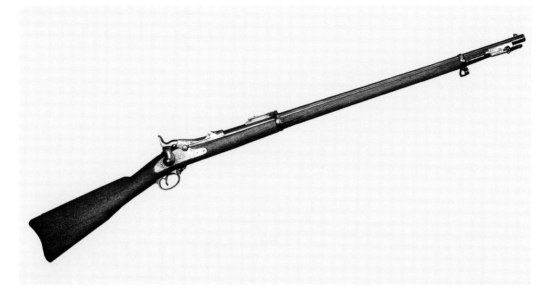

between 1886 and 1916. Other well-known models are the Conlin Model, named after the owner of a shooting club in New York and the Stevens-Gould pistol, named after an American author on weapons. In addition Stevens made a number of single-shot rifles, based on the same hinged system, often with detachable threaded stocks, the so-called Pocket Rifles.

## Springfield 1873/1884 Trapdoor Rifle

**TECHNICAL SPECIFICATIONS**

Calibre : .45-70 Government
Cartridge capacity : single-shot
Operation : single-action
Firing system : centre-fire
Breach-loading : folding lever
Length : cadet rifle: 121.9 cm (48"), rifle: 129.5 cm (51")
Barrel length : cadet rifle: 74.9 cm (29.5"), rifle: 82.6 cm (32.5")
Weight : 3.8–4.5 kg (8.5–10 lb)
Sight : graduated sight
Safety : half-cock hammer
Stock : walnut

*Detail of the Springfield 1873/1884 Trapdoor Rifle*

*Springfield 1873/1884 Trapdoor Rifle with open bolt*

*Specific details*: Originally made as the Model 1870 in a .50 calibre. In 1873 the calibre was changed to .45-70.

The bayonet mount is visible below the muzzle. Some 232,000 rifles of this type were made by Springfield Armory in the period 1884 to 1890.

The military rifle and the cadet rifle both had two barrel bands.

## Remington-Lee Model 1885 carbine

**TECHNICAL SPECIFICATIONS**

| | |
|---|---|
| Calibre | : .45-70R |
| Cartridge capacity | : cartridge holder for 5 cartridges |
| Operation | : single-action |
| Firing system | : centre-fire |
| Breach-loading | : lug |
| Length | : carbine: 110.5 cm (43.5"); rifle: 132.1 cm (52") |
| Barrel length | : carbine: 61 cm (24"); rifle: 82.6 cm (32.5") |
| Weight | : carbine: 3.2 kg (7 lb); rifle: 4 kg (8.9 lb) |
| Sight | : graduated sight |
| Safety | : rotating sear on rear of bolt |
| Stock | : walnut |

*Specific details*: This was produced by E. Remington & Sons from 1885 to 1887 and by the Remington Arms Company of Ilion, New York from 1888 to 1895. Some 10,000 of these rifles were made.

The carbine in the photograph is quite rare, as the production data of 1889 and 1893

*Remington-Lee Model 1885 Carbine*

shows that only 26 of these carbines were produced. The weapon has a detachable cartridge holder of the Lee-type, which would later also be used for British Enfield rifles.

James Paris Lee (1831–1904) was a Scotsman by birth who emigrated to Canada. After his technical education he moved to the United States. He built his first magazine rifles on a commission from the American Navy. The American Army showed little interest in his invention, but several European arms companies, such as Enfield were.

## Remington Model 1890 Police

**TECHNICAL SPECIFICATIONS**

| | |
|---|---|
| Calibre | : .44-40 Win. |
| Cartridge capacity | : 6-shot |
| Operation | : single-action |
| Firing system | : centre-fire |
| Breach-loading | : N/A |
| Length | : 325 or 330 mm (12.8 or 13") |
| Barrel length | : 140 or 191 mm (5.5 or 7.5") |
| Weight | : 1150 or 1250 g (40.6 or 44.1 oz) |
| Sight | : fixed |
| Safety | : half-cock hammer |
| Grip | : hard-wood grip plates |

*Specific details*: This was built in a small number (approx. 2000) during a short

*Remington Model 1890 Police*

period between 1891and 1894 as a competitor for the Colt 1875 Single Action. A high-quality replica is still made by Uberti-Italy in the calibres .357 Magnum, .44-40 Win., .45 ACP and .45 LC.

## Winchester Model 1892 Carbine

**TECHNICAL SPECIFICATIONS**

| | |
|---|---|
| Calibre | : .32-20, .25-20 or .44-40 Win. |
| Cartridge capacity | : tubular magazine for 13 cartridges |
| Operation | : single-action |
| Firing system | : centre-fire |
| Breach-loading | : lever-action |
| Length | : 95 cm (37.5") |
| Barrel length | : 51 cm (20") |
| Weight | : 2.7 kg (6 lb) |
| Sight | : simple graduated sight |
| Safety | : none |
| Stock | : walnut |

*Specific details*: This was made by Winchester in the period 1893 to 1941. This weapon was also called the Trapper carbine.

A typical feature is the saddle ring on the left of the action frame. The other side contains the loading gate that provides access to the tubular magazine below the barrel. The carbine was made in several versions with barrel lengths ranging from 12 to 18" (30.5 to 45.7 cm).

## Winchester Model 1892 Rifle

**TECHNICAL SPECIFICATIONS**

| | |
|---|---|
| Calibre | : .32-20 Winchester |
| Cartridge capacity | : tubular magazine for 5 cartridges |
| Operation | : single-action |
| Firing system | : centre-fire |
| Breach-loading | : lever-action |
| Length | : 106 cm (41.6") |
| Barrel length | : 61 cm (24") |
| Weight | : 3.1 kg (6.8 lb) |
| Sight | : simple graduated sight |
| Safety | : none |
| Stock | : walnut or other hardwood |

*Winchester Model 1892 Rifle*

*Winchester Model 1892 Carbine*

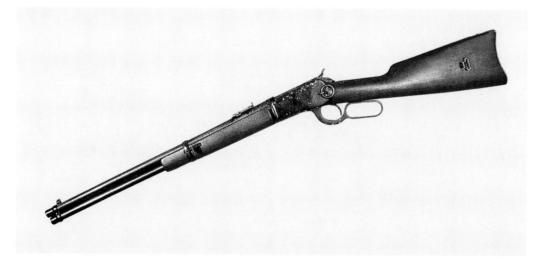

*Specific details*: This was made by the Winchester Repeating Arms Company from 1892 to 1941. This was a simple version of the Winchester M1886. This rifle was also available in the .38-40, .44-40 and from 1895 the .25-20 Winchester calibres. The short tubular magazine below the barrel is fully enclosed by the forward grip. This model was made in more versions, such as the carbine, the musket and the Take Down Rifle (which could be disassembled) in 1893.

The tubular magazine of the rifle must be loaded through the opening on the right-hand side of the action frame.

*Johnson Safety Double-Auction Revolver 1893*

## Smith & Wesson Single Shot Pistol Model 1893

### TECHNICAL SPECIFICATIONS

| | |
|---|---|
| Calibre | : .22 LR, .32 S&W of .38 S&W |
| Cartridge capacity | : single-shot |
| Operation | : single-action |
| Firing system | : rim- or centre-fire |
| Breach-loading | : N/A, hook when fitted with notched sight |
| Length | : 298 mm (11.75") |
| Barrel length | : 152, 203 or 254 mm (6, 8 or 10") |
| Weight | : 620 g (21.9 oz) with 8"/203-mm barrel |
| Sight | : adjustable |
| Safety | : half-cock hammer |
| Grip | : ebonite, walnut or ivory |

*Specific details*: The 1st Model was launched in 1893 and made until 1905 in the following quantities: 862 of the .22 LR, 229 of the .32 S&W and 160 of the .38 S&W. This model was made both in a blued and a nickel-plated version. The 2nd Model, which was produced from 1905 to 1909, was only available in a .22 LR calibre and had a 10"/254-mm barrel. It was made in a blued and a nickel-plated version and had an ebonite grip. The total quantity produced was 4615 pieces. The 3rd Model (1909 to 1923) was only available in a .22 LR calibre as well with a choice of 6, 8 or 10"/152, 203 or 254-mm barrels. 6949 3rd Models were made in total.

## Johnson Safety Double-Action Revolver 1893

### TECHNICAL SPECIFICATIONS

| | |
|---|---|
| Calibre | : .22, .32 of .38 S&W |
| Cartridge capacity | : 5-shot |
| Operation | : double-action |

| | |
|---|---|
| Firing system | : rim- or centre-fire |
| Breach-loading | : folding latch on upper bridge |
| Length | : 140 to 241 mm (5.5 to 9.5") |
| Barrel length | : 51 to 152 mm (2 to 6") |
| Weight | : 330 to 570 g (11.6 to 20.1 oz) |
| Sight | : fixed |
| Safety | : half-cock hammer |
| Grip | : ebonite or walnut |

*Specific details*: This was made by Iver Johnson Arms Inc. from 1893 to 1950. From 1883 the company was situated in Worcester and after 1891 in Fitchburg, Massachusetts.
The model shown has a 3"/76-mm barrel. Johnson also made a couple of models with concealed hammers. An action block that can be swung up is attached to the upper bridge over the cylinder. The barrel and cylinder section can then be swung forwards to load the revolver. At the same time the cases or cartridges were ejected by a star-shaped extractor. Johnson was one of the first manufacturers to apply the transfer rod safety system. The spring-loaded firing pin is mounted inside the grip section.
When the weapon is fired, the hammer hits a rod that transfers the blow to the firing pin. Only if the trigger is pulled all the way, does the transfer rod move up to be positioned between the hammer and the firing pin.
If the trigger is released halfway, the rod will move down again so that the hammer cannot reach the firing pin.

*Winchester Model 1894 Carbine*

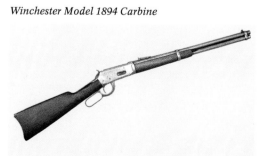

## Winchester Model 1894 Carbine

### TECHNICAL SPECIFICATIONS

| | |
|---|---|
| Calibre | : .30-30 Win. |
| Cartridge capacity | : tubular magazine for 6 cartridges |
| Operation | : single-action |
| Firing system | : centre-fire |
| Breach-loading | : lever-action |
| Length | : 96.9 cm (38.15") |
| Barrel length | : 51 cm (20") |
| Weight | : 3.1 kg (6.9 lb) |
| Sight | : simple graduated sight |
| Safety | : none |
| Stock | : walnut or other hardwood |

*Specific details*: This was made by Winchester from 1894 to 1936. Production of this type was started again in several calibres after World War II. The weapon was made in various types with a total production of over 7 million. Most carbines had a saddle ring on the left-hand side of the frame. From 1895 onwards the M1894 was also available in the .25-35 Win. calibre.

## Colt Model 1894 Bisley

### TECHNICAL SPECIFICATIONS

| | |
|---|---|
| Calibre | : .45 Colt: see Specific details |
| Cartridge capacity | : 6-shot |
| Operation | : single-action |
| Firing system | : centre-fire |
| Breach-loading | : N/A |
| Length | : 330 mm (13"): see Specific details |
| Barrel length | : 191 mm (7.5"): see Specific details |
| Weight | : 1050 g (37 oz) |
| Sight | : fixed |
| Safety | : half-cock hammer |
| Grip | : walnut grip in one piece |

*Specific details*: This was produced from 1894 to 1915. Named after the British shooting ranges where shooting competitions have been held since the 19th century. The Colt Bisley was designed as a match revolver with an extra curved grip back. The model name 'Bisley' has been stamped

*Colt Model 1894 Bisley*

| Weight | : 2.95 kg (6.5 lb) with 40.8"/103.5 cm barrel |
|---|---|
| Sight | : simple graduated sight |
| Safety | : safety latch, half-cock hammer, locking safety |
| Stock | : walnut |

*Specific details*: This was produced by Marlin in the period 1894 to 1935 with a total output of 250,000 pieces. This model was taken into production again after World War II. The first version was only made in the .38-40 and .44-40 calibres. Next to the company name it bore the inscription 'Patented Oct. 11, 1887. April 2, 1889' on its barrel and 'Marlin Safety' on the action frame. The later versions are inscribed with 'Aug. 1, 1893' and 'Model 1894', which was shortened to 'Model 94' by around 1920. All versions had round or octagonal barrels.

## Colt Model 1895/1873 U.S. Artillery 1895 Single Action Army

### TECHNICAL SPECIFICATIONS
| | |
|---|---|
| Calibre | : .45 Colt |
| Cartridge capacity | : 6-shot |
| Operation | : single-action |
| Firing system | : centre-fire |
| Breach-loading | : N/A |
| Length | : 330 mm (11") |
| Barrel length | : 139.7 mm (5.5") |
| Weight | : 1050 g (37 oz) |
| Sight | : fixed |
| Safety | : half-cock hammer |
| Grip | : walnut grip in one piece |

into the barrel. During the production period, the weapon was sold in a large range of calibres, from the .32-20 to the .455 Eley and in several barrel lengths: 4.75", 5.5" and 7.5" (120, 140 and 191 mm). The name was chosen to attract the British market, but the weapon also sold well in North America. E.M.F. Company has a beautiful replica in several calibres.

## Marlin Model 1894 Lever Action Rifle

### TECHNICAL SPECIFICATIONS
| | |
|---|---|
| Calibre | : .25-20 WCF, .32-20 Win., .38-40 Win. or .44-40 Win. |
| Cartridge capacity | : 10-shot tubular magazine |
| Operation | : single-action |
| Firing system | : centre-fire |
| Breach-loading | : lever-action |
| Length | : 103.5–123.5 cm (40.8–48.8") |
| Barrel length | : 61–81 cm (24–32") |

*Specific details*: Artillery model from 1895. After the Indian wars a great number of 1873 revolvers were worn to such an extent that they had to be refurbished. This was done by Colt and the Springfield Arsenal. The old 7.5"/191-mm barrels were replaced by 5.5"/139.7-mm barrels. This revolver is also called the 'Rough Rider'. This name came from the 1st U.S. Volunteer Cavalry

under the command of Theodore Roosevelt. The American Cimarron Firearms Company produces an authentic replica, including the proof and regiment marks.

## *Marlin Model 1895 Lever Action Rifle*

**TECHNICAL SPECIFICATIONS**

| | |
|---|---|
| Calibre | : .33 WCF, .38-56 Win., .40-65 Win., .40-70 Win., .40-82 Win., .45-70 Governm. or .45-90 Win. |
| Cartridge capacity | : 4- to 6-shot tubular magazine |
| Operation | : single-action |
| Firing system | : centre-fire |
| Breach-loading | : lever-action |
| Length | : 108–123 cm (42.5–48.4") |
| Barrel length | : 66–81 cm (26–32") |
| Weight | : 2.9 kg (6.4 lb) with 42.5"/108-cm barrel |
| Sight | : simple graduated sight |
| Safety | : safety latch, half-cock, locking safety |
| Stock | : walnut |

*Specific details*: This was produced between 1895 and 1917 with a total output of 18,000 pieces.

This model was produced with round or octagonal barrels. Some versions have a long tubular magazine that continues all the way up to the muzzle. Next to the company name it bore the inscription 'Patented Oct. 11, 1887. April 2, 1889' on its barrel and 'Model 1895' on top of the action frame.

After 1896 the barrel was also engraved with 'Special Smokeless Steel'. Many versions of this rifle were made with different engravings and/or gold-inlaid animal figures. Such an engraved and gold-inlaid rifle in calibre .45-70 Government was sold at an auction for US$ 79,750. In 1972 Marlin started producing this model again. The photograph on the next page shows a post-war model.

*Marlin Model 1895 Lever Action Rifle*

*Detail of the Marlin Model 1895 Lever Action Rifle*

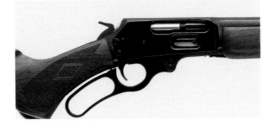

## Winchester Model 1895

### TECHNICAL SPECIFICATIONS

| | |
|---|---|
| Calibre | : see Specific details |
| Cartridge capacity | : internal magazine for 5 cartridges |
| Operation | : single-action |
| Firing system | : centre-fire |
| Breach-loading | : lever-action |
| Length | : 106 cm (42") |

*Winchester Model 1895*

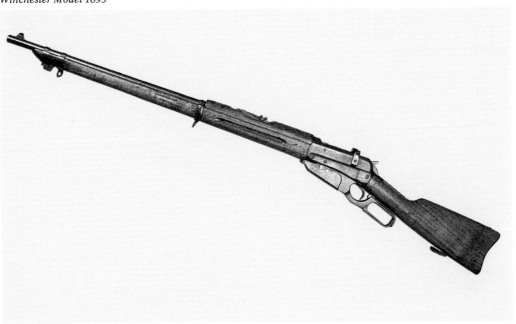

*Russian Winchester with folded lever.*

Barrel length    : 61 cm (24")
Weight           : 3.4 kg (7.55 lb)
Sight            : graduated sight
Safety           : none
Stock            : walnut

*Specific details*: This was made by Winchester from 1895 to 1931. The total quantity produced in this period was approximately 426,000 pieces. The weapon was available in the calibres .30-30 Win, .30-06, .303 British, .30-40 Krag, .35 Win., .38-72 Win., .40-72 Win., .405 Win. and 7.62 x 54R. In 1915 Winchester got a major order from Russia for 300,000 of these rifles in the Russian 7.62 x 54R calibre. This type has a bayonet lug below the barrel. The weapon in the photograph is a Russian Winchester.

## Springfield Krag-Jorgensen Model 1896

**TECHNICAL SPECIFICATIONS**

| | |
|---|---|
| Calibre | : .30-40 Krag |
| Cartridge capacity | : 5 cartridges |
| Operation | : single-action |
| Firing system | : centre-fire, bolt action |
| Breach-loading | : lugs |
| Length | : 124.7 cm (49.1") |
| Barrel length | : 76.2 cm (30") |
| Weight | : 4.1 kg (8.9 lb) |
| Sight | : graduated sight |
| Safety | : sear in top of bolt |
| Stock | : wood |

*Specific details*: This was introduced with the American military in 1896. Springfield made some 62,000 of these rifles. The weapon was derived from a first model from 1892. The modifications to this first model include the graduated sight and the stock. The M1896 was also made as the M1896 Cadet Rifle for the Military Academy in West Point and the M1896 carbine with a .22"/56-cm barrel. This weapon included some new modifications such as another graduated sight, a modified bolt lever and another forward grip.

*Springfield Krag-Jorgensen Model 1896*

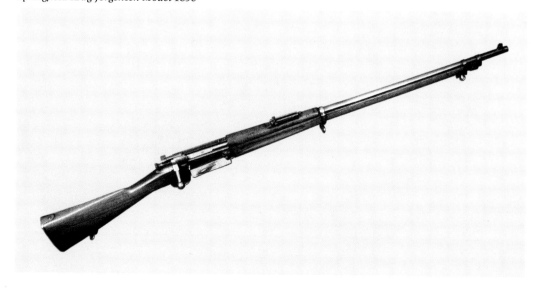

# 10 Russian firearms from 1809 to 1895

*Russian Cavalry Pistol Model 1809*

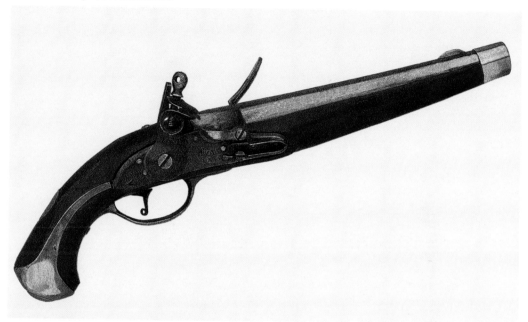

## Russian Cavalry Pistol Model 1809

**TECHNICAL SPECIFICATIONS**

| | |
|---|---|
| Calibre | : 17.8 mm (.700") |
| Cartridge capacity | : single-shot |
| Operation | : single-action |
| Firing system | : flintlock |
| Breach-loading | : N/A |
| Length | : 400 mm (15.8") |
| Barrel length | : 250 mm (9.8") |
| Weight | : 1400 g (49.4 oz) |
| Sight | : bead |
| Safety | : half-cock |
| Grip | : walnut |

*Specific details*: This was designed for the Russian Cavalry in 1808. Produced by the Russian arms factories in Izhevsk, Oloneck, Sestroreck and Tula from 1809 to 1839. The pistol was modified in 1839, one of the modifications being the removal of the front part of the forward grip below the barrel.

This was done to lower the weight of this pistol when riding on horseback. The weapon in the photograph is a specimen of the old model that was made by the arsenal in Tula in 1833. It was customary to mount a brass plate with the Tsar's initials on the neck of the stock.

## Beaumont-Adams Russian Model 1855

**TECHNICAL SPECIFICATIONS**

| | |
|---|---|
| Calibre | : .442 of .500" (11.2 or 12,7 mm) |
| Cartridge capacity | : 5-shot |

*Beaumont-Adams Russian Model 1855*

1865. This model was also made by other companies, such as Francotte in Liège, Belgium. The model in the photograph was destined for Russia as indicated by the gold engraving on top of the barrel. A bullet guide is connected to the lever on the right-hand side of the barrel. When the lever is pushed upwards, the bullet guide moves back, allowing every cylinder chamber to be loaded separately.

| Operation | : double-action |
|---|---|
| Firing system | : percussion |
| Breach-loading | : N/A |
| Length | : 290 or 315 mm (11.4 or 12.4") |
| Barrel length | : 127 or 152 mm (5 or 6") |
| Weight | : 850 g (30 oz) |
| Sight | : fixed |
| Safety | : half-cock hammer |
| Grip | : walnut |

*Specific details*: This was produced by the London Armoury Co. in the period 1856–

## Mosin-Nagant M1891

**TECHNICAL SPECIFICATIONS**

| Calibre | : 7,62 x 54R |
|---|---|
| Cartridge capacity | : 5 cartridges (internal magazine) |
| Operation | : bolt-action |
| Firing system | : centre-fire |
| Breach-loading | : lugs |
| Length | : 130.3 cm (51.3") |
| Barrel length | : 80.2 cm (31.6") |
| Weight | : 4.4 kg (9.7 lb) |
| Sight | : simple graduated sight |

*Right-hand side of the Beaumont-Adams Russian Model 1855*

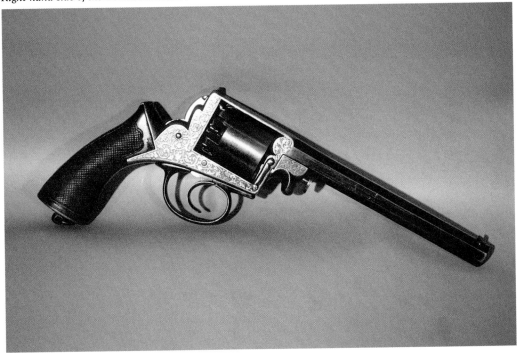

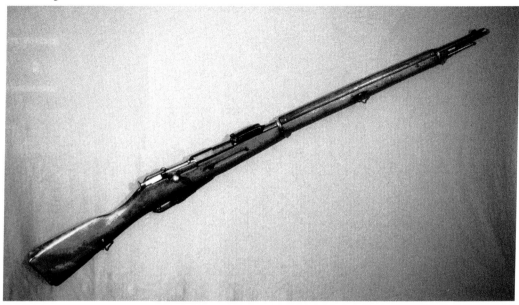

| Safety | : the firing pin tensioning knob can be rotated a quarter turn and locked after pulling it out |
|---|---|
| Stock | : walnut |

*Specific details*: Sergei Ivanovich Mosin was a Russian artillery officer who worked in the Emperor's Arsenal at Tula as a weapons engineer. Around 1885 he participated in studies into a new military rifle for the Tsar's army, who were using the single-shot Berdan rifle that had become severely outdated. The first tests were performed around 1890. In addition to a single-shot rifle designed by Mosin himself, a design by the Belgian weapons engineers Emil and Leon Nagant had been put forward as well. Eventually a compromise was decided on: a Mosin rifle with a 5-shot Nagant magazine system. However, the new rifle that was first issued to the troops in 1891 did not carry the names of its designers. The official designation was Trehlinejnaja Vintovka Obrasca 1891 Goda. Part of this name referred to the new calibre: 3-lines or .30 (7.62 x 54R). The name Mosin-Nagant only came into use much later. The rifle was produced by the

Russian arms factories Ishev Arsenal, Sestroretsk Arsenal and Tula Arsenal in the period 1891 to around 1917. More than 9.3 million of these rifles were made in total. The rifles were also produced by arms factories outside Russia, such as the French MAC: Manufacture d'Armes de Chatellerault (1893–1896) and later by the American companies Remington and New England Westinghouse (1915–1917). A typical feature is that the cartridge guide inside the magazine is stopped by a special lever during the bolt action so that only the upper cartridge is released for loading. The other cartridges are held back. This prevents the bottom side of the bolt from rubbing against the upper cartridge in the magazine. The cleaning rod has been mounted below the barrel.

## Nagant Army Revolver Model 1895

**TECHNICAL SPECIFICATIONS**

| Calibre | : 7,62 mm Nagant (.30") |
|---|---|
| Cartridge capacity | : 7-shot |
| Operation | : single- of double-action |
| Firing system | : centre-fire |

| | | |
|---|---|---|
| Breach-loading | : | N/A |
| Length | : | 235 mm (9.3") |
| Barrel length | : | 114 mm (4.5") |
| Weight | : | 770 g (27.2 oz) |
| Sight | : | fixed |
| Safety | : | when opened loading gate blocks hammer |
| Stock | : | nut |

*Specific details*: Designed by the Belgian engineer Nagant the first batch was for the Russian army produced in Liège. The Russian state factory in Tula made them from 1896 to around 1933. When the hammer is cocked, the cylinder slides forward to rest against the rear of the barrel. The cartridges are longer than the cylinder (1.7 mm), so they protrude. This means that the front of the case is inside the adapter cone. A longer cartridge and cylinder that slides forward ensure a gas-tight construction that seals the space between the cylinder and the barrel almost completely. Because the cylinder is moved forward before the cartridge is fired, the hammer has been fitted with an extra long firing pin to ensure a good contact with the cartridges. Initially soldiers were given single-action Nagant revolvers, while the double-action revolvers were for the officers. This was a service weapon until after World War II.

# Register

*Colt Navy London Model 1853*

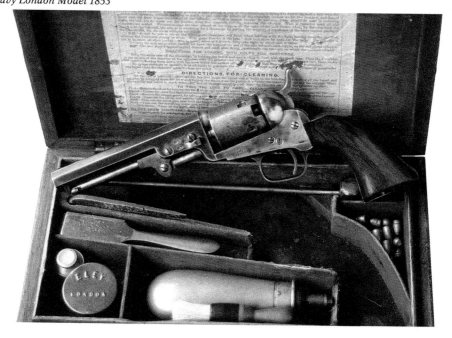

# Information on the internet

*www.amazon.com*
books on antique firearms

*www.armsandarmourauctions.com*
sales of antique firearms over the Internet

*www.atozstuff.com/links*
links to Internet sites on antique firearms

*www.collectorsfirearms.com*
sales of antique firearms

*www.gunhoo.com*
links to a large number of Internet sites on antique weapons

*www.gunindex.com*
links to a large number of Internet sites on antique weapons

*www.gunshop.com*
sales of new and antique firearms

*www.hogarth.com*
Internet museum of antique weapons

*www.liongate-armsandarmour.com*
sales of antique weapons over the Internet

*www.militaria-online.com*
for collectors of militaria

*www.oldguns.com*
the Antique Firearm Network/research centre

*http://oldguns.net/*
Antique and Collectable Firearms and Militaria Headquarters

*www.rebo-publishers.com*
publisher, also of books on firearms and knives

*www.shilohrelics.com*
sales of antique firearms over the Internet

*www.win.bright.net/~gundoc*
sales of antique firearms

# Acknowledgements

I would like to express my special thanks to my wife, Annelies Hartink, for her indispensable help in proof-reading all texts, for her patience with me, and for her devotion to our family, so that I could devote myself fully to writing this book.

In addition I would also like to thank the following people for their expertise and for making their arms collections available to be photographed:
Mr. Verschoor of the Verschoor arms shop in 's Gravendeel, the Netherlands,
Mr. J. Winters of the "De Donderbus" arms shop in Rotterdam, the Netherlands,
Mr. A. Bode (arms collector),
Mr. F. Vink (active recreational shooter of historical firearms),
Mr. J.A.F. Verdick of Langerak, The Netherlands (for being my right hand during all the photography work).

Finally I would like to thank the following companies for their cooperation. Without their assistance this book might not have been produced at all, and it would certainly not have been so beautiful:

– Cimarron Firearms, P.O. Box 906, Fredericksburg, TX 78624-0906 (USA)
– De Donderbus, Oostzeedijk Beneden 231a, 3061 VW Rotterdam (NL)
– Marlin Firearms Co., 100 Kenna Drive, North Haven CT 06473-0905 (USA)
– Navy Arms Company, 689 Bergen Blvd., Ridgefield, NJ 07657 (USA)
– Uberti, Via G. Garducci 41, I-25060 Ponte Zazano-Brescia (I)
– Verschoor Wapenhandel, Schenkeldijk 9, 3295 EC 's-Gravendeel (NL)